Hugo Haase

Hugo Haase:
Democrat and Revolutionary

KENNETH R. CALKINS

1979
Carolina Academic Press
Durham, North Carolina

Printed in the United States of America

Carolina Academic Press
P. O. Box 8971, Forest Hills Station
Durham, North Carolina   27707

To Jill

Contents

PREFACE

Until the present effort, no scholarly biography of Hugo Haase has been attempted, and in general works he has been treated cursorily at best. This is in large measure traceable to the fact that Haase was the champion of a lost cause. Rising to leadership in the German Social Democratic Party (S.P.D.) at a time when internal tensions were already threatening to tear it apart, he refused to deviate from his commitment to the traditional principles of that party despite the momentous changes brought about by war and revolution. As a result of this commitment, Haase chose first to defy the majority of his colleagues in the leadership of the German movement and then to play a leading role in splitting that movement. The Independent Social Democratic Party (U.S.P.D.) which grew out of this division was to a considerable degree Haase's creation, and, for a time, it appeared to give promise of triumphing over the old party. It, too, however, was torn by many of the tensions that had so crippled the S.P.D. and not long after Haase's death, it collapsed. Haase, like the party he had helped to create, was then left without any established group that had a vested interest in preserving his memory.[1]

Another factor that has undoubtedly contributed to Haase's relative obscurity is the paucity of biographically revealing documents. Unfortunately, most of his private papers were lost when his son fled from Germany just prior to the Second World War. Nevertheless, with the kind assistance of many of his relatives, and by making extensive use of the papers and memoirs of his associates as well as the minutes of many of the meetings he attended, it has been possible to develop a reasonably complete picture both of the man and of his work. The result will, hopefully, serve both as a useful case study in what Peter Gay has called the "dilemma of democratic socialism" and as a revealing portrait of one of that movement's most attractive leaders.

I have been assisted in the preparation of this biography by a number of generous individuals, none of whom, however, should be held responsible for whatever defects are to be found in the finished product. As noted above, I have enjoyed the aid and support of many members of the Haase family. In its early stages the work benefited from the kind assistance of Wilhelm Matull of Düsseldorf and the expert advice and suggestions of Prof. Dr. David W. Morgan of Wesleyan University. More recently the manuscript was read by Prof. Dr. Gerald Feldman of the University of California and was improved as a result of his criticisms. Throughout its preparation I have profited from the advice of Prof. Dr. S. William Halperin of Wayne State University. But my greatest debt is clearly to Dr. Walter Friedlander, Professor Emeritus of the

University of California, and Dr. Ernest Hamburger of New York City. It was their many helpful suggestions, their constant encouragement and support, and their extraordinary patience which more than anything else made the completion of this work possible.

In an effort to provide a more complete picture of Haase's personality, I have appended to the biography itself the recollections of three individuals who knew Haase well. I am indebted to Dr. Friedlander, Dr. Hamburger and Dr. Peter Fleischmann for providing these statements and particularly to Dr. Friedlander for suggesting this approach and arranging for them to be written.

Except for a few additions and minor changes which I have made in response to recent publications, the text remains essentially the same as that which was published in German translation by Colloquium Verlag, Berlin.

Hugo Haase

CHAPTER I

FROM DISTANT KÖNIGSBERG

East Prussia, the province in which Hugo Haase was born and lived most of his life, was by no means devoid of a radical tradition despite its reputation as an area dominated by the conservative Junker establishment. In Königsberg, in particular, the Kantian spirit lived on, and the city contributed its full share of leaders to the German left. The political atmosphere within which Hugo Haase was to mature was created by men of the stature of Johann Jacoby and Julius Rupp, veterans of 1848 who late in their lives moved beyond liberalism to Social Democracy.[1]

Haase was not, however, directly exposed to this radical heritage until he moved to Königsberg to begin his university studies. He was born in 1863 in the much smaller and more provincial city of Allenstein, the eldest of ten children. His father, a shoemaker at the time, soon found it necessary to give up his trade and move to Wormditt where he established himself as a relatively prosperous merchant.[2] He had great hopes for his eldest son, and when Hugo was not promoted into the upper form of the local school at the age of eleven, he sent him to Rastenburg to attend the *Gymnasium* there. The move was obviously a wise one, for he graduated first in his class.[3]

Although as yet extremely naive concerning the implications of his decision, Haase had already resolved during his final year in the *Gymnasium* to study law. As he later recalled in a letter to his fiancee, "I glowed . . . with enthusiasm for the legal profession. I could think of nothing finer than to intervene with all my strength so that justice would triumph and the unjustly persecuted would find protection and security."[4] This fervor, however, was rapidly dampened by the uninspiring reality of legal study at Königsberg. He found himself more attracted to the courses in economics and philosophy which he pursued incidentally to his principal course of study. Yet he persisted in his determination to enter the legal profession, hoping that actual practice would prove more rewarding than the petty theorizing which seemed to dominate his formal studies. This expectation was justified, for once Haase had rid himself of his adolescent naivete, his practice proved both successful and personally rewarding.

As a student in Königsberg, Haase gave practical expression to his idealism by becoming a leader of the "Free Student Association," which had been formed in opposition to the older drinking and dueling fraternities. It was also

[3]

while studying at the university that he began to move toward Social Democracy. Drawn by his studies of Marxist literature and repelled by the class rule that manifested itself so much more blatantly in East Prussia than in Germany's southern and western provinces, Haase joined the Social Democratic Party (S.P.D.) after passing the first of two state examinations required of lawyers in Prussia.[5]

At first the young jurist devoted himself merely to routine work within the party, yet his decision to join the Social Democratic movement could not but have an immense impact upon his life. The S.P.D. still labored under the weight of Bismarck's persecutory socialist law, and as East Prussia's only Social Democratic lawyer, Haase would have found it difficult to escape the attention both of his party comrades and of the state authorities, even if he had wished to do so. He very quickly established a reputation as an able defender of the poor and the politically persecuted. Even after the fall of Bismarck and his laws, there were more than enough political cases to keep him busy, especially when these were added to his flourishing civil and criminal practice.[6]

Haase's success soon drew the wrath of the state prosecutor's office down upon him. In 1892 the State's Attorney opened proceedings against the young lawyer before the court of honor of the bar association, charging him with, among other things, having maintained a close relationship with several well known Social Democrats, having spoken for the party in various public meetings, and having repeatedly defended Social Democrats in the courts. "Such encouragement of Social Democratic endeavors," complained the lengthy accusation, "is irreconcilable with the position of a lawyer and severely damages the honor of the profession." When Haase's peers returned a verdict of not guilty, the State's Attorney's office appealed the case to the court of honor of the imperial high court of justice. Even this body, however, declared Haase innocent of most of the charges against him, finding him guilty only of denigrating the police by denouncing their red-baiting.[7] Both the persistence of the state in its efforts to discredit Haase and the difficulty it experienced in achieving the most limited success speak well for his effectiveness.

In spite of his open association with the Social Democratic cause and his explicitly Marxist analysis of the prevailing system of "class justice" in Prussia, Haase was not the kind of provocative revolutionary liable to alienate his professional colleagues unnecessarily. He was no fiery orator; speaking with a pronounced East Prussian accent and in a voice that was often marred by hoarseness, he sought to convince his audience, both in court and in political meetings, by closely reasoned argument and well marshalled facts rather than by rhetorical brilliance. A short, somewhat stocky man with a high forehead and a broad face punctuated by light blue eyes, an angular nose and an unpresumptuous mustache, Haase radiated the image of the cultured middle-class professional, even while addressing the roughest workers' rally.[8] In court, he was liable to cite Kant or even Treitschke in support of a client. Although he often sought to drive home a political point in the course of a trial, Haase generally maintained an acceptably respectful demeanor toward the judges and other court officials.[9] This was not simply a matter of good tactics. In his theoretical discussions of justice in the capitalist state, Haase like most other Social Democrats consistently directed his criticism against the institutions rather than the men who were caught up in the system and could not be expected to act differently than they in fact did.[10]

This tendency to focus on issues rather than personalities was characteristic of Haase throughout his life. Usually warm and friendly in his relationships with colleagues and friends, he rarely allowed himself to be carried away by feelings of personal rancor, even toward his bitterest political opponents.[11] He had little in common with the ascetically inclined revolutionaries to be found on the extreme left with of the S.P.D. He was, rather, an individual who obviously enjoyed life immensely, at least until the war and his political responsibilities began to weigh heavily upon him. He found particular pleasure in such varied activities as travel, long walks in the countryside and evenings spent reading poetry with family and friends.[12]

Haase's marriage to Thea Lichtenstein in 1891 proved extraordinarily successful in spite of the fact that it began under somewhat inauspicious circumstances. Thea was, like himself, the offspring of a middle class Jewish family, and both sets of parents were deeply upset by the young couple's adamant refusal to participate in a religious wedding. It was typical of Haase, however, that he sought to ease his parents' qualms by vigorously denying any lack of respect for their beliefs and by asking his cousin, a cantor, to deliver a secular address at the beginning of the marriage festivities.[13] After the wedding, he was scrupulously considerate of his parents' sensitivities, maintaining a kosher household whenever they visited him.[14]

Thea Haase shared her husband's avid interest in politics as well as his active social conscience. Her brother, Max Lichtenstein, was a leading member of the left liberals in Königsberg.[15] Despite their political differences, the two brothers-in-law soon became good friends.[16] Thea also shared her husband's intellectual interests. She was actively involved in the party's educational programs in Königsberg.[17] Even during the war, the Haase household in Berlin was frequently the scene of informal meetings at which the classics of German philosophy were discussed.[18] It was perhaps above all because of these many common interests that the practical difficulties which Haase's increasing involvement in the Social Democratic movement inevitably brought with it placed no perceptible strain on his marriage.[19]

The impact of Haase's Jewish upbringing is difficult to assess, but despite his early rejection of his parents' religious beliefs, one cannot escape that impression that this element in his background exerted a significant and lasting influence upon his life. Haase was, of course, just one of the small but impressive band of Jewish intellectuals and professionals who moved beyond liberalism to Social Democracy during the pre-war era.[20] For such men, the decision to espouse the cause of the proletariat must have been primarily ideological, and grounds for such a decision are clearly to be found in both the ethical precepts of Judaism and the historical situation of the German Jewish community. Not only did the basic humanitarian idealism of Social Democracy have much in common with the central ethical precepts of the Jewish religion, but the socialist program seemed to speak directly to the condition of the German Jews whose legal emancipation had only recently been completed. Like the Social Democratic worker, the Jew often felt alienated from a society which refused to grant him full equality of opportunity and social acceptance. And it was, of course, only natural that many idealistic Jews felt a particular bond with a group which was persecuted by that society. Finally, the internationalism of the S.P.D. cannot but have appealed to the large number of Jews who were repelled by the increasingly aggressive chauvinism of Wilhelminian Germany.[21]

It is, of course, extremely difficult to document the impact of such general influences upon a specific individual. In Haase's case, however, there is evidence to suggest that he never completely broke with his Jewish heritage. He was one of the relatively few Jewish Social Democratic leaders who never formally severed their ties to the Jewish religious community.[22] He listed himself as a Jew in the official Reichstag handbook throughout his career. Moreover, he continued to maintain close relationships with his parents and with other relatives and friends who remained active and religiously committed Jews. Finally, although it is impossible to document any direct relationship, his attitudes on many issues conformed to what might be expected of a politically and socially concerned Jew during this period in German history. His quest for justice through law, his consistent humanitarianism and internationalism, his identification with the persecuted and oppressed, even his rather abstract and legalistic interpretation of socialist theory were, no doubt, all at least partially conditioned by his Jewish heritage.[23]

Within the party Haase's intellectualism and essentially bourgeois way of life did not, as might have been expected, seriously detract from his growing influence. Any resentment which these may have generated was more than compensated for by his forthright theoretical radicalism and by widespread gratitude for his willingness to serve the poor without thought of compensation. Haase's relative financial success also caused little jealousy, for it enabled him not only to remain independent of party subsidies as he gradually increased the amount of time he devoted to party affairs, but also to give generous assistance to his comrades at times of special need.[24] Moreover, his continuing interest in economics and philosophy placed Haase in a position to exercise a growing intellectual influence within the party. It was as a leader of the "Kantian Reading Clubs," organized by the young Ludwig Quessel in the 1890s, that he helped to bring Otto Braun, the future Prime Minister of Prussia, into the party.[25]

In the 1890s, with the fall of Bismarck and his anti-socialist law and the accelerating industrialization of Germany, the S.P.D. made great strides forward in most parts of the Reich. Although progress was made especially difficult in East Prussia by its largely agrarian economy, its backward political and social structure and its proximity to czarist Russia, the party was able to move slowly forward even there. The East Prussian situation was further complicated by the tendency of potential party leaders to move away to the more advanced industrial centers.[26] Under these circumstances it was only natural that Haase, a young and successful lawyer respected by both workers and bourgeoisie within and outside the party, should be drawn toward the center of the political stage.

In 1894, at the age of 31, Haase was elected to the City Council of Königsberg.[27] To serve as Königsberg's first Social Democratic city councilor was, however, no easy task. Gustav Noske, who was elected to the council in 1899, later noted that the prevailing three-class electoral system insured that the body would be "nothing more than a large clique gathered to protect the interests of houseowners." "I sat across from a closed phalanx of representatives of various interests," Noske recalled, "who differed in nuance, but were equally insensitive to even the most moderate social demands of the working population." Noske concluded his comment by remarking that during the two years he served on the council, he probably worked harder than at any other time during his very active career.[28]

The hard work and frustration involved in city council membershp were, however, not wholly without compensation, for the position enabled Haase to enhance his reputation among local Social Democrats. When Karl Schultze, who had represented Königsberg in the Reichstag since the party first conquered the seat in 1890, died in 1897, it was therefore not surprising that the party chose Haase to succeed to Schultze's mandate. Haase's victory in the by-election thrust him onto the national stage for the first time.

The Wilhelminian Reichstag did not, of course, enjoy the power and prestige of parliaments in the western democracies. The Bismarckian constitution precluded a truly parliamentary regime. Nevertheless, it seemed to not a few observers at the turn of the century that basic constitutional changes were quite possible. The rapidly growing Social Democratic delegation reflected this kind of optimism as it gradually ceased to view the Reichstag merely as a sounding board and began to focus its attention increasingly upon using it to achieve concrete, if limited, improvements for its constituents. Large numbers of Social Democrats came to believe that the Reichstag was becoming the agency of a peaceful revolution, and membership in the Reichstag therefore became increasingly prestigious.

Nevertheless, election to the Reichstag could be a very frustrating experience. This was, of course, especially true for the younger, less experienced deputies who entered the Reichstag full of great expectations about the roles they were going to play, only to discover that the reins of power could only be grasped after much further struggle, if at all.[29] In accordance with Bismarck's efforts to insure that the Reichstag would be dominated by the wealthier classes, deputies were not paid by the state until 1906. This meant that there often was not even a quorum of that august body present in Berlin. Furthermore, inasmuch as the S.P.D. paid its deputies whenever they were in the capital on Reichstag business, the party made every effort to keep its members at home except when absolutely necessary. This practice not only degraded the office of deputy but also reinforced the tendency of the delegation to fall under the domination of a relatively small number of leading figures who planned parliamentary tactics, spoke for the party on most important occasions, and occupied the most important committee positions.[30]

Under these circumstances, the young attorney from distant Königsberg found himself relegated to a relatively minor role. Haase is rarely mentioned in the minutes of the S.P.D. Reichstag delegation meetings, and his rather infrequent speeches on the floor of the Reichstag were largely confined to matters specifically related to his special concern, legal affairs.

Nevertheless he soon established a reputation as an able parliamentarian. His speeches in the Reichstag showed a sure, if unspectacular, competence. Firmly in control of his facts, often conciliatory in tone, yet consistently radical in his basic philosophy, Haase exhibited from the beginning the qualities which would carry him to the chairmanship of the party nearly a decade and a half later. Frequently referring to his own experiences as a practicing lawyer, he avoided any hint of the melodramatic. He often sought to play the practical politician, pointing out how Social Democratic aims could be at least partially reconciled with the programs of the liberal parties and stressing that though his party sought and fully expected eventually to achieve a basic reorganization of society, it was also eager to gain as many immediate improvements as possible. At the same time, Haase made enough references to the fundamental tenets of Marxism and laid enough stress on the necessity of eventual revolutionary change to avoid being identified with the growing revisionist-reformist element in the party. Thus Haase's role in the Reichstag established him clearly as a member of that rather amorphous group , usually called

Marxist centrists, from which national party leaders almost without exception were chosen after the turn of the century.[31]

Moreover, not all of Haase's interventions on the Reichstag floor were of a minor nature. In 1904 his role in a *cause célebre,* the "Königsberg Conspiracy Trial," drew the spotlight of national and even international attention to the deputy from Königsberg, who was the leading defense attorney in the case. The affair involved the prosecution by the Prussian government of a number of German citizens for smuggling political literature into Russia. The charges ranged from conspiracy to insulting the Czar and committing high treason against the Russian government. Haase was immediately called in to represent several of the accused and continued to lead the defense through the long months of investigation and trial which followed. The spectacle of the Prussian government prosecuting German citizens for treason against the Czar, plus the flagrantly high-handed conduct of the Prussian officials in the case, made it a political issue of the first magnitude. With the help of August Bebel, the S.P.D.'s most prominent leader, Haase carried the matter to the Reichstag floor in a series of speeches in January and February, 1904, which aroused considerable excitement both in the Reichstag and among the public at large.

These speeches were obviously designed to serve both offensive and defensive purposes. The S.P.D. could not but view the case as the possible beginning of a new attack upon the legal rights of the party, for the prosecutors claimed that the smugglers, most of whom were party members, were engaged in transporting "anarchist" literature of the most inflammatory sort. The memory of Bismarck's use of such scare tactics to obtain support for his anti-socialist legislation was too fresh to allow the Social Democratic leaders to view these new developments with tranquillity. Actually, the great Social Democratic electoral victory of 1903 may have convinced the government that the revival of such legislation might become a necessity. Haase therefore went to great lengths in his speeches to dissociate both German and Russian Social Democracy from any advocacy of terrorist policies. He further pointed out that inasmuch as all those involved in the Königsberg case were expressly opposed to terrorism, any terrorist leaflets found among the literature being transported by the defendants could in all probability be traced to Russian agents intent on halting the distribution of even the more moderate Social Democratic and liberal materials.

But it was a spirit of vigorous attack that dominated Haase's Reichstag speeches. Citing specific details, even giving the names and aliases of reputed Russian agents, Haase launched a devastating assault upon the Prussian and Imperial governments. He accused them of turning over innocent freedom-loving youths to Russian "barbarism" and of allowing the rights of German citizens to be trampled on to such an extent that the country was now experiencing a "frightening Russification of [its] public life." Repeatedly appealing to his audience's patriotism, he countered the ministerial attacks upon Social Democratic radicalism by declaring that the S.P.D. would do everything possible to restore and preserve the good name of Germany which had been so severely compromised by the government's efforts to return to the shameful period of the Holy Alliance.[32]

This offensive was not without effect. Liberal and Center Party deputies demanded on the floor of the Reichstag that the government answer the Social Democratic charges. Although this additional opposition was by no means as firm as that of the S.P.D., it was apparent that the government had been thrown onto the defensive.[33]

The trial did not take place until July, by which time the prosecution's case had been thoroughly discredited in the eyes of most liberals and moderates.[34] Haase's speeches at the trial, although focused upon the specific details of the matter at hand, touched repeatedly on the broader political questions treated in his Reichstag statements.[35] Once again they were widely reported. Although only three of the nine defendants were acquitted, the others being convicted on the minimal charge of conspiracy, the victory for the Prussian government was clearly pyrrhic at best. The inadequacies of the Prussian legal system had been subjected to devastating criticism, sympathy had been aroused for those struggling against the Russian autocracy, and the grim realities of Russo-German cooperation against the forces of progress had been revealed to a shocked, even incredulous public.

For Haase, the trial marked an important step forward. Not only had he achieved widespread national recognition for the first time, but his close cooperation with Bebel in the Reichstag debates on the case had served to cement an increasingly friendly relationship, a relationship which would prove decisive in determining the future course of Haase's career.

Haase's political activity was not, of course, confined to the Reichstag and the courtroom during these years. Beginning in 1897 he attended the majority of the annual national party congresses as an official delegate. As in the Reichstag, his role was in the early years a relatively modest one. He participated only occasionally in the formal debates,[36] and it was not until 1906 that he was called upon to deliver a major address. Thereafter, however, he asserted himself with increasing vigour on a wide variety of topics.

The title of Haase's speech to the 1906 congress, "Penal Law, Penal Procedure and Punishment," sounded anything but promising, but he succeeded in turning what could well have been a dry and technical lecture into a broadly conceived and emphatic indictment of the entire social order. He began his address with a brief analysis of the origins of judicial systems. "The needs of society determine the content of penal laws," he declared. "The criminal code appears clearly as the superstructure which raises itself on the basis of the whole system of productive relationships." In the case of a capitalist state such as Germany this meant that the entire legal system was oriented toward defending the interests of the ruling classes. The S.P.D. could expect to gain increasing support for the struggle it was obligated to carry on against this system, Haase predicted, for the system failed to change with the social conditions out of which it had sprung, and as the working class became more influential the contradictions between the existing legal norms and the sense of justice of the great mass of the people would be more and more keenly felt.

The basic premises of Haase's speech were thus Marxist. Like so many of his "orthodox" colleagues, however, once he moved beyond the theoretical aspects of his analysis Haase focused his attention largely upon reforms of the kind that many liberals, let alone revisionist Social Democrats, would have endorsed. His demands for equal justice and more humane laws and penal practices project the image of a Kantian believer in the liberal *Rechtsstaat* much more clearly than that of a revolutionary Marxist.

When Haase turned to the more general problem of increasing criminality, he returned to standard Marxist concepts. This development could not be traced simply to economic factors in the limited sense, he declared, but to "the economic structure of society and to the division of the entire society into classes which results from this structure." Any attempt to solve the problem of criminality without attacking these fundamental causes would be useless. But the conclusions he drew from this analysis once again were limited to demands for immediate social reforms such as the introduction of the eight-hour day, better schools, cheaper homes and a more responsible tariff policy that could very well have been made by his revisionist colleagues.[37]

The combination of traditional Marxist revolutionary theory and ethical humanism so strikingly apparent in this speech was to remain characteristic of Haase's thought throughout his career. He had developed a vision of a future society in which the classical ideal of justice for all, augmented by the insights of modern social democracy, would finally be realized. He was convinced that this goal was realistic and that the instrument of its achievement would be the revolutionary working class. The fact that he also demanded short term reforms did not make him a revisionist, but rather reflected his practical approach to politics and his humanitarian concern about the immediate plight of his fellow man. Indeed, in this respect, Haase's position was not unlike that of the leading exponent of "orthodox" Marxism, Karl Kautsky.[38] Moreover, a similar mixture of revolutionary theory and reformist practice had been formally incorporated in the German Social Democratic Party's program at Erfurt in 1891.[39]

Indeed, that Haase already stood rather to the left of the orthodox center than to the right of it is indicated by a letter which he wrote to his wife while at the congress. Although he praised the unusual spirit of unity that had dominated the discussions, he complained that this spirit had led the executive committee to espouse a highly questionable policy of appeasement on the volatile issue of the general strike. Led by Bebel, the committee had asked the congress to declare that a resolution passed the previous year which explicitly sanctioned the use of the general strike was consistent with a statement passed by the Congress of Unions which repudiated "all efforts to settle on a specific tactic by propagating the general strike." "The executive committee," Haase wrote, "thus demands that we commit intellectual hara-kiri."[40]

Haase's defeat in the Reichstag elections of 1907 did not constitute a major personal setback inasmuch as it was the direct result of a temporary conservative-liberal alliance against the S.P.D. and the Center on the colonial issue, and his fate was shared by a large number of his Social Democratic colleagues.[41] Indeed, his role as a party leader continued to expand. In August of that year he attended the Congress of the Second International at Stuttgart. The most important matter considered was the question of what the members of the International should do in case of war. The issue was difficult to resolve, for the Germans, representing the strongest party in the International, resisted demands made above all by the French that specific steps be outlined that every party would be obligated to take if war should threaten.[42]

Although Haase made no speech on this issue, he was called in to help draft an effective compromise resolution.[43] The result was a strong if somewhat vaguely worded declaration that would be repeatedly cited by Haase and his followers during the First World War. "If the outbreak of war threatens," the resolution declared, "the working classes and their parliamentary representatives in the participating countries must . . . utilize whatever means appear most effective to them" to prevent it. "Should war nevertheless break out," the resolution continued, "it is their duty to intercede for its swift conclusion and to make every effort to utilize the economic and political crisis caused by the war to arouse the people and thereby accelerate the dissolution of capitalist class rule."[44]

In several letters to his wife written at the congress Haase indicated how central the issue of international peace had become to his thinking. His enthusiasm for the spirit of amity and solidarity that prevailed was obviously immense. Yet he was highly critical of the German delegation which, he complained, was dominated by the unionists. The majority of his colleagues, he felt, had too little respect for theory. He was therefore delighted when his delegation's overly moderate resolution on the issue of colonialism was defeated by the congress.[45] In another letter he gave further evidence of his critical attitude toward the revisionist elements in the S.P.D. In describing a private conversation with a fellow German delegate, he claimed to have convinced her "that people who again and again cast doubt on the principles of the party, who do not know how to integrate the individual phenomena of social life into a single point of view, and who express in their publications other views than those that have been basic to the party's great achievements, should not occupy positions of trust as representatives of the party. . . ."[46] Haase clearly shared the increasing concern of many of his fellow left centrists about the drift of the party toward reformism for its own sake. And it was because of this concern that he gradually allowed himself to be drawn into the leadership of those who, although intent on maintaining party unity, were adamantly insistent upon the necessity of preserving the traditional theoretical foundations of Social Democracy.

Haase's increasing stature was indicated by the fact that he was asked to deliver the major address on party reorganization at a congress of the Prussian S.P.D. in November 1907.[47] More important, he played a significant role at the national congress of 1908 where he intervened with considerable effect in the long simmering controversy over the party's relationship to the youth movement. For some years proletarian youth groups had been springing up outside of the party structure.[48] Their independence and radical proclivities had aroused increasing uneasiness among party and particularly union leaders. The passage in April 1908 of a repressive law regulating rights of association and assembly throughout the Reich created an opportunity for these leaders to intervene in the affairs of the bourgeoning youth organizations, ostensibly to defend their younger comrades, but in fact to establish firm adult control over them. By the time the party congress met, the trade unions had already taken vigorous action against the movement,[49] thus alerting those in the party who were sympathetic to the youth to the dangers facing their proteges.

A resolution on the issue that had been proposed by the executive committee had been widely criticized as simply another effort to throttle the independence of the youth, and a lively debate broke out at the congress.[50] Haase, who throughout his life evinced a particular interest in young people, intervened to propose that a special committee be appointed to discuss and revise the executive committee resolution.[51] His suggestion was accepted and a committee was appointed under his chairmanship that included a majority of members who shared his own sympathies for the youth movement. The new draft was, indeed, a compromise, for it made no provision for the creation of an independent central organization for young people, but it did allow for the maintenance of separate local youth groups which were to be permitted to direct their own affairs with the assistance of local youth committees set up by the party and the unions. In reporting to the congress for his committee, Haase emphasized that the new draft sought to make it completely clear that the party would not try to curb the independence of the youth movement. Moreover, he urged that those chosen to assist the youth should avoid the schoolmaster's approach; rather, they should seek to "immerse themselves in the youthful soul" and "work lovingly with the young people." Although many of the more conservative delegates undoubtedly had serious reservations about this approach, Haase's speech was received with lively applause, and the revised resolution was accepted unanimously.[52]

The most provocative issue to be dealt with at the meeting, however, was raised by the action of the Social Democratic deputies in the Bavarian and Baden state parliaments who had voted in August for their respective state budgets. By doing so they had violated a resolution passed by the 1901 congress which permitted such an endorsement of the existing regime only under very exceptional circumstances.[53] The debate on the issue lasted several days and generated considerable excitement. Haase wrote to his wife that if the minority had not utilized such "extortionate tactics" a compromise could have been reached which would have preserved the majority point of view. "But if the majority allows itself to be intimidated now," he added, "it will mean not only a triumph for the resivionists. . . . but above all the establishment of the rule of a small group over the entire party." This, he warned, could very well lead to the atomization of the party. "The thought of a party conflict is not a pleasant one," he concluded, "but it cannot prevent me from thinking and acting responsibly."[54]

At the close of the debate a resolution was passed by a large majority which explicitly declared the action of the southern deputies to be irreconcilable with the policy established by previous congresses. It confirmed the earlier policy statements and added that an exception would be allowed only if the rejection by Social Democratic deputies of a state budget would lead to the adoption of a budget less advantageous to the working classes.[55] Despite this apparently decisive defeat, however, a spokesman for the rebellious revisionists immediately rose to read a statement signed by sixty-five delegates which, although it conceded the competence of the congress to decide questions of national policy, reasserted the right of deputies in state parliaments to formulate their own local strategy and tactics.[56]

This sequence of events was symptomatic of the mounting tension within the S.P.D., and Haase, as an increasingly well known and respected spokesman of the left centrists, could hardly have avoided involvement in the resulting internal strife. Indeed, his involvement in this struggle helped to catapult him into the leadership of the national party. In August 1910 the Social Democratic deputies in the parliament of Baden again threw down the gauntlet to the party majority by voting for the state budget. Just a few weeks later the issue became the object of lively debate among German delegates to the

Copenhagen meeting of the International. The radicals at Copenhagen agreed to convene a meeting of sympathetic colleagues on the day before the national congress was to open at Magdeburg. A commission of seven, of which Haase was a member and his friend Wilhelm Dittmann the chairman, was established to make the necessary arrangements.[57]

On September 17 some 210 delegates gathered in a Magdeburg hotel. Dittmann opened the meeting with a short speech declaring that the left had in recent years facilitated the machinations of the right wing leaders by neglecting to organize itself for effective action. After a discussion which indicated that Dittmann's views were widely shared, the delegates assigned to the commission of seven the task of directing left wing strategy on the crucial budget issue.

When the revisionist leaders began collecting signatures at the congress for a motion to assign the question to a study commission, the commission of seven countered by circulating an amendment to the resolution brought in by the executive committee on the issue. Whereas this resolution simply repeated the earlier condemnations of the tactics of the southerners, the amendment was designed to put teeth into the resolution by declaring that those who violated it in the future would "thereby immediately place themselves outside the party." The amendment was quickly endorsed by more than 200 delegates.[58]

The principal speeches on the issue were delivered by Bebel, who spoke for the resolution proposed by the executive committee, and Ludwig Frank, a rising young star within the party, who defended the Baden deputies. Bebel demanded the condemnation of the rebels, but his remarks lacked the bitterness of his earlier attacks on the revisionists. Frank's speech was also relatively mild in tone, and it appeared for a time that the issue would be resolved with a minimum of fireworks.

But the ensuing debate soon made it apparent that the left was no longer willing to temporize. Among the most spirited of the critics was Haase, who declared in an impassioned speech that Frank had not made any definite statement concerning the future behavior of the Baden deputies. "The party comrades throughout the country and the majority of the delegates present here," he asserted, "are not in a mood simply to listen to beautiful speeches or to have paper resolutions drawn up. Rather, they want a guarantee that we will not fall into such party squabbles in the future and that the congress will be recognized by all as the highest authority." They did not wish to throw their friends in Baden out of the party, Haase continued, but the situation had to be clarified. The basic question was whether the majority should rule. To acquiesce in the action of the Baden deputies would be to plunge into a "topsy-turvy world." That could not be permitted. The motion to refer the matter to a study commission was therefore totally unacceptable. The tactics of the southerners were not, as they had been described, "completely new and modern." Rather, they were the "jagged, rusty weapons with which the National Liberals had hurried from defeat to defeat." If the southerners felt that they were correct, they could try to bring about a change of policy through discussion and the usual modes of democratic procedure. In the meantime a decision had to be reached so that the party could return to its united struggle against the common enemy.[59]

The following morning Bebel met with the commission of seven to discuss their amendment. He objected to it because it implied that members could be expelled from the party without having been given the benefit of the normal procedures set up for that purpose. The commission members replied that they considered the amendment simply to mean that future refusal to abide by the decision of the congress would be grounds for the initiation of such procedures, but when the party chairman insisted on his objections they agreed to accept his suggestion that the executive committee simply make a formal statement that it agreed completely with the intent of the sponsors of the amendment and would interpret its own resolution in this light. The commission delegated Haase to work out the wording of this declaration with Bebel.[60]

After Bebel had included in his closing speech the statement that he and Haase had drafted, the latter rose to withdraw the radical amendment, declaring that he and his friends were interested in achieving their goal rather than in debating questions of form.[61] Frank, however, refused to be satisfied with this compromise. His closing speech bristled with disdainful remarks about the "retreat" of Haase and his friends and included the flat statement that "none of you can tell us today what will happen on the occasion of future budget votes. That depends on circumstances."[62] These remarks of course provoked a heated reaction from the majority. Haase immediately asked for an overnight adjournment to allow for informal discussion of Frank's attack, but his request was ignored.[63] After a series of personal remarks by various delegates, the meeting was adjourned for an hour.

Haase and his friends gathered for a hurried meeting and after a lively debate decided to propose a new amendment to the effect that Bebel's statement would be declared a formal resolution of the congress.[64] When the session was resumed, the delegates first passed the executive committee's resolution by a large majority. When the radicals insisted upon an immediate vote on their new amendment, a large number of the southern delegates left the hall. Haase then made a short speech justifying the amendment on the basis of Frank's refusal to make any commitment regarding future action. When viewed as a whole, he declared, Frank's declaration had to be considered "a slap in the face of the great majority of the convention. . . ."[65] The amendment was then passed by a margin of 228 to 64.

At the last party congress before his election to the co-chairmanship of the S.P.D., Haase thus emerged as a leading spokesman for those who viewed with alarm the growing campaign to revise the basic principles of the party. His allegiance to these principles, as defined in the Erfurt Program and as reasserted and refined by party congresses and orthodox theoreticians, would serve as the basis of his political thought and action for the rest of his life.

Despite his aggressive role in the attack on the revisionists, however, Haase continued to be known as something of a moderate. On several important occasions during his rise to prominence he had intervened as a mediator, and even at Magdeburg he had been open to compromise in form if not in substance. Dittmann later recalled that "among our radical friends Haase was considered, next to Bebel, the most competent and at the same time the most conciliatory leader of the left wing of the party, and he was similarly assessed on the right."[66] Moreover, despite the efforts of the executive committee to achieve a compromise solution to the budget issue, when this proved impossible several of its most important members such as Friedrich Ebert and Hermann Müller had also voted for the amendment brought in by Haase and his friends. The question was one which so obviously involved basic principles that the center, as on crucial occasions in the past, had once again united with the left wing.

Haase had thus succeeded in avoiding the isolation which eliminated the more intransigent leaders of the left from consideration for positions in the national party leadership while simultaneously gaining increased respect among this very important group. At the age of forty-seven he found himself a central figure on the national stage, one of those who would have to be considered should the party find itself faced with the necessity of choosing a new national leader.

CHAPTER II

THE CALL TO BERLIN

On January 31, 1911, Paul Singer, who for many years had shared the co-chairmanship of the S.P.D. with Bebel, died. His death brought to a head a long festering leadership crisis within the party. He had been born into a petty bourgeois family, but had early amassed considerable wealth through success in the business world. Despite his proven business acumen and his bourgeois way of life, however, Singer continued to manifest the lively interest in politics he had developed as a follower of Johann Jacoby. At first privately, then openly, he followed Jacoby and his circle from left-wing liberalism into the S.P.D. And like many who came to Social Democracy from this quarter, he generally aligned himself with the left wing of the party. A member of the Reichstag since 1884, he soon was elected co-chairman of the party as well as of the Social Democratic Reichstag delegation. Like Bebel, he was able to work for the party without remuneration.[1] He was also, like Bebel, a personal friend of Hugo Haase.[2]

His death was not altogether unexpected. He had been ailing for some time, as had Bebel and another older member of the executive committee, Karl Gerisch. The physical disabilities of a large proportion of the executive committee members, combined with the increasing complexities involved in directing a rapidly growing mass movement, had made the problem of reforming and strengthening the party leadership a matter of widespread concern for some time. In 1905 the party congress had endorsed a plan for reorganizing the executive which at that time was still being run essentially as it had been when the party was a relatively small organization trying to operate under government persecution. In that year Friedrich Ebert was added to the committee and, with the assistance of Herman Müller, who was elected in 1906, he was able to reconstruct the executive on something approximating modern lines.[3] Indeed, the illness and increasing age of the other committee members meant that Ebert and Müller soon became the dominant figures in day-to-day party operations.

Although the efforts of Ebert and Müller, together with further organizational innovations introduced by the congress of 1909, helped to alleviate some of the most immediate problems facing the party, their very success led to serious misgivings on the part of many on the left who viewed the new men

[18]

as highly competent bureaucrats who threatened to stifle completely the revolutionary fervor of the movement. A generation gap began to manifest itself. The old established leaders who were generally acceptable to all elements within the party were losing control.[4] Their places were being taken by a new breed of "organization men" who, although they had not yet made common cause with the revisionists, nevertheless seemed totally unsuited to direct a movement committed to the eventual overthrow of existing society.

Thus, there was considerable sentiment even before Singer's death for the addition of members to the executive committee who would more clearly represent the traditional philosophy of the party. This feeling was further stimulated by the success of Haase and his friends at the Magdeburg congress.[5] The death of Singer merely provided an opportunity for this sentiment to congeal and focus on a specific course of action. And the fact that it was Singer, considered even more than Bebel the bulwark of the old radicalism, who had passed away made it even more imperative for those who stood generally on the left to demand that his replacement be someone who enjoyed their confidence.

The selection of an appropriate candidate, however, proved to be no easy task. The party simply did not have any more figures like Bebel, who clearly towered over other potential leaders. This situation was partly a result of the recent political fractionalization of the party. Ludwig Frank, for instance, whom some viewed as one of the party's most promising politicians,[6] was absolutely unacceptable because of his close association with the minority reformist wing. On the other hand, the extreme left had no figures of sufficient stature to overcome the increasing isolation of that group. This fact would be made more than ever apparent at the coming congress when Bebel would made a final and decisive break with Rosa Luxemburg, intellectually the most impressive leader on the extreme left.[7]

In this situation the logical place to look for a national leader was, of course, the center, and the most highly respected centrist leaders were generally to be found within the executive committee. Several of the members of that body, however, were, as we have noted, either too old or too ill to qualify. Among the younger members, Friedrich Ebert did show considerable promise, especially as a possible compromise candidate. On the decisive questions he had usually voted with the "principled" left against the revisionists, yet as a competent administrator and practical politician he had considerable appeal for the right wingers. They sensed that he basically sympathized with their approach. Many on the left, however, undoubtedly sensed this too. He was, after all, a member of the new bureaucracy who tended to be more concerned about immediate practical problems than about purity of doctrine. Although apparently seriously considered, Ebert himself recognized that the time was not ripe and declined to seek the position.[8]

It was under these circumstances that Haase's candidacy developed and gradually assumed for many leaders the proportions of a virtual necessity. The suggestion that he should join the national leadership had been made at least as early as 1909. In a letter to Haase in February of that year, Karl Kautsky, the editor of the party's theoretical journal *Die Neue Zeit*, asked him if there was any possibility of his moving to Berlin. "I recognize very well," he wrote, "that it would involve a great financial sacrifice on your part, but if you were active at the center of the movement you could now accomplish things of world-historical significance. . . . Tell me yourself who else could replace Bebel in the leadership of the party."[9]

Kautsky's suggestion was based upon more than this close personal friendship with the East Prussian. His deep respect for Haase's ability and judgment is clearly reflected in the repeated appeals for advice that he addressed to him at that time concerning his controversy with the executive committee over the publication of his pamphlet *The Road to Power*. Kautsky turned to Haase in the first instance, of course, because of his proven skill as a jurist, for the executive committee's objections turned on the question of whether the pamphlet, in which Kautsky argued that revolution was both a very real and an imminent possibility, would be liable to bring down the wrath of the authorities upon both its author and the party. But Kautsky appealed to his friend for political and personal counsel as well, for the dispute raised questions that ranged far beyond mere legal technicalities. None of his other friends, he declared in one of these letters, so successfully combined "the lawyer with the friend and the party comrade."[10]

Moreover, in addition to enjoying Kautsky's personal respect and sharing his theoretical orthodoxy, Haase tended to agree with his misgivings concerning the present leadership of the party. Thus, at one point in this correspondence Haase wrote that he was filled with uneasiness by the way in which the executive committee was open to outside influences that were trying to lead it into "a calm, easy-going course" (*sanftes Fahrwasser*). The committee's treatment of Kautsky, Haase complained, was just one of several recent actions that "must arouse serious concern."[11] On March 18, the anniversary of the street fighting of 1848 in Berlin, he wrote that it was "not very encouraging" to have to concern oneself on such a day with the question of whether it was still permissible for German Social Democrats to speak of "the expectation of proletarian revolution."[12]

For the time being, however, Haase remained unconvinced that he could help solve the leadership problem himself. "Your proposal that I should become a candidate for the executive—and I say this without any false modesty," he wrote several months later, "stems from an overestimation of my person." But he did promise to discuss the matter more fully with Kautsky later.[13]

This modesty and relative lack of political ambition were to prove major obstacles throughout Haase's career. He failed, however, to convince Kautsky, and at this juncture Kautsky was a figure of great importance. Although often maligned, he remained the party's best known and most widely respected theoretician. He was also at the very center of party activity, constantly conversing with party leaders in Berlin and corresponding with those in the provinces. His endorsement could therefore be of very real significance.

More important, by 1911 Bebel had also concluded that Haase should be elevated to the leadership of the S.P.D. Thus, the most eminent political leader and the most influential theoretician of the party were prepared to throw their weight behind the lawyer from distant Königsberg when the leadership crisis became acute. Within a few days after Singer's death both men appealed to Haase to abandon his reservations and become a candidate for the position now available.[14] Once again, however, Haase hesitated. "For the moment I must refuse," he wrote Kautsky on February 12. "I have explained the grounds [for my decision] in a detailed letter to Bebel which you will no doubt see."[15] But his refusal was not categorical, and the two leaders therefore continued to hope that it might be withdrawn.

In the same letter Haase suggested that his associate in Königsberg, Otto Braun, should replace Singer on the executive committee. Braun, who during the war was to become one of Haase's severest critics, was at this time considered a left centrist and therefore appeared to be an appropriate substitute for Haase himself. Haase, who had helped to bring Braun into the Social Democratic movement in the early 1890s, praised him as "very intelligent, consistently far-sighted, theoretically well-grounded, and gifted with journalistic talent."[16]

This suggestion appealed, if not to Bebel and Kautsky, at least to many of ·the radicals who were eager to obtain a swift decision in their favor. The party's control commission, which was dominated by the left, had the legal right to fill vacancies in the executive committee between conventions. On February 12 Klara Zetkin, a left wing member of this commission, wrote Wilhelm Dittmann regarding the leadership crisis and asked him to indicate immediately whether he would be available as a candidate.[17] Dittmann replied that he did not want to be considered, adding that in his view the situation should be resolved at the forthcoming congress in the fall. Furthermore, he felt that Haase, "for whom Bebel, who values him highly, will undoubtedly also intervene," would be the best man for the job.[18]

Despite Dittmann's advice, the control commission did act at once, electing Braun to replace Singer. They did this, however, without consulting the executive committee, which expressed such indignation that Braun withdrew his candidacy. A major criticism of Braun's candidacy came from Bebel who insisted that the new party chairman should be financially independent of the party as he and Singer had been. This view apparently was shared by many of those who feared the growing influence of the professional functionaries.[19] Thus, Haase's suggestion was rejected but a few weeks after it was made. Moreover, Bebel's insistence that the new chairman must be financially independent further limited the number of possible candidates. Haase, as an eminently successful lawyer, could be expected to develop a new and profitable practice if he were to move to Berlin, thus satisfying this further requirement.

Dittmann's support was also not insignificant in the further development of Haase's candidacy. He immediately wrote to several members of the commission of seven which had played such a role in organizing the left at Magdeburg and which remained an active and potentially powerful force in internal party politics. Dittmann's suggestion that Haase be chosen to fill Singer's place met with general agreement. He also addressed a long letter to Haase urging him to become a candidate.[20]

The prospect of Haase's candidacy did not go unopposed. In a letter written to Kautsky in August, Bebel cautioned that he could not guarantee that Haase would be elected by a large majority. Yet, he added, "the more his candidacy is fought by the opposition, the more necessary it is that he accept, even if he is elected by a relatively small majority. In a fight one cannot set conditions for victory; one must take risks when the interests of the party require it."

Bebel predicted that opposition could be expected from both the right and the left. Since Magdeburg, he wrote, Haase and the old radical warhorse, Georg Ledebour, were the potential candidates most hated by the revisionists. He thought that they might try to nominate Hermann Molkenbuhr, an older and relatively moderate member of the executive committee, for whom there was even some support in the executive committee itself. He had sought to head off this maneuver by writing to Molkenbuhr of his own objections to his candidacy.

There was also a very real danger, Bebel continued, that the extreme left would put up its own candidate. He had heard the names of Ledebour and "even Dittmann" mentioned. If that were to occur, he speculated, the revisionist candidate would be certain to win, whoever he might be. Luxemburg had written him months before expressing her opposition to Haase and he had answered her appropriately. "It is possible," he concluded, "that if Rosa's and Klara's (Zetkin) intelligence and judgment are conquered by their passion and blind hate, this will be the result. I believe them capable of such stupidity."[21]

It is probable, however, that by August 5, when Bebel wrote this letter, the danger from the left was already long past. In June, Luxemburg had written Dittmann of a visit to Königsberg where she had discussed the leadership question with Haase at some length. This letter provides no evidence of active opposition on her part to Haase's candidacy. In it she noted that Bebel and many others were supporting him and gave the impression that the matter would be resolved as far as she was concerned by Haase's own decision.[22]

In the meantime Haase continued to hesitate, although by this time he had retreated considerably from his earlier attitude. In her letter of June 17 to Dittmann, Luxemburg predicted that she would receive a definite answer from Haase within two weeks. On July 26 Dittmann finally received a long and generally positive reply to his earlier letter, but Haase still refused to commit himself. "It is not indifference that has caused me to delay my answer so long," he wrote,

but indecisiveness regarding the question which you and a number of other comrades whom I regard highly have put to me. I confess that in March, after lengthy consideration, I rejected the candidacy for the executive committee which had been offered me, above all because I did not feel myself equal to the task. In the meantime, I have been urged from various quarters to abandon my refusal in the interests of the party, since it would be difficult to find a more suitable candidate and since my reservations are not well founded. This has led me to make repeated self-examinations, which have been made even more difficult by the fact that I am closely and happily tied by many bonds to Königsberg and that moving my home to Berlin will require the foundation of a new economic existence and will necessitate a complete change in my family's standard of living. Payment for my party activity is out of the question for me. Comrade Bebel advised me to become a lawyer in Berlin, and this way out could certainly be followed. I have not yet reached a decision, since I still must discuss the matter with a friend who will visit me next week.

Apparently this friend was not negatively disposed toward Haase's candidacy, for the definitive answer was now not long in coming. When Bebel wrote to Kautsky on August 5, he still had no word from Königsberg, but on that same day Haase wrote to Kautsky, "I have . . . succumbed to your and Bebel's attacks, however much I tried . . . to defend myself against them." Even this reply, however, reflected a certain hesitation and lack of self-confidence. "I am, to be sure, convinced," he added, "that in this position I can be of some service to the entire party. Whether my energy will be sufficient or whether it will be too quickly consumed is a question about which I am in doubt." He appended a final plea that if Kautsky should discover some other candidate before the convention, he should intervene for him decisively.

Kautsky's enthusiastic reply left little doubt that this request would lead to no practical result. "It is high time that a man of strong intelligence and energetic personality should finally once again come into the executive," he wrote. "In the past year it has become a universal laughing stock. . . . Bebel himself will have a completely different effect when he is no longer isolated. . . . You two united will give the entire executive a different complexion." The party secretaries were, despite their numerous weaknesses, generally "intelligent and useful" men, he added—and "under good leadership they will accomplish a great deal."[25]

The question of Haase's candidacy had finally been settled, but few thought that his election would completely solve the leadership problem. Haase, Dittmann and other leaders of the left had for some time been agitating for an expansion of the executive committee as well as for a reorganization of the party structure aimed at insuring a closer relationship between the executive and the membership.[26] As the party congress approached they once again mobilized the commission of seven, and again it was on the whole successful in achieving its goals. The original reluctance of the executive committee was overcome,[27] and the congress voted to add two secretaries to it. The question of fundamental reorganization was referred to a study commission which was directed to report to the next convention.[28] Moreover, Otto Braun and Phillipp Scheidemann, who were elected to fill the new secretaryships, were both at the time believed to stand left of center and apparently enjoyed the full support of the commission of seven.[29] Somewhat surprisingly, they also received the votes of the extreme right.

Haase's candidacy, on the other hand, was still considered too provocative to permit any compromise. Instead of bringing in a candidate from their own ranks, however, the revisionists shrewdly threw their weight behind Ebert. When he found his name on the list of candidates, Ebert himself immediately rose to declare that he would under no circumstances run for the chairmanship. He urged his supporters to vote rather for Haase. His plea was, however, answered by the reformist labor union leader Carl Legien, who maintained that he could see no real reason for Ebert to refuse to become a candidate. He praised him highly, noting his long experience in the executive committee and stressing that he had proved himself an effective mediator between the various factions within the party. He further pointed out that the congress had just appointed a commission to plan a reorganization of the leadership structure and that at such a time it was particularly important to elect men who had been actively engaged in the operation of that structure. He therefore urged all those who had intended to vote for Ebert not to be deterred from doing so by Ebert's attempt to withdraw his candidacy.

Richard Lipinski, a member of the commission of seven, then plunged into this unusual debate. He did not praise Haase. Instead, he sought to counter Legien's argument regarding Ebert's importance to the forthcoming discussions of reorganization. The election of Ebert, he pointed out, would preempt the right of the commission to consider carefully whether the party should abandon its practice of electing only unpaid chairmen.

Bebel too then entered the discussion, asserting that whether Legien could understand Ebert's grounds for refusing to become a candidate was of little importance. The decision, after all, lay with Ebert himself. He reported that Ebert's candidacy had been discussed by the executive committee and the control commission some time after Singer's death, but that even at that time Ebert had categorically refused to become a candidate. Moreover, Ebert himself had asked him to stress that his activities as a mediator had been conducted with the full support of his colleagues on the executive committee and therefore deserved no special commendation.

Concerning Haase's candidacy, Bebel observed that he himself had conducted the negotiations and that Haase had only consented to run after repeated efforts on his part to make clear the reasons that motivated the executive committee in supporting his candidacy. He noted further that Haase's move to Berlin would entail considerable financial and personal sacrifice on his part, but that despite this fact he had agreed to serve without salary. He answered the charge that a full-time chairman was needed by pointing out that, despite his legal practice, Haase would be able to visit the party offices daily, an arrangement which would constitute a considerable improvement over past practices.

The revisionists were not yet satisfied, however. Karl Ulrich, of Offenbach, intervened to pinpoint more clearly the right wing's objections to Haase. Touching explicitly on "the purely personal side" of the question, he declared that he and a large number of other delegates had come to the conclusion that "in Ebert we would have a better, a more reliable chairman in view of the immense task of holding the party together as a unity." The reference was obviously to Haase's recent leadership of the left center alliance, and Bebel felt called upon once more to rise to the defense of his friend. "I know what Ulrich is referring to with this remark," he asserted.

In his place I would not have hesitated to express it openly here. I declare further that I find such reservations on the part of Ulrich and his friends completely natural, but I believe nevertheless that he draws the wrong conclusions from Haase's conduct at the Magdeburg convention. Everyone who knows him well knows that he is an unusually conciliatory man who would like nothing less than to provoke differences.

He added that the executive committee laid great weight upon the fact that Haase was an excellent lawyer, whose advice would be extremely useful. In the last analysis, however, he recognized that those who had reservations about Haase would not now be convinced by his arguments and he knew that

Haase's supporters would not abandon him. When the matter was brought to a vote, this prediction proved to be correct. Of the 393 votes cast, Haase received 283 and Ebert 102.[30]

Haase's election represented a temporary return to the traditonal left-center alliance against the right.[31] But the revisionist demonstration against Haase was conducted with a studied restraint usually foreign to such confrontations in the past. Dittmann viewed their opposition as directed primarily toward strengthening Ebert's position as the prospective successor to Bebel.[32] In any case, their relative moderation during the debate, combined with their support of Braun and Scheidemann, indicated that the right wing leaders were eager to avoid the kind of clash that might once more have cemented the left and center securely together. Unfortunately for Haase, they were largely successful in this. As George Kotowski has pointed out, the elections at the 1911 congress "were the last victory of the organized radicals."[33]

Haase thus assumed his party's highest office under somewhat inauspicious circumstances. Openly opposed by the growing right wing, his candidacy had been endorsed by many on the extreme left only because of that group's increasingly apparent isolation. He had, to be sure, received the enthusiastic support of the most important leaders of the center, but many of their colleagues presumably shared at least in part the reservations of the revisonists concerning the potential divisiveness of Haase's radicalism and only supported him out of loyalty to Bebel and because of the lack of a suitable alternative. Although well known to most party leaders for his success as an attorney and his increasingly active role in internal party politics, he had not yet developed a secure reputation among the masses of the party faithful. He remained for many simply a provincial politician as yet untested as a national party leader.

Moreover, he was hampered by his own serious reservations concerning his ability to succeed in his new position. He possessed little of the firm self-confidence that was so important an element in Bebel's character. And he must have been aware of the fact that his mandate was both weak and unclear. Supported by the center as a conciliator who could maintain the fast crumbling edifice of party unity, he was endorsed by the left and left-center primarily because he was determined to preserve traditional principles against the rising tide of revisionism. His position, in short, reflected the basic quandary confronting the party as a whole. Despite its growing numerical strength, the S.P.D. was increasingly divided and confused about its mission. The very process by which Haase was selected indicates how unclear the party leaders were as to their ultimate goals. He was chosen as much for negative as for positive reasons. In a very real sense his candidacy represented one of the final thrusts of a centrism that was rapidly losing its viability.

If he were to have any success at all, Haase needed time to prove his leadership ability in the day-to-day affairs of the movement. But time was the all-important factor in this perspective, and sufficient time was not available. Within less than two years after his election the party would find itself deprived of its one tried and universally respected leader, Bebel, who was also Haase's most effective source of support. A year later it would be forced to confront, in the World War, the greatest challenge ever faced by Social Democracy, and that challenge would inevitably force its leaders to abandon the increasingly shaky tightrope of centrism.

CHAPTER III

THE CRISIS FORESHADOWED

The S.P.D. emerged from the elections of January 1912 as by far the strongest party in Germany. More than a third of the voters had cast their ballots for Social Democratic candidates, and despite the inequitable distribution of electoral districts, the party had won 110 seats in the Reichstag, nineteen more than its nearest rival. This success, though widely predicted, had an immense impact upon both the supporters and the enemies of Social Democracy. The inexorable progress of the proletariat toward the attainment of political power, predicted so long before by Marx, had apparently been dramatically confirmed. The defeats of 1907, which in any case had been accompanied by another increase in the total number of votes garnered by the party, now appeared only a momentary aberration in the upward spiral of Social Democratic success. And the scale of the victory could not but lead to the escalation of the political struggle to a new level. "The party of four million cannot be ignored by the ruling regime," predicted Kautsky in his analysis of the election results.

It must either make concessions to the party or declare a war to the death against it. We will be the winners in either case. For the class whose interests our party defends is the only class which steadily grows. And in all of the questions on the agenda, and about which the electoral campaign was fought, we represent, together with the interests of the proletariat, those of the entire nation. It will therefore not be long before the great majority stands behind us.[1]

The tremendous enthusiasm with which the victory was greeted was, however, tempered from the beginning by a consciousness among at least some Social Democratic leaders that with success would necessarily come both new dangers and new responsibilities. The possiblity of a "war to the death" could hardly be viewed with equanimity by those charged with the practical direction of the party. Thus Bebel wrote to Adler on the day of the general election that he did not share Kautsky's optimism. "The better the election goes for us," he predicted, "the worse will become the general situation. We may then experience some remarkable things. Our opponents will not go under without defending themselves."[2]

Moreover, such a drastic change in the political situation would necessarily bring into much sharper focus the fundamental tactical questions so long debated on a largely abstract level by a party grown accustomed to the idea of achieving real power only in the indefinite future. It was no longer possible to insist that the party should simply attend to its routine organizational tasks aimed at achieving limited gains within the context of the unshaken old regime. The possibility of the S.P.D. breaking out of its traditional isolation, already exploited with some success in the sourthern states, would now have to be considered seriously on the national level. On the other hand, the widespread belief that the old regime was not likely to acquiesce peaceably to a substantial accretion of power to the S.P.D. gave new immediacy to the contrary emphasis upon the efficacy of mass, even revolutionary action. The traditional centrist position which had so long sought to reconcile these divergent views faced the prospect of erosion. The centrifugal forces of extreme right and extreme left could now be expected to demand with increased vehemence that a basic decision, so long postponed, should finally be made. The gravity of this problem was sensed by Bebel, who thus concluded his letter of January 12 to Adler: "We will have a remarkably mixed group in the [Reichstag] delegation and the reins must be taken firmly in hand. Yet I expect that it will be more the stupidity of our opponents than our own skill and insight that will bind us together."[3]

Until the war actually forced the issue, Bebel's prognosis proved essentially correct. The leaders of the old regime indicated, on the one hand, little interest in fostering the kind of compromise that might have led the S.P.D. to adopt a frankly evolutionary policy, while on the other hand they also avoided the kind of extreme provocation that might have evoked a revolutionary response. Despite this temporary reprieve, however, it became increasingly apparent that the new situation still further limited the opportunities for flexible and creative guidance by the party's centrist leadership. Even more than before, they were compelled to concentrate their energies on the single problem of maintaining party unity.

Haase was one of the many former deputies returned to the Reichstag by the massive victory of 1912. As co-chairman of the party, however, he now played a role very different from that which he had played as a provincial lawyer during his earlier terms. He was immediately elected by his colleagues to the co-chairmanship, with Bebel and Molkenbuhr, of the greatly expanded delegation. As such he now was often delegated to represent the S.P.D. in negotiations with other parties. He also became a member of the more important commissions where much of the work of the Reichstag was actually transacted. Finally, his increasing importance was reflected in his much more frequent and more important interventions on the floor of the Reichstag itself.

One of the first issues that Haase was called upon to deal with in his new capacity involved the efforts of the Social Democrats to obtain the election of

one of their number to the presidium of the Reichstag. The three co-chairmen of the delegation were directed to carry on negotiations toward this end with the Progressive, National Liberal and Center Parties. The very fact that the S.P.D. seriously claimed the right to such a position reflected both the party's new sense of power and its openness to fundamentally evolutionary tactics. The results of this effort, however, made it apparent that the road ahead was not to be an easy one. Although the Social Democratic candidate, Scheidemann, was indeed elected to the provisional presidium, the National Liberal and Center Parties soon withdrew their support, and in the elections to the permanent presidium a few weeks later he suffered defeat.

The Scheidemann candidacy was an issue of relatively little consequence in itself, but the Social Democrats' temporary success and ultimate failure in the matter were symptomatic of the essential weakness of their position. The political isolation of the S.P.D. had obviously not been overcome by its electoral victory, and as long as this was the case, the party appeared, at least to those who rejected outright revolutionary action, to have no alternative but to continue its frustrating policy of criticizing the existing regime without any serious hope of materially influencing it. "Whoever assumed that the massive demonstration of the people in the elections . . . would lead to an about-face in politics was deeply disappointed," reported the Reichstag delegation to the 1912 party congress.[4]

Indeed, the entire Reichstag session of the spring of 1912 proved to be a particularly barren one. The only concrete achievement from the Social Democratic point of view was the passage of a moderate revision of the criminal code. Otherwise, the general tendency seemed largely regressive. This was above all true concerning one of the central issues of the recent campaign, the accelerating arms race.[5] As party and delegation chairman and as one who was rapidly establishing himself as an expert in international affairs, it was Haase who was chosen to make the principal speech against a government demand for further military expansion. His vigorous attack upon the military authorization bill, however, fell largely on deaf ears,[6] and the bill passed easily with liberal support.

The enthusiasm generated by the victory of January had, therefore, been considerably dampened by the time the first session of the new Reichstag ended in May. The sense of frustration, even of stagnation, which was to haunt the party during the immediate pre-war period had already begun to manifest itself. This feeling of malaise was reinforced by the continuing leadership problem. Here too, Kautsky's predictions of a few months before proved unduly optimistic. Bebel's physical disability, though interrupted by short periods of partial recovery, continued to plague both the Reichstag delegation and the executive committee. The election of Haase did not, as Kautsky had hoped, solve the problem. Although there is no evidence to suggest incompetence on his part, it is clear that Haase found himself in no position to provide the kind of forceful leadership that Kautsky and others were seeking.

His move to Berlin in the spring of 1912 was, of course, distracting. The establishment of a new law practice required both time and energy.[7] Furthermore, although Haase was well acquainted with many national as well as local Berlin party leaders, the development of firm relationships of mutual trust and friendship with these men was of necessity a gradual process. Moreover, although Haase and Bebel remained on very friendly terms, their partnership did not prove to be as fruitful as Kautsky had predicted. Writing to Victor Adler in May 1913, Kautsky reported that although Haase was a splendid fellow and worked very well in the executive committee, he was unfortunately unable to impress Bebel as Singer had done.[8] A month later Kautsky again praised Haase as "a very good leader" and by far the most capable member of the executive outside of Bebel, but complained that he did not have enough authority to exercise really effective leadership. He blamed this situation on the fact that Haase was still too little known outside of his own circle and that he was neither a brilliant nor a moving speaker.[9]

Under these circumstances it is not surprising that Ebert continued to dominate much of the work of the executive committee. Haase, who could only spend an hour or two a day in the party offices and was at times called away from important meetings by his other responsibilities, was in no position to compete effectively with the experienced fulltime professional.[10] Furthermore, Haase, as a theoretically oriented intellectual, found himself isolated in a committee dominated by pragmatic relatively uneducated bureaucrats who naturally enjoyed a close rapport with Ebert. His only consistent ally was Luise Zietz, and her energies were fully engaged in organizing activities for the rapidly increasing number of women in the movement.

This situation was further exacerbated by Bebel's death during the summer of 1913 and Ebert's subsequent election to the co-chairmanship of the party with Haase. Ebert and Haase were unable to work well together. Although there is little evidence to suggest that they differed openly at this point on theoretical issues, Kautsky reported to Adler in October 1913 that Ebert was jealous of his colleague and had complained that Haase was inclined to act too independently.[11]

Haase's elevation to the party-chairmanship tended to exclude him from active participation in the factional strife that continued to manifest itself within the party. It was an established policy that executive committee members should try to avoid open involvement in intraparty disputes,[12] but Haase may well have gone unusually far in this direction in an effort to overcome his earlier reputation for partisanship. Certainly this, along with the relative weakness of his position in the committee, would help to explain the fact that his influence is extremely difficult to trace during the final years before the war.

In keeping with his policy of internal neutrality, Haase did not attend a meeting of some thirty radical deputies at Eisenach called by his old friends Gustav Hoch and Georg Ledebour to consider the report of the reorganization commission prior to the 1912 party congress.[13] Moreover, as a presiding officer at the congress itself, he often found it necessary to censure the more vituperative outbursts of some of the left-wing spokesmen. Apparently his efforts to assume a relatively non-partisan role were successful, for in 1912 he was reelected to his post with a majority only slightly smaller than that of Bebel.[14]

Perhaps the high point of the congress was Haase's speech on imperialism, a topic very much on party members' minds during these final years before the war. He devoted the first part of his address to a rather dry description, replete with elaborate statistics, of the recent growth of international trade and the concomitant expansion of imperialistic pretensions on the part of the major industrial powers. He described these developments in terms of the by now familiar argument that imperialism represented the highest and final stage of capitalism, but he emphasized that the age of imperialism was fraught with grave danger, for it was characterized not only by world-wide economic competition, but also by the willingness to resort to brute force to achieve economic goals. There was, therefore, a natural tendency for international tension to increase, for armaments races to develop, and a very real possibility that the ultimate result would be war.

There were few within the ranks of Social Democracy who would have challenged Haase's analysis to this point, but the question had now to be raised: must this process of necessity continue to its apparently logical conclusion, the collapse of the capitalist system in the catastrophe of world war? This question had recently been hotly debated in the party's press and was obviously of considerable practical as well as theoretical moment.[15] Haase, at least, was deeply enough impressed by the persuasiveness of this argument to devote much of the latter part of his address to its refutation.

In his attack on the pessimists' position, the predominance of humanitarian and ethical considerations in Haase's thought once again became clearly apparent. Admitting, indeed stressing, the great danger of world war, he nevertheless emphasized that Marx and Engels had often warned against the simplistic acceptance of a fatalistic philosophy of history. He pointed out that despite the fact that the Social Democrats had always recognized the tendency of capitalism to exploit the working classes, they had never slackened their struggle to attenuate the effects of this exploitation, and this fight had been remarkably successful. Just as the proletariat had been able to make its power felt at home, so the growing forces of international socialism should continue to strive to counteract the ominous drift toward world war. To be sure, the general tendency of the capitalist system was toward such a conflict, yet there were also contrary tendencies which could be utilized by an alert socialist movement. The imperialist phase of capitalist development had, for instance, increased the economic interdependence of the ruling classes. Many of the great industrial magnates were not unaware of this fact, and several of them had sought to work for peace during recent international crises. Moreover, if a part of the burden of the arms race could be shifted to the possessing classes, as was already to some degree the case in England, their enthusiasm for the crassest sort of imperialistic adventurism could be expected to diminish significantly.

The nature of modern warfare also gave the proletariat an effective weapon against uninhibited jingoism, Haase argued. It was widely recognized by military experts that the élan of the masses would play a very significant role in any future conflict, and the various governments would act with greater circumspection if they realized that their troops would participate in any future conflict only against their will. They were also not unaware of the fact that military defeat would in all probability drive large numbers of people into the ranks of Social Democracy. Thus, it would be absurd to allow the ominous development of imperialistic competition simply to take its natural course.

It was undoubtedly true that permanent peace and the end of exploitation would not come until the capitalist system had collapsed before the onslaught of international socialism, but until that victory was achieved it was their duty to promote international ties, to strengthen their political and economic organizations and to do everything in their power to reduce the dangers inherent in imperialism.[16]

Thus Haase had again deduced essentially reformist tactics from what appeared to be fundamentally revolutionary premises.[17] As Carl Schorske has pointed out, his formula for the party's policy in international affairs closely paralleled that already being pursued on the domestic scene.[18] Moreover, this point of view was obviously shared by a large majority of party leaders, for Haase's speech was greeted by prolonged and stormy applause, and in the subsequent debate he was supported by representatives from nearly every point on the political spectrum within the party.[19]

Yet there remained an articulate minority on the extreme left that had no intention of being stilled by this demonstration. The attack on Haase's speech and the resolution which he had introduced in conjunction with it was led by Paul Lensch, a Reichstag deputy and editor of the *Leipziger Volkszeitung* who had recently been carrying on a running debate on the issue with Karl Kautsky in the pages of *Die Neue Zeit*.[20] He was particularly critical of Haase's position insofar as it raised hopes of international agreements to limit arms production. This point of view, he declared, was utterly utopian and was symptomatic of the basic difference between his own position and that of Haase. The arms race was, he maintained, a natural and necessary outgrowth of existing economic conditions. The course of world history could not be altered. Capitalism without the use of force was unthinkable.

Furthermore, the "contrary tendencies" cited by Haase were illusory. In fact, bourgeois resistance to imperialism was declining. The only genuine contrary tendencies were to be found in the international socialist movement, and it opposed the whole capitalist system rather than such specific manifestations of it as the arms race. To be sure, the party should make use of bourgeois peace proposals such as those put forward by the English government, but far from viewing them optimistically as Haase had one, they should be recognized for what they were, selfish efforts to maintain the status quo. It was unfortunate but nevertheless true that almost all progress within a capitalist society had to be made in ways which Social Democrats abhorred. Thus, the building of large national armies, while indeed increasing the danger of war, simultaneously created the material basis for the militia system which socialists demanded. Disarmament, on the other hand, would inevitably lead to the creation of a praetorian guard, a development which the party could not condone. In this specific case, therefore, there was no reason why the S.P.D. should try to obstruct the course of history. In the last analysis the progress of imperialism must necessarily sharpen the class struggle and thus prepare the way for the final victory of socialism. It was toward this end, he concluded, that the S.P.D. should direct its activities, for to be prepared for the final conflict would be all-important.[21]

The criticism voiced by Lensch and his friends represented the kind of doctrinaire revolutionism which gained widespread acceptance within the left wing of the opposition during the war when the course of events seemed to lend the impressive weight of observable fact to theoretical logic. The acceptance of such an approach in 1912, however, would have necessitated a radical break with the whole trend of pre-war Social Democratic thought and practice both within Germany and in the International as a whole. Thus Lensch's attack received but little support, and Haase's resolution was passed against only three negative votes and two abstentions.[22]

The peace issue continued to serve as a focal point of party activity during the remaining months before the war. The Balkan disturbances of 1912 elicited a much more energetic response from the International than had the Moroccan crisis of the previous year. Moreover, on this occasion it was the usually cautious Germans who at several points seized the initiative in pressing for early and effective action. Any attempt to ascribe this striking change in attitude on the part of the S.P.D. solely to Haase's presence on the executive committee would clearly be unjustified, but that it was an important factor cannot be doubted.

Soon after the party congress, Haase headed a German delegation to a meeting of the International Bureau summoned to Brussels to discuss the situation. Meeting at a moment when war had broken out in the Balkans, the Bureau decided to convene a special congress of the International at Christmas time in Basel to deal with the crisis. When the danger appeared to be moving toward a new peak shortly thereafter, the congress was, at the suggestion of the Germans, moved up to November 24 and 25.[23]

The weeks preceding the congress were marked by a series of well-coordinated and often massive peace demonstrations in major cities of most of the nations represented in the International. In a letter to friends in Königsberg, Haase described one such demonstration in Berlin's Tempelhof Park in which more than 200,000 people participated. As the members of the immense crowd raised their hands to proclaim their opposition to war, the sun broke through the cloudy skies to illuminate the scene, creating an "unforgettable" impression.[24] The enthusiasm and sense of purpose that was built up during these weeks within the ranks of international socialism had seldom if ever been equalled.

The Basel Congress itself was conducted in this same spirit. It was in effect an international demonstration. All of the major decisions had been worked out in the International Bureau before the congress convened.[25] As vice president of the congress and spokesman for the German delegation, Haase was called upon to address the delegates on two occasions. In the course of these speeches, both of which were greeted by stormy applause, he presented essentially the same point of view he had so recently expressed at the party congress, but he did so in far more vivid and dramatic terms. He spoke of the "revolutionary thoughts and feelings" that filled their hearts and minds, but which were directed "not toward destruction but toward peace and international reconciliation."[26] He described the suffering of the victims of the Balkan Wars in moving terms, but declared that there as elsewhere the ranks of Social Democracy would continue to grow until one day they would be able to rebuild at least in part what now was being destroyed. He stressed the danger of a world war and cautioned that the diplomats could not be depended upon to prevent such a catastrophe. But, he declared, the international proletariat would make its power felt. While explicitly recognizing that that power had limits, he emphasized that it was nevertheless a factor that could not be lightly pushed aside. After the great world-wide demonstrations of the proletariat, the rulers must realize that they could never convince the workers to go into battle with the enthusiasm so necessary in modern warfare.[27]

Speaking for the German delegation, he reiterated the central point of his argument against the spokesmen of the extreme left at the party congress. The German proletariat, he declared, was convinced that its most important task was to spread its own enthusiasm for peace to other levels of the population. They would demand that the German government call a halt to the provocative acts of its Austro-Hungarian ally, and they would work for the establishment of a relationship of mutual understanding between France, Germany and Great Britain, "the strongest bearers of civilization and human progress." With this declaration of western solidarity he coupled an attack upon the "internally rotten" Russian autocracy, an expression of the Russophobia so long nurtured by the S.P.D. and of special moment to an East Prussian such as Haase. He promised, finally, that the Germans, "using the methods which our conditions . . . permit," would do everything in their power to maintain world peace.[28]

The manifesto passed by the congress reflected the great sense of urgency that dominated the proceedings. It was formulated in unusually vigorous and militant terms. One segment that was crucial from Haase's point of view endorsed his position that the socialist movement should look beyond the proletariat for allies in the struggle against war. Still more important in the long run was the inclusion of a categorical statement that any future war must be considered imperialistic in character and dealt with accordingly.[29] The Basel manifesto would thus serve as a primary source of support for Haase and his colleagues in the opposition during the war.

Long after the delegates had left Basel, the member parties of the International continued their efforts to influence their governments. Although it is extremely difficult to determine what impact these activities actually had upon the torturous course of European diplomacy, it is quite apparent that many socialist leaders, Haase among them, were convinced that they had been indeed significant, and this conviction undoubtedly contributed to the new "wave of optimism" that swept through the International in 1913.[30]

Yet the socialist peace campaign was not without its political perils during these tense months. In spite of the fact that the S.P.D. had never claimed that it would try to halt a war by direct action—indeed, it had been the German party that had objected most vigorously to the enunciation of such a policy by the International—the majority parties in the Reichstag neglected no opportunity to embarrass the Social Democrats by imputing such designs to them. The Basel Congress and the campaign that accompanied it provided the occasion for new attacks of this kind in the Reichstag. In the course of a foreign policy debate early in December 1912, Haase had to accept the unpleasant duty of responding to a blunt assertion by a spokesman of the Center Party that the S.P.D. planned to halt any war by fomenting revolution. In his reply,

Haase quoted Lassalle's dictum that revolutions cannot be "made" at will and Kautsky's declaration in *The Social Revolution* that no Social Democrat could desire a war even in order to bring on the final revolution. When pressed further by interjections from the floor, Haase declared explicitly that "none of us thinks in terms of making a revolution in order to prevent war." Indeed, he went on the assert that the German party even opposed the use of a mass strike for such purposes.[31]

This explicit denial of all the threats contained at least by implication in the manifestoes of the International was no doubt considered a political necessity by most party leaders, but it could not but have been greeted with serious misgivings by those, both at home and abroad, who had long been critical of the timorousness of the German Social Democrats. Once more Haase had been compelled by his new position as a national leader to draw a clear line between himself and many of his colleagues and friends within the party and the International.

Despite such irritating incidents, however, the spirit of Basel continued to pervade the International. The emphasis at the congress upon the necessity of achieving amity among the western European nations, which was so basic to Haase's pacifism, appears to have made a particularly strong impact. Even the pointed and strikingly perceptive attacks upon the nationalistic tendencies to be found within the S.P.D. made by the French Socialist Charles Andler early in 1913[32] failed to substantially diminish the atmosphere of good will that had developed between the French and German parties. Writing to his son, who was in France at the time, Haase defended his party vigorously against Andler's charges. He accused the Sorbonne professor of providing ammunition for the chauvinists. "If any party has consistently and realistically fought against militarism and imperialism . . . ," he wrote, "it is German Social Democracy. . . ."[33]

In the same letter Haase reported the publication on March 1 of a joint manifesto of the French and German parties against the arms race. He described the manifesto, which had been proposed by the S.P.D., as "a brilliant witness to the basic agreement of both parties."[34] A few weeks later another effort to promote Franco-German amity was launched by several Swiss political leaders. Acting in the spirit of Basel, the leaders of both socialist parties agreed to the Swiss suggestion that an interparliamentary conference be called that would include non-socialist as well as socialist deputies. In a joint statement by the S.P.D. and its sister party in France vigorous support was promised for "all efforts by bourgeois groups and parties" directed against chauvinistic agitation, expansionist politics and the arms race.[35]

Haase played a leading role at the conference, which met on May 11 in Bern. He delivered a major address and was elected co-chairman with the French Senator Paul Henri Benjamin d'Estournelles de Constant. The participants met in a friendly atmosphere and produced a broadly worded statement in which they promised to work for the reduction of armaments and to strive to overcome the misunderstandings and conflicts that had arisen between the two countries. They also decided to establish an interparliamentary committee to continue and expand the work begun at the conference.[36] The Bern conference, however, could hardly be considered an unqualified success. Out of the total of 155 deputies who participated, only thirty-four were Germans, and, of these, twenty-eight were Social Democrats. In striking contrast, many of the French deputies were non-socialists.[37] The frustrating isolation of the S.P.D. had once again been made abundantly apparent.

Even the party's one apparent parliamentary success of 1913 was far from an unmixed blessing. Owing to the fact that the government's demand for further expansion of the military establishment was coupled with proposals for the introduction of direct taxation, long a principal plank in the Social Democratic platform, the Reichstag delegation found itself in the unenviable position of having to decide whether it should help to secure a breakthrough on the tax issue at the expense of accepting at least partial responsibility for the continuation of the arms race. That it finally chose to do so once again indicated the limitations of its pacifism.

When the military bill was placed before the Reichstag, Haase again led the Social Democratic attack upon it. His arguments largely paralleled those he had expressed in his other anti-war speeches. On this occasion, however, he emphasized with particular vehemence the danger of tying German policy to that of Austria-Hungary and predicted that any attempt to go to war in support of the "stupidity and lust for power of the Austrian politicians" would "unleash an outburst of indignation such as we in Germany have never yet experienced." He admitted that chauvinists were active in France just as in Germany, but, quoting from the joint manifesto of the French and German socialist parties issued just a few weeks previously, he proudly pointed out that French Social Democrats, like their German comrades, were vigorously engaged in agitation for peace. The international situation, he insisted, gave no grounds for such an immense increase in German military might. The bill was therefore obviously designed not to serve defensive purposes, but rather to support the aims of the imperialists and to strengthen the representatives of the status quo. Once again he countered the charge that the S.P.D. wanted to leave the nation defenseless by claiming that it actually sought to increase its military potential through the institution of a militia system, a system which, however, was useful only for defensive purposes. He concluded by dramatically quoting from one of Fichte's "Speeches to the German Nation" in which he had urged the creation of an "empire of justice" characterized by "freedom based on the equality of all. . . ."[38]

Just as in 1912, however, Social Democratic oratory could do little to hinder the rapid passage of the military bill, supported as it was by every other party in the Reichstag. Regarding the military bill itself, therefore, the party was forced into its traditional position of vain protestation against the inevitable. This situation was radically altered, however, when the debate moved on to the question of determining how the new expenditures were to be met. The problem of maintaining a principled position in the world of practical politics, so long debated primarily in relation to the party's role in the southern Landtage, now had clearly to be faced on the national level.

The resolution of this fundamental and in many ways portentous question proved to be difficult in the extreme. In the course of the long and at times heated debate in the delegation meetings of the early summer a wide variety of points of view were expressed. The majority insisted that the delegation was obligated to support the new direct taxes, especially inasmuch as at least one of these, a property tax, was in danger of defeat if Social Democratic support should be withheld. The party could not turn away from this opportunity for a major victory, especially in view of the fact that the passage of the military bill itself could not be prevented.

The opposition to this point of view ranged from those who maintained that the S.P.D. must remain true to the principle "for this system, not one man, not one penny" to those who took a largely tactical position, arguing that the delegation should at least vote against that part of the tax bill which would be certain to pass even without Social Democratic support. The final decision was reached on June 26 by a vote of fifty-two to thirty-seven with seven abstentions, whereupon the delegation unanimously agreed that the minority would, as in the past, support the majority position. Representatives of the various points of view then were selected to draw up a joint statement which was read by Haase in the Reichstag on June 30.[39] "The military bill has become law," he declared. "Thus we stand now only before the question: who will bear its costs? We have constantly demanded that the burden of arms not be placed upon the propertyless classes." In order to prevent the introduction of other, less fairly assessed taxes and in the belief that the new taxes represented a step in the right direction, he continued, the S.P.D. would support them. "In so doing," he concluded, "we are moved by the conviction that the more direct involvement of the possessing classes in bearing the costs of the arms race . . . will help to cool their ardor for it and thus will simplify our struggle against militarism."[40]

The role of the Social Democratic delegation in securing the passage of the new taxes was, of course, viewed by many as a major victory. The party seemed finally to have begun the process of breaking down the isolation that had insured its impotence in national affairs. Many others, however, were deeply troubled by the party's involvement in the arms race, and not a few were convinced that the S.P.D. had allowed itself to become entangled in an inexcusable compromise with the existing system. Far from providing a satisfactory resolution of the matter, therefore, the statement read by Haase in the Reichstag unleashed a spirited debate in the party press which set the stage for a lengthy reiteration at the national congress in September of the arguments already presented within the Reichstag delegation. The strength of the opposition was indicated by the fact that a resolution sustaining the action of the delegation was opposed by 140 delegates.[41]

Unfortunately, it is impossible to determine where Haase stood on this crucial issue. Although many of his friends and future associates in the wartime opposition voiced vigorous criticism of the delegation's policy during the debate at the party congress, others did not,[42] and Haase himself was prevented by illness from attending. From one of his letters to his son, written during the spring of 1913, it is at least apparent that he hoped that the delegation would be successful in shifting the burden of the arms race onto the possessing classes,[43] but this does not mean that he would necessarily have supported any given tactic to achieve this end. Whatever action he may have in fact taken, it is clear that his decision cannot have been an easy one.

Moreover, the bitter feelings aroused by the controversy over the military bill must have contributed significantly to the rapidly growing sense of malaise with which Haase and his colleagues in the party leadership now had to contend. This feeling was further aggravated by a stagnation in membership growth, increasing labor troubles, a series of defeats in Landtag elections[44] and perhaps most important, the death of Bebel during the summer of 1913. Bebel had, of course, long been failing, but he nevertheless still represented the last remaining tie with the party's former sense of unity and purpose. He was the last figure of sufficient stature to stand somewhat above the increasing turmoil of intraparty strife. The situation was still further complicated by Haase's severe illness which prevented him from playing any sort of directive role during much of the summer and fall of 1913.

The election of Ebert at the 1913 party congress to fill the vacancy created by Bebel's death could, of course, do little to improve the situation. Despite his proven competence as an administrator and organizer, Ebert was in no position to bridge the widening fissures within the S.P.D., to reendow it with the sense of unity and purpose it so desperately needed. Moreover, his relationship with Haase was, as has been suggested, already far from exemplary. Their partnership was anything but propitious at such a moment.

Not long after the party congress, Haase's position was made still more difficult by the election of Philip Scheidemann to replace Bebel as co-chairman of the Reichstag delegation. Scheidemann's election appears particularly portentous in retrospect because of the circumstances surrounding it. In two ballots which were taken on December 2, 1913, Ledebour, the candidate supported by the left, appeared to be the winner by a margin of one vote.

Objections were raised, however, because of his failure to receive an absolute majority, and after a long discussion, it was decided that a new election should be scheduled for some later date.[45] When a third and final ballot was taken on December 10, Scheidemann was declared the winner by a majority of three votes.[46] It is unlikely that the tempestous Ledebour would have been able to play a really decisive role even as co-chairman with Haase of the delegation.[47] Nevertheless, it is at least conceivable that the course of the wartime crisis might have been significantly altered by his election, for not only would Haase have had an ally, however troublesome, in a position of some power, but it would also have meant that Scheidemann, who proved to be one of the most effective leaders of the majority faction, would then have found it more difficult to assert himself in the delegation.

Despite its recent electoral victory, the S.P.D. was thus plagued during the years immediately preceding the war by a number of increasingly serious problems. As a fundamentally centrist leader striving simultaneously to maintain both unity and principle, Haase symbolized the basic fragility of the imposing party structure. As long as the S.P.D. was able to avoid a major crisis, he could function with a certain degree of effectiveness. The controversy over the military tax bill of 1913, however, had already indicated that any crisis which unmistakably challenged the traditional principles of the S.P.D. was certain to shake it to its core and in the process to make the centrist's position extremely difficult, if not impossible to maintain.

CHAPTER IV

THE UNEXPECTED CATASTROPHE

Despite the widespread feeling of dissatisfaction and aimlessness that had developed within the S.P.D., the early months of 1914 brought no hint of the impending threat to the party. Indeed, during that winter and spring the party was moved by a new sense of militancy, provoked largely by a number of apparently threatening moves on the part of the government. In November, 1913, the arrest of a number of civilians by an army officer in the Alsatian town of Zabern had created a major scandal which aroused the indignation of Germans far beyond the ranks of the S.P.D. and was utilized by the party with considerable success in its anti-militarist agitation. Despite the disclaimers of Bethmann-Hollweg, the Zabern affair seemed to many to lend further weight to the fear that the growing military machine would be eventually used to repress the "internal enemy." The trial and conviction in February of Rosa Luxemburg for having reputedly urged soldiers to mutiny was also considered provocative even by many who had little personal sympathy for the fiery revolutionary. The refusal of the government to introduce further social legislation and the continuing failure of the Prussian regime to fulfill the Kaiser's pledge of 1908 to reform the Prussian suffrage system caused even the normally moderate union leaders to issue strong protests.[1] The new militancy was reflected in the Reichstag and the Prussian Diet, where the Social Democratic representatives engaged in unusually vituperative clashes with the right wing parties. The revived feeling of alienation from the regime and all that it represented was dramatized by the demonstrative refusal of Social Democratic deputies to rise for the traditional tribute to the Kaiser with which the Reichstag session was closed in May.[2]

Ironically, one of the principal concerns of the Social Democratic leadership during the last months before the war was the forthcoming congress of the International which was scheduled to convene in Vienna in August and which its organizers hoped would serve as another dramatic demonstration of the unity and militance of international socialism. At the suggestion of the S.P.D., one of the principal topics on the agenda was "Imperialism and International Courts of Arbitration," and Haase had been asked to prepare one of several reports which were to serve as the basis of discussion on the issue. He completed a summary of his report in May which was subsequently circulated in printed form by the International Bureau.[3] Its basic thesis was very similar to that which he had presented at the party congress of 1912. After a strongly worded and apparently quite pessimistic description of the evolution of imperialism, he concluded with several paragraphs in which he argued even more optimistically than heretofore that though imperialism as a system could only be overcome by the defeat of capitalism, its impact could "very well" be moderated by the "watchfulness and energy of the working classes." He went on to stress the recent improvement in Anglo-German relations which he attributed both to the activities of the International and to the gradual recognition by the ruling classes that their own interests would thereby be served. Though less sanguine about the current state of Franco-German relations, he promised that the workers of both countries, supported by the entire International, would redouble their efforts to bring about a reconciliation. Moreover, unlike the resolution of 1912, this report did not end on a militant note, but rather concluded with the simple statement that socialists everywhere would work for peace and against war in accordance with the principles enunciated at Stuttgart, Kopenhagen and Basel.[4]

Perhaps the most difficult political problem facing the congress was raised by the renewed proposal of Vaillant and Kier Hardie that the International pass a resolution threatening to call a general strike in case Europe should be faced by an immediate threat to the peace. In a letter to Vaillant written in May, Haase reported that his party's executive committee had discussed this proposal at length, but had again concluded that the Germans could not support such a resolution. Indeed, he added, with some exaggeration, that this opposition was related so directly to the German political situation that no important differences of opinion had arisen in the S.P.D. concerning the issue. In the first place, he argued, even if a general strike could be seriously contemplated, it would be foolhardy to inform the authorities in advance, for the immediate response of the government would be to destroy the trade unions. Furthermore, it would be a mistake to hurl threats which could not in fact be carried out. Despite its rapid growth and apparent strength, the German movement, clearly the most powerful in the International, had not yet even succeeded in organizing the railroad and munitions workers, certainly the key groups in any strike against war. Neither the French nor the German party had, furthermore, succeeded in their efforts to slow the recent acceleration of the arms race. How then could they speak of proclaiming a general strike, an action of infinitely greater magnitude and difficulty than the electoral and agitational campaigns they had engaged in for this much more moderate purpose? Finally, he asked, what should be done in case a country with a strong labor movement should be attacked by one in which the workers as yet wielded little influence? Should the more highly developed movement in such a case call a general strike and in so doing perhaps insure the defeat of its own homeland by an aggressor nation? For all of these reasons, Haase concluded, the S.P.D. could not go beyond the Basel resolution which allowed each national party to choose its own most appropriate means of resisting war. He therefore urged Vaillant not to force the German party into the position of having to oppose his resolution.[5]

Haase's apparent moderation may appear somewhat surprising in one so soon to be identified with radical opposition to the German war effort. Yet, although the temperance of his language was at least in part motivated by the widespread fear of government sanctions,[6] his optimism concerning the international situation was apparently genuine and, of course, was at this time shared by many far beyond the ranks of Social Democracy. Moreover, his cautious approach toward direct action was quite in keeping with the attitude he had expressed heretofore and with his actions during the war and even during the revolution itself. This attitude, however, did not prevent him from reacting swiftly and vigorously to the crisis when it came. When the news of the assassination of Archduke Francis Ferdinand, successor to the Austro-Hungarian throne, struck the world, Haase was among the first of the Social Democratic leaders to sense its full significance.

On June 29, the day after the assassination, the party's executive committee met to discuss its possible repercussions. In his introductory remarks, Haase stressed that the Sarajevo incident would very likely bring Europe to the brink of war and that under these cirumstances there was a strong possibility that the International Congress would be jeopardized. He therefore urged the committee to authorize the presentation of a formal request to the Austrian party for assurances that the Austrian government would in no way interfere with the meeting.

Ebert disagreed vehemently with Haase's analysis of the situation. He insisted that his colleague's pessimism was unfounded. He did not believe that the assassination would lead to a severe international crisis, and in any case, he felt that the Austrian government would have no reason to interfere in the affairs of the International. After considerable debate, the majority supported Haase's position and approved a motion made by Scheidemann to urge that a meeting of the International Bureau be convened to consider the matter.[7]

The atmosphere of relative calm and restraint which seemed to pervade the halls of European diplomacy during the first weeks of July appeared to substantiate Ebert's optimism, and many party leaders felt no particular need to interrupt their normal vacation plans.[8] The German Social Democrats, like most other Europeans, were therefore stunned by the news of the vicious Austrian ultimatum which was presented to the Serbian government late on July 23.[9]

The party's executive committee found itself facing the unexpected crisis minus Ebert, Molkenbuhr, and Scheidemann, three of its most important members, yet it was impossible to wait for their return before taking action. On July 25 the committee issued a proclamation drafted by Haase.[10] The strongly worded protest condemned the action of the Austrian government as a "frivolous provocation." The demands made upon Serbia were so brutal that they could only be intended to bring war. "The class conscious proletariat of Germany," it continued,

voices in the name of humanity and civilization a flaming protest against this criminal action of the warmongers. It urgently demands that the German government exert influence on the Austrian government to preserve peace, and, in case the shameful war should not be prevented, insists that it refrain from any warlike intervention.

Having thus censured the Austrian government, the proclamation concluded with a dramatic appeal to party members to express immediately their "unshakable will for peace" in mass meetings.

A grave hour has come, graver than any in decades. Danger is on the march! World War threatens! The ruling classes, who in peacetime gag, despise and exploit you, want to use you as cannon fodder. Everywhere the ears of the autocrats must ring with the cries: We want no war! Down with war! Hurrah for the international brotherhood of peoples![11]

On July 26, Haase and Ebert were invited to the Prussian Ministry of the Interior for a discussion of the situation. Since Ebert had not yet returned to Berlin and Molkenbuhr and Scheidemann were absent as well, Haase asked Otto Braun to accompany him. The government was obviously deeply concerned about the S.P.D.'s reaction to the approaching conflict, and this meeting was part of a concerted effort to insure that the party would do nothing to interfere with the process of mobilization.[12] In the course of the discussion Haase and Braun were informed that the peace demonstrations planned by the party would not be suppressed, but that the government was afraid that these might be conducted in such a way as to encourage the Russian panslavists in their agitation for Russian support of Serbia. The two men were also told that the government would honor its commitment to support Austria if the Russians gave the Serbians military aid. Haase replied that the S.P.D. rejected such an interpretation of the German-Austrian alliance, which in its view was purely defensive in character and therefore would in no sense be binding if the Austrians chose to initiate a conflict with Serbia. The spokesmen for the government retorted that neither the foreign office nor the other parties in the Reichstag could accept the Social Democratic interpretation of the alliance.[13]

The size and enthusiasm of the crowds that participated in the Social Democratic peace demonstrations on July 28 seemed to offer grounds for hope that the German government would be so impressed that it would restrain its Austrian ally.[14] But the socialists were by this time not the only group that had taken to the streets to express its views. The excited throngs of singing, chanting jingoists were only temporarily thrust aside by the solemn masses of the party faithful.

Nevertheless, when Haase left with Kautsky on July 28 to represent the S.P.D. at an emergency meeting of the International Bureau in Brussels,[15] he was apparently still optimistic regarding the ability of international socialism to deliver the world from the impending catastrophe. Although he was obviously impatient to return to Berlin, Haase played a very active role in Brussels. When Victor Adler confronted the assembled group of socialist leaders on the morning of the twenty-ninth with an extremely pessimistic report in which he concluded that the Austrian party could do virtually nothing to influence its government,[16] Haase was extremely aggravated. He intervened in the discussion to read a telegram from Berlin describing the massive demonstrations that had taken place in that city on the previous day.[17] Later he specifically criticized Adler for his passivity and resignation.

In replying to Adler, Haase was compelled to deal with arguments similar to those he himself had used in his letter to Vaillant in May. He refused to accept Adler's statement that any action by the Austrian party would endanger its very existence, insisting that if the Social Democrats now actively resisted the conflict, they would find public opinion on their side after the war was over. He also rejected Adler's argument that resistance would encourage Austria's enemies. On the contrary, he declared, demonstrations by the proletariat would have a braking effect on every government.

Turning to the situation in Germany, Haase remained remarkably sanguine both about the intentions of the government and about the militancy of the S.P.D.[18] He insisted that neither the great industrialists, nor government circles, nor even the military wanted war and even argued that it was possible that Bethmann-Hollweg had not been consulted concerning the Austrian ultimatum to Serbia. He added, however, that if Russia attacked, Germany would also necessarily become involved. The S.P.D., he promised, would continue its activities. Indeed, it would strengthen its demonstrations and give them an even more vigorously pacifistic character.[19]

Like most of the participants in the Brussels meeting, Haase obviously was still operating on the assumption that, as in 1912, preventive measures would be successful. He thus focused his attention primarily upon the forthcoming congress which he envisioned as a second Basel. It was at Haase's suggestion that the congress was moved up to August 9 and was transferred to Paris.[20] Haase also successfully proposed that the topic "The War and the Proletariat" be placed at the head of the agenda.[21] It was this confidence in both the basic sanity of most important European governments and the power of the International that largely explains the startling fact that those at Brussels never seriously considered what they would do if the Paris congress could not take place. The issues which a few days later would be hotly debated in the national parties simply were not raised. The representatives at Brussels contented themselves with the publication, again at Haase's suggestion, of a generally worded statement that the parties they represented would continue and even increase the pressure they were exerting on their governments to localize and hopefully halt the developing conflict.[22]

At a mass meeting on July 29, Haase and Jean Jaurès succeeded in conveying something of their confidence and enthusiasm to an enormous throng. Speaking with his arm around Haase's shoulders, the great French protagonist of international understanding declared with passion that "we recognize only one alliance, that which binds us to the human race." Haase, in a speech highly critical of the actions of both the Austrian and the German governments, seconded Jaurès' sentiments and warned grimly, "Our enemies should take care! It could happen that the people, tired of so much suffering and so much oppression, will finally rise up and establish a socialist state."[23]

Yet, although the delegates returned home from Brussels filled in most cases with new enthusiasm for their cause, they still had no effective plan for dealing with the on-rushing crisis. The leaders of the International had failed to make use of their final opportunity to replace words with deeds. Their brave and well-meant phrases would be drowned out within a matter of days by the roar of cannon and cries of nationalistic fervor.

While Haase was in Brussels, the government continued its efforts to insure that the S.P.D. would do nothing to interfere with the approaching mobilization. On July 28 Bethmann-Hollweg phoned to invite Haase to discuss the situation with him in the chancellery. Upon learning that the party chairman was on his way to Brussels and that Ebert had not yet returned to Berlin, the Chancellor called upon the right-wing leader Albert Südekum to act as an intermediary between himself and the S.P.D. executive committee. Bethmann talked with Südekum for several hours, impressing upon him the fact that he was doing everything in his power to prevent war, but that the danger of a world conflict was both real and immediate.[24] Südekum reported the results of this discussion to Ebert, who had in the meantime returned from his vacation, and to a number of other leaders who had gathered at the party headquarters. On the strength of these conferences he told the Chancellor that the government need fear no direct action by the S.P.D. in the form of strikes or sabotage which might endanger efficient mobilization. The executive committee members also recognized the necessity of avoiding any ambiguous statements which might be misused by the war parties in the potentially

belligerent countries. Finally, he noted that the Chancellor's efforts to communicate directly with the party leadership had been received with grateful
and sympathetic understanding.[25]

As a result of the response of the S.P.D. leadership, obtained at a moment
when Haase was unable to make his influence felt,[26] the Chancellor felt able to
assure the Prussian cabinet on July 30 that "nothing special need be feared
from the Social Democratic executive committee. . . . Either a general strike,
a partial strike or sabotage is out of the question."[27] On the following day the
war ministry issued the following statement to its commanders: "According to
reliable information, the Social Democratic Party firmly intends to act as all
Germans should under the present circumstances."[28] Long before the world
was shocked by the news of the S.P.D.'s acquiescence in Germany's war
policy, the basis of what was to become a formal *Burgfrieden* (domestic peace)
had already been established.

It was as yet, however, by no means certain that the S.P.D. would go
beyond the purely negative action of assuring the government that no effort
would be made to interfere with German mobilization. An attempt to call a
general strike in case of war had, after all, long been rejected as impracticable
by most Social Democratic leaders. Of much greater actuality was the question of whether the S.P.D. would support the war effort, and this was as yet
unresolved when Haase returned to Berlin on July 30. By then the Austrian
declaration of war on Serbia had made it fully apparent that the world stood on
the brink of war. Meeting that afternoon under Haase's chairmanship, the
executive committee reacted to the widespread fear that the government
would soon take decisive action against the Social Democrats by voting to send
Ebert and Braun into exile with a substantial portion of the party's funds.
Ebert thus was unable to play a significant role in the crucial events of the next
several days.[29]

Formal discussion of how the party should react to the expected demand
for war credits was finally initiated on the following day at a meeting of the
executive committee and the leadership of the Reichstag delegation. Haase
opened the debate by referring to a Reichstag speech given by Eduard David
late in 1912 in which he had emphasized that the S.P.D. regarded Germany's
treaty obligations to Austria as strictly defensive in character.[30] From this
Haase concluded that in the present situation the delegation must of necessity
vote against any request for war credits. David replied that this position was
no longer tenable. If war should come, the Social Democrats would have to
vote for the necessary credits. Only Ledebour and Wengels fully supported
Haase's point of view, although a number of those present felt that a policy of
abstention would be acceptable if pursued in cooperation with other members
of the International.[31]

During the meeting an incident occurred which revealed how much more clearly and passionately committed Haase was at this point than most of his colleagues. Friedrich Stampfer, a leading Social Democratic journalist whose column was published by many of the party's papers, had distributed an article entitled, "To Be or Not to Be," in which he vigorously argued that party members must be prepared to defend the Reich in case of war. Heinrich Ströbel, the acting editor of *Vorwärts* and later an active leader of the opposition, strongly objected to Stampfer's column, and the matter was referred to the executive committee. According to Scheidemann, the text of the article was read over the phone to the gathered party leaders. After hearing only the first sentences, Haase sprang up excitedly and protested against its publication. Despite the fact that the majority of those present were already or soon would be in essential agreement with Stampfer, Haase was able to obtain general support for his demand that the article be recalled.[32]

The appearance of renewed internal strife over the question of the party's proper relationship to the nation at war was, of course, not wholly unexpected. Kautsky had written to Adler on July 25 that the most difficult problem to be faced during the emerging international crisis would be to maintain the unity of the party.[33] For the moment, however, the future battle lines remained obscured by confusion and indecision. Many Social Democratic leaders were as yet uncertain as to what position they should take.[34] The reluctance of others to take a clear public stance was undoubtedly governed primarily by tactical considerations. The meeting on July 31 thus broke up without any decision having been made other than to send Hermann Müller to Paris with an extremely vague mandate to try to organize some kind of coordinated action by the French and German parties.[35]

On August 1, however, as the news of Jaurès' assassination was followed by that of the German declaration of war on Russia and French mobilization, a new sense of urgency developed. During the day the S.P.D. leaders turned in earnest to the task of defining the party's position on the voting of war credits. In the morning Eduard David discussed the matter with Scheidemann, who as co-chairman of the Reichstag delegation could be expected to play a key role in the decision-making process. Scheidemann at first appeared to favor a policy of abstention, but during the course of their conversation David was able to convince him that the delegation should vote for the credits.

Continuing his efforts to round up support for his position, David found that Haase's friend Luise Zietz, the women's representative on the executive committee, was unshakable in her conviction that the party should reject the government's demand. Later in the day, David spoke to Haase, who was at the time working with Kautsky on a statement opposing the voting of the credits, and tried in vain to convince him of the necessity of a positive vote.

Haase insisted that such a step would be "the greatest misfortune which could possibly befall the party." Moreover, according to David, the chairman was still convinced that no majority could be obtained in the delegation for such a policy.[36] Shortly before suppertime, David met with a half dozen of his revisionist colleagues and found them to be in complete agreement with his own position on the issue of war credits. This group decided to invite several other sympathetic deputies to a meeting on the following day to work out a statement supporting their point of view. On his way home after this day of vigorous campaigning, David passed among the excited crowd gathered before the palace to hear a speech by the Kaiser, a speech in which the monarch made the declaration which he would repeat in the Reichstag a few days later: during the forthcoming struggle he would recognize no parties, only Germans.[37] Even as the Social Democratic factions jockeyed for support, the government thus continued to build the foundations of its projected *Burgfrieden*. On that same day, Reichstag deputies throughout the Reich received telegrams summoning them to an emergency sesesion on August 4.[38] The internal as well as the external crisis had become acute. A decision had finally to be made.

August 2 brought a further intensification of the struggle among the party leaders in Berlin. At a combined meeting of the executive committees of the party and of the Reichstag delegation, Haase again pleaded for the rejection of war credits. He sketched out a proposed speech defending this position and was vigorously supported by Ledebour. David, however, spoke at length against the chairman's position, and after a tense debate, during which at least one deputy broke down in tears, the delegation leaders voted by a majority of four to two to recommend the voting of the credits. After a break for dinner, the group met late into the night in an unsuccessful attempt to reach agreement on the text of a declaration to be read in the Reichstag. They finally adjourned to await a decision by the entire Reichstag delegation which had been summoned to gather in Berlin on the following day. Haase was delegated to speak for the minority position at that meeting while David was assigned the task of defending the point of view of the majority.[39]

As the moment of final decision approached with the issue apparently still very much in doubt, the process of building the basis for a *Burgfrieden* continued. Social Democratic leaders were being swayed above all by the government's efforts to portray the impending conflict as a defensive struggle against the Russian autocracy they had so long been taught to hate.[40] Even as Haase and his colleagues debated the stand to be taken by the S.P.D. in the Reichstag, a conference of union leaders was voting to break off all movements for higher wages for the duration of the war.[41]

The night of August 2 was a troubled one for supporters of both positions on the issue of war credits. The long and heated debates had served to clarify the issue for the Berlin party leaders, but the opinions of the large number of deputies who had not yet reached the capital were as yet unknown. The traditional strength of the radicals within the party seemed to indicate that the credits might well be rejected. Yet as early as August 1, non-socialist papers had begun to predict that the S.P.D. would support the war,[42] and as the deputies began to assemble on the morning of the third, it soon became apparent that this prediction was well-founded. Although many representatives were still missing from the short morning session, David reports that he experienced an immense feeling of relief as he learned that a number of the radicals had decided to abandon their old intransigence.[43]

The morning session was cut short after a number of routine matters had been dealt with in order to allow Haase and Scheidemann to attend a noon meeting of party leaders with representatives of the government. At this meeting, Bethmann-Hollweg read the speech he had prepared for the following day's Reichstag session. The party leaders then discussed the appropriate procedures for conducting the extraordinary session. Haase and Scheidemann pointed out that the S.P.D. had not yet decided how it would vote and insisted that the party would in any case have to present a statement explaining its position. They agreed, however, to communicate the text of the S.P.D. declaration to the leaders of the other parties in advance so that they could respond if they thought it necessary to do so. Haase further promised that the Social Democratic spokesman would in all probability simply express the S.P.D.'s refusal to accept any responsibility for the policies which had led to war.[44]

After lunch the decisive debate began under Scheidemann's chairmanship. David insisted that the time had come for the S.P.D. to rid itself of its traditional prejudices. Germany was being invaded from East and West. The defeat of Russia would mean the destruction of the Czarist autocracy. The S.P.D. could not allow itself to be eliminated from consideration at such a moment. A negative vote would bring the destruction of the Social Democratic organizations, while a positive vote would immeasurably strengthen the position of the party. The government would then no longer be able to treat the Social Democrats as outsiders, and the end of the war would bring a wave of democratization. Haase then spoke for the minority and was vigorously supported by a number of the well known radicals. Haase's friend Kautsky, concerned as ever to find a compromise which would preserve party unity, proposed that the S.P.D. vote for the credits only if the government agreed to certain specific conditions concerning the conduct of the war, but this suggestion was generally viewed as wholly impracticable.[45]

The arrival of Hermann Müller from Paris during the debate added to the general excitement, but he could only report that no agreement on common action had been reached with the French party. It was his impression that the

French socialists would vote for war credits in the Chamber of Deputies. Müller's report obviously constituted a blow to the hopes of Haase and his friends, but there is no evidence that it exercised any significant influence on the ultimate outcome of the debate. When a poll finally was taken, David's confidence was shown to have been well founded. The delegation voted by a margin of seventy-eight to fourteen to support the government's demand for war credits.[46] A dramatic indication of the radical change that had taken place within the party as a result of the war crisis was the decision, made shortly thereafter, to rise for the *"Kaiser Hoch"* during the following day's session. This complete reversal of a policy proclaimed just two months earlier was justified by reference to the fact that the *"Hoch"* would now be directed toward *Volk* and fatherland as well as the Kaiser,[47] but the incident made it clear to all that the psychological as well as the practical basis for a *Burgfrieden* had already been established. David tersely recorded his reaction to this final victory in his diary: "I look at the Dittmanns, the Hochs, and the Geyers and laugh."[48]

The delegation met again on the morning of August 4 to approve the final text of a statement which had been worked out by a commission assigned the task on the previous day. The efforts of Haase and his friends to alter the statement substantially were unsuccessful.[49] The atmosphere of tension and confusion which pervaded the meeting became glaringly apparent when the question was raised as to who should read the declaration in the Reichstag. When Scheidemann explained that in keeping with Haase's expressed wish and in agreement with the executive committee of the delegation he had himself consented to read it, a storm of indignation burst forth. In response to heated demands made with special vehemence by Haase's radical friends that Haase read the statement, the party chairman at first emphatically refused, insisting that it conflicted with his convictions. When his refusal was greeted by renewed stormy objections on the part of what was apparently the large majority of the delegation, however, Haase finally agreed to sacrifice his own feelings for the sake of party discipline and unity.[50]

As Liebknecht later reported, this incident was apparently viewed by many of the radicals as a new victory for their cause.[51] In fact, however, it definitely added to the confusion of the public when news of the S.P.D.'s decision burst upon an incredulous world. Haase's son reports that this was the one political decision that his father later regretted.[52] In the midst of this stormy debate, Haase apparently also declared that as a result of his recent experiences he would give up the delegation chairmanship "as soon as calmer times return."[53] It is unclear whether the declaration represented a carefully considered decision or whether (this seems more probable) it was simply a temperamental outburst caused by the tension of the moment. In any case, it offered further evidence of the overwhelming sense of anguish and disappointment with which Haase viewed the collapse of his dream.

During the first of the two sessions of the Reichstag that afternoon, Bethmann-Hollweg read his often cited speech defending the German position and proclaiming the unbreachable unity of the German people in the face of their enemies.[54] A number of the social Democratic deputies joined in the demonstrative applause which repeatedly interrupted the speech, and thus brought on a new conflict when the delegation met again during a short recess which preceded the actual voting of war credits. The indignant reaction of the radicals to this patriotic demonstration resulted in a scene in which several of the deputies very nearly came to blows.[55] As chairman, Haase demanded that such behavior not be repeated and was supported by a large majority of the delegation.[56]

The delegation also agreed at this time to change the text of its statement, which in its original form had expressly declared that the party would resist any attempt by the government to expand the conflict into a war of conquest. Bethmann-Hollweg had objected during a meeting with Haase prior to that day's first session that this passage might be misunderstood by the English who had not yet entered the war. In its revised form the statement merely included a general condemnation of all wars of conquest.[57] It is interesting to note that the German violation of Belgian neutrality, which had been frankly admitted by the Chancellor in his speech, played no role in determining the position of the S.P.D. It is difficult to believe, as some historians insist,[58] that Haase and Scheidemann knew of the government's plans in this regard even before the delegation took its decisive vote on the issue of war credits. It is more probable that the reference to the invasion of Belgium was added to Bethmann's speech after he had discussed it with the party leaders on August 3.[59] Even if this was the case, however, it is certainly indicative of the general confusion surrounding the events of August 4 that no one, not even the arch-radical Liebknecht, suggested the addition of some reference to the Belgian invasion to the S.P.D. declaration after the Chacellor had delivered his speech. Haase later reported that within twenty-four hours the executive committee deeply regretted this oversight.[60]

Despite its calculated restraint, the S.P.D.'s statement was greeted with immense enthusiasm when it was read by Haase in the Reichstag. The apparently abrupt reversal of the nation's greatest party made a tremendous impression upon a people grown accustomed to the existence of a seemingly unbridgeable cleavage in their ranks. Now that ominous gap, the importance of which had so often been emphasized by both Social Democratic theoreticians and apologists for the status quo, seemed miraculously closed in the crucible of war. The *vaterlandslosen Gesellen* had finally joined the fatherland in its hour of need. Eduard David noted in his diary that as he walked that evening he almost broke into tears. He could now die in peace, he wrote, knowing that he had done a great service to both his people and his party.[63] Unfortunately we have no comparable document describing the feelings on that historic evening of David's principal opponent, the Social Democratic leader, who in the course of but a few hours had seen his party and his people carried over the precipice despite his frenzied efforts to prevent such a catastrophe.

CHAPTER V

WALKING A TIGHTROPE

The decision of the S.P.D. to vote for war credits on August 4, 1914, was viewed by much of the world as a gross betrayal of its traditional principles. Yet there is much to be said for the point of view, expressed perhaps most cogently by Arthur Rosenberg,[1] that the decision to vote the credits not only represented a completely logical policy for the minority of revisionists, but also lay well within the Marxist theoretical framework still accepted by the majority of the party. Marx and Engels had by no means ruled out participation in wars between capitalist states. They rather urged that each situation be judged on its individual merits and had indeed at first supported the German side in the Franco-Prussian war, believing that the defeat of Napoleon and the achievement of German unification would serve the interests of the proletariat. Furthermore, Social Democratic leaders had often declared that they had no intention of leaving Germany defenseless against foreign invasion. The fact that in 1914 such an attack was threatened by the Russian autocracy, a traditional object of vilification above all by the radical wing of the party, lent added weight to this oft-repeated pledge. The character of the war was therefore the principal question at issue from the very beginning, and it was only as increasing numbers of party members began to suspect that German policy was moved by aggressive intent that the opposition within the party reached truly substantial proportions. There were, moreover, other very powerful traditions which tended to militate against the expression of open opposition by a radical minority group within the party. It was, after all, the radical wing which had insisted most vehemently upon the maintenance of party discipline when the revisionists had been in the minority. Now, when many of these same radicals found themselves in the minority, it was obviously difficult for them to urge a breach of the very discipline they had been so concerned to impose but a few years previously.

Finally, the deepening concern of the centrists to preserve the unity of the party served as a very powerful motivation for both the most prominent leaders of the opposition such as Haase and later Kautsky and the outstanding apologists for the position of August 4 such as Ebert, Scheidemann, and Müller, to make every effort to limit the deeply divisive debate on the war issue to the inner circle of the party leadership. It is only by keeping these factors in mind that one can properly understand why the impassioned

[55]

struggle which preceded the action of August 4 did not immediately produce a major crisis within the party.

If the policy of August 4 and the subsequent virtually unanimous public support of that policy by the S.P.D. leadership is therefore fully comprehensible within the context of the party's history, this is certainly far less true of the simultaneous establishment of the so-called *Burgfrieden* between the S.P.D. and its sworn enemy, the Prussian-dominated German state. It was this acceptance of an unconditional peace with the state which, as Rosenberg suggests,[2] represented a truly radical break with the traditional policy and philosophy of the S.P.D. Yet it is interesting to note in this connection that even Kautsky, who during the debates before August 4 had urged the setting of conditions for S.P.D. support of the war effort and who as the party's most influential theoretician had always insisted upon consistent and explicit opposition to the capitalist state, at first appeared publicly to support the *Burgfrieden*. Thus, in several articles published in *Neue Ziet* in August and September, the spokesman for Marxist orthodoxy repeatedly declared that as long as the homeland was in danger, the only relevant question was that of victory or defeat and that therefore for the time being all differences must of necessity be suppressed. "The critique of weapons has begun," he wrote immediately after the decision of August 4 was made, "and therewith is the weapon of criticism stilled."[3]

Kautsky's position was, of course, based on the widespread assumption that the war would be short. The *Burgfrieden* would thus be only a temporary truce, which when peace came would be dissolved by revived and amplified manifestations of class differences. The party, whose organized might had been preserved by the truce, would then be in a position to exploit these differences in new and perhaps decisive attacks upon the defenders of the status quo.

For many other prominent Social Democrats, however, including not a few who had hitherto counted themselves among the radicals, the war and its acompanying *Burgfrieden* aroused an immense sense of relief from the isolation they had felt as members of what had become virtually a Social Democratic sub-culture.[4] "We German Social Democrats," wrote the former radical Konrad Hänisch,

have learned to consider ourselves in this war as part, and truly not the worst part, of the German nation. We do not want to be robbed again by anyone, from the right or the left, of the feeling of belonging to the German people. . . . We have given up . . . this [our] . . . inner resistance, which for decades dominated us, consciously or unconsciously, against the German idea of the state because we could no longer honestly maintain it.[5]

The fact that enormous numbers of party members shared at least to some extent the views so dramatically expressed by Hänisch represented the decisive shift in the orientation of German Social Democracy at this time rather than the mere decision of the Reichstag delegation to vote war credits on August 4. The minority of revisionists and reformists had, of course, long striven for the amalgamation of the party into German society, but they had always been blocked on the one hand by the majority's adherence to the "orthodox" Marxist prejudices against accepting a positive relationship to the capitalist state and on the other hand by the unwillingness of the classes controlling that state to actively seek Social Democratic support. Now it appeared that these obstacles had been overcome by the necessities of national defense and that the party could therefore begin to play a constructive role within the context of the German nation. Had not the Emperor himself declared that he now "knew no parties," and had the party leadership not voted overwhelmingly to support the Emperor in his efforts to defend the fatherland?[6] Only time with its accompanying military defeat, revolution and counter-revolution would prove the essential shallowness of this analysis, and even then by no means to everyone's satisfaction.

In the meantime, it was the representatives of the extremes of both right and left who most clearly recognized the significance of this fundamental shift in the orientation of the S.P.D. On the right, Eduard David and several of his revisionist friends rapidly developed an aggressive program designed to insure the permanence of their victory on August 4. Meeting frequently to plan their strategy, they actively sought on the one hand to increase their influence within the centrist leadership and the party press and on the other hand to convince the government of the great gains to be secured by offering substantial consessions to the Social Democrats.[7] Even the hitherto sacrosanct unity of the party could, from their point of view, quite justifiably be sacrificed if that were necessary to achieve their goal of a Social Democratic Party that had become a fully integrated part of German society.[8]

The leaders of the extreme left also soon came to the conclusion that August 4 represented a decisive turning point in the history of German Social Democracy. For them, however, the policy enunciated on that day proved the total bankruptcy of the party's traditional policy. After a brief period of confusion and dismay, they too began to organize an active campaign to secure support for their point of view that the time had come for the organization of a frankly revolutionary movement. If they were somewhat more hesitant than David and his friends to contemplate an immediate split in the party's ranks, it was only because they recognized that for the time being they were tactically in a very weak position.[9]

In the face of the confusion that reigned among the acknowledged leaders of the party and the agitation by extremists of right and left for a radical reorientation of its traditional policy, the difficulties inherent in Haase's centrist position soon became glaringly apparent. Despite his total rejection of the policy of August 4, his actions continued to be governed by his belief in the necessity of maintaining party unity. His role as chairman and leading spokesman of a party whose policies he deplored, of course, proved to be extremely embarrassing. For the time being, however, he chose to place his organizational responsibility above his opposition to the course the party had embarked upon, and it was only as the expected early end of the conflict failed to materialize that the paradox inherent in his position became intolerable.

Even Haase's relationship with his allies on the extreme left frequently was the source of acute embarrassment, for he was separated from them by more than his sense of responsibility to the existing party structure. Of course, he shared with them in a general way the orthodox Marxist view of the causes of the war. The holocaust had been brought on by the nemesis inherent in the capitalist system. The war was therefore a travesty on the rights of the working classes who had no interest in it and who nevertheless would be compelled to bear the brunt of its burdens. Yet from the beginning, Haase drew from this analysis conclusions that were very different from those of Liebknecht and his friends. Liebknecht, after his momentary "error" of August 4, quickly came to the conclusion that the war had created a revolutionary situation in which the whole colossus of the capitalist system should and could be brought crashing to the ground. From this perspective, the hallowed unity of a party which had failed to fulfill its historical mission could hardly be considered a fundamental barrier to the unleashing of the final conflict which would usher in a new and better world order.

In contrast to this militantly revolutionary attitude, Haase's letters and speeches of this period suggest that his fundamental motivation was a humanitarian concern to bring the awful destruction of the war to an early end. Despite his Marxist phraseology, Haase was much more interested in preventing futher bloodshed than in using the chaos brought on by the war to foment revolution. His tone, if not his vocabulary, was much more that of a liberal pacifist than of a revolutionary. His criticism tended to be directed not so much against the capitalist system as against the German militarists who, in his opinion, bore the major share of the immediate responsibility for bringing on the war. Haase's internationalism, his readiness to condemn his own fatherland and to play down the misdeeds of both the governments and the socialist parties of the *entente* powers, served as a focal point of the criticism leveled against him by his opponents both within and without the party.[10]

From Haase's point of view, therefore, the coming of the war did not require any fundamental revisions of either tactics or theory such as those suggested by the extremists of both right and left. On the contrary, in his mind the most important task at hand was to lead the S.P.D. back to its pre-August position. The conflict was, to be sure, a result of capitalistic folly, but if the party would only return to its old policy of consistent opposition, it might well be able to pressure the German government into accepting a reasonable peace. For a man of Haase's pacifist inclinations it was impossible to conceive of "using" the terror of world war even for the most laudable of ends. He did not, of course, like so many of his colleagues, give up all thought of revolution, but its prospect remained for him distant and unreal. For the time being, the one reasonable goal of international socialism had to be the achievement of peace. Viewed from this perspective, his own immediate responsibility as chairman was not to develop some new tactic or analysis, but rather to maintain the unity and thereby the strength of the party while seeking through every means at his disposal to lead it back to its proper path, a path which, after all, had been repeatedly outlined at national and international congresses.[11]

Among the most formidable of the obstacles Haase faced was the *Burgfrieden* that had been quickly established within the party. Such an agreement to restrict internal debate severely limited his ability to agitate effectively for his point of view. It was only very slowly that the rank and file party members could even be made aware of the fact that their chairman did not personally espouse the position which he had felt himself compelled to enunciate publicly as the official spokesman of the S.P.D. Moreover, his effort to maintain a centrist position at a time when the crisis had caused a significant number of his colleagues to urge a radical revision of traditional policies made him extremely vulnerable to distrust and eventually to open attack from both right and left.

Haase's principal field of activity between Reichstag sessions was of course the executive committee. His position in this body after August 4 was hardly enviable, his only support on most important issues coming from the lone female member Luise Zietz and the elderly Wengels. As early as August 8, Scheidemann complained to David that Haase was engaged in trying to sabotage all "positive proposals" in the committee.[12] A few days later, he declared flatly that the chairman was becoming "impossible."[13] As Haase continued his determined opposition to the policies of the majority, the other principal centrist leaders gradually moved toward an acceptance of the right wing's analysis of the new political situation. Scheidemann clearly took the lead in this movement toward the right, but Ebert also soon found it increasingly difficult to maintain his neutrality. Personal differences, already apparent before the war, played a significant role in the process of disintegration which rapidly eroded the unifying central core of the S.P.D. As early as mid-September Ebert and Haase became involved in an altercation which very nearly degenerated into physical violence. The immediate cause of this particular incident, an effort undertaken by Ebert to discipline an outspoken radical without having first consulted Haase, was symptomatic of the collapse of the cooperative spirit which alone made effective collegial leadership of the party possible.[14]

The press, of course, played a key role in the developing struggle within the party. From the beginning a large majority of the Social Democratic papers enthusiastically endorsed the policy of August 4. Indeed, many went far beyond the measured tones of the Reichstag declaration in their patriotic support of the German war effort. Some of the most important journals, however, including the *Vorwärts*, refused to be swept away by the general war fever. The control of these papers became a focal point of the struggle for power within the party. The editors of the *Vorwärts* expressed their opposition to the policy of August 4 in a memorandum to the executive committee drafted that very evening.[15] Although the paper could not, because of the strict censorship imposed by the government, make its opposition directly and clearly known to its readers, the fundamental disagreement which had developed between the executive committee and the party's central organ could not long remain hidden and necessarily became a source of extreme tension within the party leadership.

Haase, whose position paralleled in many ways that of the editors of the *Vorwärts*, was intimately involved in the ensuing conflict. From the first days of the war he made a practice of visiting the editorial offices every evening both in order to give legal advice and undoubtedly also to discuss the political situation with the editors, several of whom later became his close associates in the U.S.P.D.[16] The point of view of the editors, which soon became apparent to the paper's readers, was a constant source of friction in the executive committee, and, of course, much of the blame for their heresy was placed on Haase's shoulders. But when Haase, perhaps in an effort to still some of this criticism, later urged Scheidemann to replace him as the executive's link to the paper, the latter obdurately refused.[17]

Despite the discomfiture caused by the attitude of the editors of the *Vorwärts*, the executive committee continued to try to defend the rights of its organ when it was attacked by the government censors. Indeed, according to Scheidemann, the committee was more vigorous in its opposition to the increasing heavy-handedness of the censors than the editors themselves.[18] Moreover, the centrist leaders were also concerned about the extremes to which some of the right-wing papers were going in their enthusiasm for the early German victories. Haase was thus able at an editors' conference held late in September to obtain majority support for the dispatch of a memorandum to all papers cautioning them to keep in mind their Social Democratic principles despite the distracting and confusing circumstances of the moment.[19]

Despite the growing friction within the S.P.D., the relatively peaceful course of a meeting of the party council late in September indicated that the majority of the party leaders still hoped to avoid an open confrontation on the war issue. Ebert opened the meeting with a report on the condition of the party after two months of war. He emphasized the massive efforts of the S.P.D. to prevent the outbreak of hostilities, noted the executive committee's attempts to restrain the inappropriate enthusiasm of some Social Democratic editors, and explicitly declared that the party was unequivocally opposed to the aims of the annexationists. He added, however, that he did not yet consider the situation appropriate for large-scale agitation on the issue.[20] The discussion which followed revealed undertones of dissension within the leadership, but no real debate on party policy developed. This was perhaps due above all to the moderation of Haase, who declared his support for the *Burgfrieden* within the party, insisting that the policy of August 4 should not yet be publicly criticized and cautioning members of the Reichstag delegation not to provoke polemics on the issue. Moreover, he criticized the practice, which had been engaged in by spokesmen for both the extreme right and extreme left, of undertaking political tours in Germany and abroad without consulting the executive committee. He urged that foreign trips be limited to executive committee members, who were in a position to speak for the party as a whole. He reiterated Ebert's condemnation of annexationist propaganda in somewhat stronger terms, but unlike Ebert, who had been extremely critical of the socialist parties abroad, he pleaded for the maintenance of the tradition of solidarity within the International and urged that all attacks on foreign parties be avoided.[21]

The first wartime meeting of the party council, which would later become a principal scene of internal conflict, thus passed without serious incident. It was not long, however, before the centrist leadership had to face a far more difficult test of their will and ability to hold the party together. Within little more than a month preparations for the second session of the wartime Reichstag began during which the Social Democratic delegation would again be asked to vote for war credits.

On November 5 Haase, Scheidemann and David were invited to attend a meeting at the chancellery where they were formally informed of the government's intentions.[22] Later in the month the leaders of the Reichstag delegation met several times to discuss the situation. Apparently realizing that he could not hope to gain majority support for a simple negative vote on the credits, Haase proposed a variety of alternatives which, from his point of view, would have represented an improvement over the policy of August 4. At the first of these meetings he suggested that the delegation agree to vote for credits only if the amount requested by the government were cut in half. This would have forced the Chancellor to summon the Reichstag again within, at most, a few months. David vigorously opposed Haase's proposal, asserting that it would weaken the position of the party and be viewed abroad as a sign of German weakness. Everyone except Ledebour agreed with David, and the suggestion was defeated.[23] At a later meeting Haase, reviving Kautsky's ealier proposal in a new form, urged that a positive vote by the S.P.D. be made contingent upon the government's agreement to renounce publicly all annexations. Again, he was decisively defeated.[24]

In the meantime, a number of the factional leaders had also been actively preparing for the approaching Reichstag session. After a series of preliminary meetings, David and his friends succeeded in gathering some twenty-six sympathetic deputies for a strategy session on the eve of the first meeting of the delegation. Among other things, this group decided that if the opposition deputies should speak out in the plenary session contrary to the decision of the delegation, then, as David dramatically expressed it, they should be prepared to "shake them off."[25] While the right wing faction was thus preparing to exercise as much influence as possible over the course of the forthcoming session, Karl Liebknecht was striving to persuade the opposition deputies to undertake just the kind of action David and his associates were preparing to resist. Although he was ultimately unsuccessful in his efforts, at one point it appeared that as many as nine deputies might join him in breaking the delegation's unit voting rule.[26]

As the second major test of the S.P.D.'s position on the war approached, therefore, the danger to party unity had become very real. Two relatively small but increasingly influential groups had already come to the conclusion that a split was not only ultimately inevitable but necessary and desirable. Moreover, the official truce within the party was visibly disintegrating. During November the policy of August 4 was more and more frequently the subject of lively discussions in party meetings throughout the Reich. The centrists who dominated the executive committee were well aware of the danger. Late in November Victor Adler, who was close to the German centrists, wrote to Kautsky that Hilferding and others had been talking of a possible division in the ranks of the S.P.D. Adler was deeply concerned about these reports, although he professed to believe that such a catastrophe would not be allowed to occur.[27] Adler's concern was well justified, for even Ebert, though still striving to maintain an attitude of at least formal neutrality, told David that he was prepared, if the opposition should vote openly against the war credits, to initiate an all-out attack upon them, an attack which would inevitably bring the party to the brink of disintegration.[28] Under these circumstances, it was Haase who held the key to the immediate fate of the S.P.D.

Haase's position was in some ways stronger at the end of November than it had been in August. The four intervening months had given a number of

important Social Democrats an opportunity to reevaluate their positions in
the light of facts which had become known concerning both the causes of the
war and Germany's actual military situation. Perhaps the most influential of
the additions to Haase's still small group of supporters was Kautsky, who on
August 4 had only very reluctantly supported the party's position. By November he had changed his mind. Writing to Victor Adler at that time, he declared
that he was very happy that he now was in full agreement with Haase, "who
among the leaders here is by far the best and wisest."[29] Dittmann was also
moving toward acceptance of Haase's point of view, although he did not as yet
go so far as to oppose the voting of war credits. Writing to the executive
committee of the delegation in mid-November, Dittmann urged that vigorous
demands be voiced during the new session for social and economic reforms.
More important, the delegation should be prepared to make a powerful plea
for an immediate peace. The danger of invasion had clearly been eliminated,
"and Germany's position insures us an honorable peace. Thus, our situation is
now very different from what it was on August 4."[30] Support was not only
forthcoming from Haase's associates among the left centrists. Dismayed by
the destructiveness of the war and increasingly dubious about Germany's role
in its inception, Eduard Bernstein, the foremost exponent of revisionism, was
also by this time moving rapidly toward the opposition camp.[31] There is little
reason to doubt that many lesser figures had also lost their early enthusiasm
for the war. Nevertheless, despite this significant increase of open and potential support for the opposition, it was apparent long before the delegation
convened that the shift in sentiment was by no means substantial enough to
endanger the position of the majority.[32]

When the Social Democratic deputies gathered in Berlin on November
29, therefore, it was a foregone conclusion that the party would support the
government by granting war credits. But it was also clear that, contrary to the
wishes of David and his friends, a Social Democratic spokesman would again
read an explanatory statement in the Reichstag, for the executive committee
of the delegation had already decided to recommend this procedure. The
struggle within the delegation would therefore necessarily center upon the
text of this statement as well as upon the possibility of a public minority vote
by the opposition.

The first day of the meeting was devoted almost entirely to a discussion of
the issue of war credits. Scheidemann opened the debate by outlining what
was to become the standard argument for continuing to support the war effort.
The situation since August 4 had changed, to be sure, but for the worse.
Although the German armies had succeeded in turning back the first invasion
attempts, the Reich now found itself threatened by even more enemies than
before. The situation remained so desparate that not only would it be

"impossible" to refuse to vote new war credits, but it would also be the gravest folly even to demand limited concessions such as the elimination of martial law and censorship.[33]

As the major spokesman for the opposition, Haase answered Scheidemann's arguments. Scheidemann was incorrect, he insisted, in trying to tie the issue of war credits to the question of victory or defeat. As far as he knew, no member of the opposition hoped for the defeat of Germany. The vote in the Reichstag would rather be considered as what it in fact was, a political act. It had nothing to do with the obligation to defend the fatherland. The S.P.D. lacked confidence in the government and must express its fundamental opposition to that government through its votes in the Reichstag. Scheidemann and others who constantly attacked the actions of the other parties in the International were playing into the hands of the German imperialists. It was the obligation of the S.P.D. to fight against German imperialism, not to join the German imperialists in attacking the imperialism of other countries.[34]

The debate continued essentially along these lines, but in keeping with the general recognition that a decision in favor of war credits was a foregone conclusion, no vote was taken. Toward the end of the discussion, a commission was named to work out a statement to be read in the Reichstag. The commission did not meet until the morning of November 30. In the meantime the three co-chairmen of the delegation conferred with Bethmann-Hollweg. The Chancellor read excerpts from the speech he planned to give in the Reichstag and painted a gloomy picture of Germany's military position. When he was informed that the Social Democrats had as yet made no decision regarding the voting of war credits, but that in any case they would read a statement on the issue, he pleaded with the party leaders to urge the delegation to give up this plan. If they insisted on issuing a declaration, they should refrain from making any plea for an early peace.[35]

The commission had before it three drafts, one drawn up by Haase, another by the well-known revisionist lawyer and journalist Wolfgang Heine and a third by Hoch, a centrist who tended to sympathize with Haase's position.[36] Haase's draft, obviously an attempt by the opposition to make the best of a bad situation, expressed the S.P.D.'s wish for an early peace and explicitly demanded that the German government declare that it would welcome any offer by neutral countries to mediate between the warring powers. It further condemned every effort to turn the struggle into a war of conquest and declared that the party expected the government to live up to Bethmann's promise of August 4 to make full restitution for the unjust invasion of Belgium.[37] This statement was, of course, completely unacceptable to the majority of the commission. It was only after hours of heated discussion, however, that a draft was accepted which largely conformed to the outline proposed by Heine.[38]

The commission completed its work a quarter of an hour before the delegation convened again. After Haase had described in some detail the meeting with the Chancellor, the commission's draft statement was read. Several amendments were immediately proposed by Hoch and Haase's friend Oscar Cohn which would have restored the key points of Haase's draft. After considerable debate, these amendments were defeated, receiving the support of between twenty-nine and thirty-four deputies. To the dismay of Heine and David,[39] however, Scheidemann at this point introduced a compromise resolution which provided that if Bethmann should try to justify the German breach of Belgian neutrality in his Reichstag speech, the S.P.D. would formally declare that it continued to support the Chancellor's statement of August 4 in which he had admitted that the attack had been an unjust, if necessary act. This motion was easily passed. The delegation then voted by a margin of eighty-two to seventeen to again support the government's request for war credits and accepted the commission's draft statement seventy-four to twenty-two.[40] The opposition had thus made only a minor numerical advance since August 4, although the more substantial votes for the strengthening of the declaration indicated that a considerable number of delegates were gravitating toward it.

At this point the precariously maintained discipline within the delegation was threatened directly by the radical Alfred Henke, who moved that the opposition be allowed to vote against the war credits in the Reichstag. In the excited debate which ensued, Haase intervened decisively against the motion. "It would," he declared,

represent the end of all discipline, the disintegration of the delegation. The minority must follow the will of the majority. That has always been the practice in the party, and at the present time it is impossible to make a new decision in this matter.

"We cannot," he concluded, "take up the struggle after the war with a broken battle line."[41] Apparently impressed by these arguments, Henke withdrew his motion. It was renewed by Liebknecht, who defended it by adducing the obligation of every politician to express his view openly. In the face of Haase's impassioned appeal for the preservation of party unity, however, Liebknecht could make little headway with such arguments, and the motion received only seven votes. When Liebknecht then moved that the Reichstag statement be made "in the name of the overwhelming majority," Haase again expressed his opposition, and the motion was rejected. The meeting was then adjourned.[42] The first formal attempt to split the ranks of the Social Democratic Reichstag delegation had thus been defeated, largely through Haase's intervention.

The danger was, however, not to be so easily dispelled. The S.P.D. statement was, as in August, immediately communicated both to the government and to the leaders of the other parties. On December 1 it became known that both the government and the other parties were dissatisfied with the statement and that, as a result, the non-socialist parties planned to issue their own statement to counter that of the Social Democrats.[43] This development unleashed a new and extremely heated debate within the ranks of the S.P.D. At a meeting on the first of the leaders of all of the delegations with representatives of the government, the S.P.D. declaration was criticized sentence by sentence. Haase defended the statement and insisted that it could not be altered. That evening the issue was raised during a meeting of the executive committee of the delegation. When Scheidemann proposed that a number of changes be made, Haase heatedly declared that they could under no circumstances give in to the pressure of the other parties. He would not agree to such a step even if the division of the party were to be the result. Scheidemann and David attacked Haase's point of view while Ledebour supported it and Ebert sought to mediate.[44]

It appeared at this point that an absolute stalemate had been reached, and both sides began to prepare for the showdown which would take place during the meeting of the entire delegation scheduled for the following morning. Late that evening a group of David's friends met to discuss the situation. David reported Haase's threats and urged the group to refuse to capitulate. They must insist on acceptance of the necessary changes, he argued, and if they gained the support of the majority, they should simply allow the opposition "to raise the flag of rebellion." If Haase should gain the support of the majority, however, they would be forced to give in, since they had already voted for the statement as it stood. Most of those present accepted David's point of view, and he returned home convinced that he would now finally have an opportunity to expose Haase's machinations to the full view of all.[45]

While the right-wing leaders were thus planning their strategy for the expected confrontation, the opposition did not remain inactive. When it became known that the majority might agree to the proposed changes, Hoch called a meeting attended by some thirty deputies. This group agreed that if the majority did capitulate, they would read the original version of the S.P.D. statement in the Reichstag, thus publicly revealing the lack of unity which existed within the party.[46]

It thus appeared during the night of December 1–2 that the decisive crisis was in the offing, the crisis which Haase and the other centrist leaders had so long sought to avoid. While both sides prepared for the approaching showdown, Haase once again struggled with his conscience. During the executive committee meeting, Scheidemann had been called out by a government representative who urged him to bring Haase to another meeting with Bethmann-Hollweg. Although Scheidemann objected that such a meeting would be useless, he finally agreed. It was after 10 P.M. when the two Social Democratic leaders reached the Chancellery, and the discussion which ensued lasted until almost midnight. Bethmann insisted again that he had done everything possible to avoid war and predicted that the S.P.D.'s declaration would be interpreted abroad as an attribution of all responsibility for the war to the German government and the non-socialist parties. Haase left the meeting without having made any final decision as to whether he would modify his position.[47]

Whether this discussion with the Chancellor made any decisive impression upon Haase or whether he was motivated by his continuing concern to preserve the unity of the party is impossible to determine, but in any case, when he appeared for the meeting of the delegation the next morning, he declared to Scheidemann that, after a sleepless night, he had decided to propose certain changes in the text of the Social Democratic statement.[48] After reporting his decision to his surprised opposition colleagues, Haase began the meeting with a description of the various negotiations which had taken place during the previous twenty-four hours. He concluded this report by declaring that in his opinion the party could not give up its planned statement, that it could not allow the content of its statement to be determined by the other parties, and that it could not allow its fundamental position to be obscured. He added, however, that he thought a satisfactory solution to the problems which had arisen could be achieved if the statement were made more precise in a number of places. He then outlined his proposed changes, the most important of which rephrased the reference to Belgium in such a way that it merely stated that the facts which had become known since August 4 did not in the opinion of the S.P.D. provide sufficient grounds for departing from the position enunciated by the Chancellor on that day regarding the invasion of Belgium and Luxemburg.[49]

David was absolutely dumbfounded by this unexpected turn of events. In his opinion, the new wording was in some ways worse than that of the original draft.[50] Nevertheless, after Scheidemann, Ebert, and Molkenbuhr had intervened in support of Haase's proposals, the debate was quickly terminated, and the revised statement was accepted by an overwhelming majority.[51] David had thus been prevented from launching his attack on Haase, and those on the left who had hoped for a decisive showdown had been frustrated. The center had once again congealed at the decisive moment and the disruption of the party had been forestalled. When the question was raised as to who should read the statement in the Reichstag, Haase at first refused to be considered, but after several members of the party executive committee as well as a number of the radicals heatedly urged him to do so, he again acquiesced.[52]

It should be noted that at the last minute Haase agreed to still another concession to the government and his opponents in the S.P.D. After Scheidemann had once more discussed the matter with the Foreign Secretary, von

Jagow, he persuaded Haase to read the passage concerning Belgium as a kind of introduction to the official declaration rather than as an integral part of the statement itself.[53] The statement in its final form declared that the S.P.D. continued to support the point of view it had expressed on August 4. The fundamental cause of the war lay in the clash of economic interests. The party had opposed the war until the last possible moment, but inasmuch as the borders of Germany still lay under the threat of foreign invasion, the Social Democratic deputies would again vote for war credits. The S.P.D. remained convinced that the continued development of the peoples of Europe would only be possible if every nation respected the integrity and independence of every other. The party therefore demanded, as on August 4, that the war be brought to an end as soon as security had been achieved and Germany's opponents were ready to conclude a peace which would make possible the establishment of friendly relations between Germany and her neighbours. The party condemned the efforts by small groups in every country to propagate mutual hatred among the peoples of Europe. As long as the war lasted every effort should be made to ease the suffering of the participants. The S.P.D. expected the government to express its trust in the German people through concrete acts. The continued maintenance of martial law and the limitation of civil rights, especially freedom of the press, was unjustified. The S.P.D. demanded that the government act immediately to rectify this intolerable situation.

The Social Democratic declaration was answered by a statement read in the name of all of the other parties. This statement, which was greeted by stormy applause, declared that in the present situation the welfare of the fatherland stood above all other considerations. In the war which had been forced upon Germany, the non-socialist parties asserted their determination "to hold out until a peace has been won that will justify the tremendous sacrifices of the German people and provide for a lasting defense against all possible enemies."[54] It represented just the kind of veiled justification of annexations which many of the Social Democratic deputies had warned against while arguing for a revision of their own statement. On the other hand, it also appeared to prove the contention of Haase and his friends that the war had become a war of conquest for Germany.

Karl Liebknecht was, of course, undeterred by his failure to persuade anyone to join him in voting against the war credits, and he carried out his act of defiance alone. Although from the long range point of view Liebknecht's act must be considered an important turning point in the history of German socialism, to many contemporaries it did not seem particularly significant. It was, to be sure, the occasion of considerable excitement in the Reichstag, including a number of outraged catcalls from right-wing Social Democrats, but it was so much less than what had been anticipated during the critical days that preceded the session that it came as something of an anticlimax.[55]

The S.P.D. thus survived its second major crisis of the war largely by virtue of the fact that Haase continued to place his immediate organizational responsibilities above his oppostion to the policy of August 4. As the crisis had unfolded, however, the difficulties inherent in Haase's position had become still more fully apparent. His problematical role as a mediator both between the Social Democratic Reichstag delegation and the government and between the leadership of that delegation and his allies in the opposition had proved to be particulary trying. Moreover, although the fact that his behavior had at times tended to be somewhat indecisive and confusing was, under the circumstances, quite understandable, it did not bode well for his future as the leader of what was eventually to become a revolutionary movement.

CHAPTER VI

COLLAPSE OF THE CENTER

As the new year began, Haase continued to uphold essentially the same position he had developed in August. During the previous five months, he had consistently defended his view that the war was being waged by Germany with aggressive intent and that the S.P.D. had flagrantly violated its fundamental principles by agreeing to support the war effort and by yielding to the government's desire to establish a domestic political truce for the duration of the conflict. If anything, these views seemed to Haase to have been amply confirmed by the course of events.[1]

While refusing to be shaken in his original analysis of the war and of his party's relation to it, however, Haase had also continued to hold fast to his organizational principles, the cardinal axiom of which was that the unity of the party had to be preserved at all costs. Thus, while acting as the principal spokesman of the opposition within the S.P.D., he had simultaneously insisted upon the minority's strict adherence to the democratic principle of majority rule. But as the early months of 1915 passed without any significant change in the military situation and the centrifugal pressures within the S.P.D. continued to mount, Haase was finally compelled to begin the fundamental, if gradual, reevaluation and revision of his views which would constitute the central theme of his political life during the next two and one-half years.

To a very considerable degree, of course, the problems which Haase now had to face had existed in a latent form from the moment he stepped into the leadership of the party. He had been elected to the chairmanship as a representative of the center, as a conciliator who, it was believed, was well equipped to maintain party unity against the attacks from left and right which had developed well before German Social Democracy met its supreme test in the World War. When the war began, however, he found himself the leader of a left-wing minority while continuing to represent both the party as a whole and its Reichstag delegation as titular head.

One solution to this dilemma would, of course, have been for Haase to have revised his position on the war issue so that it more nearly conformed to that of the majority. He was, however, so deeply committed to this position that this was impossible. There is no evidence that he at any point even considered such a compromise. His views concerning the war remained essentially the same from August 4 until its conclusion in 1918. Another way out would have been for him to have resigned his chairmanship as soon as it became apparent that he no longer enjoyed the support of the majority of the Social Democratic leadership. This was the solution which men like Heine and David obviously hoped for and indeed considered mandatory for a man of principle.[2] Here again, however, Haase considered himself obligated to reject any compromise. He was certain that his position accurately reflected the program so laboriously formulated by the S.P.D. in its national congresses and that his resignation from the party chairmanship would therefore have constituted a betrayal of the mandate he had been given by the representatives of the party as a whole. He repeatedly offered to give up his chairmanship of the Reichstag delegation, but, significantly, this challenge remained unaccepted for nearly seventeen months, despite the continuous private complaining of the majority leaders.[3] Undoubtedly, this refusal to force the issue indicated that many members of the majority shared Haase's conviction that he represented a last tenuous link holding the party together, in spite of, or even because of his espousal of the minority point of view.

At the beginning of 1915 Haase thus found himself in the highly uncomfortable position of defending posts which had already in effect been lost.[4] Until that time he had sought to make the situation at least tolerable by refraining from participating in any of the public polemics which were erupting with increasing frequency.[5] In January, however, the party council officially ended the internal truce which had, in any case, become by that time little more than a farce, and henceforth Haase found himself drawn ever more deeply into the struggle.[6] Indeed, before long he began to feel that his role as the leader of the opposition required the fullest possible exploitation of his polemical talents. His attitude toward the war thus gradually began to take precedence over his role as defender of party unity.

This development, of course, could not but further exacerbate his relationship with his colleagues in the executive committee and in the leadership of the Reichstag delegation. Furthermore, his position as party chairman made him the natural focal point of the antagonism now generated in both the extreme right and left wings of the party. David and his friends could and did fulminate with great zeal and indignation against Liebknecht's misdeeds, but it was becoming increasingly apparent that Haase was their *bête noire* because he represented a much more serious obstacle to their plans for a fundamental revision of the party's orientation. On the other hand, Liebknecht and his friends exhibited precious little gratitude for Haase's efforts to defend them from the most extreme repercussions of their increasingly defiant attitude toward the party leadership. It was in 1915 that the extreme left unleashed its campaign of vilification against Haase and his friends which would by the end of the year lead them to brand the "social pacifists" as even more dangerous to the true socialist faith than the "social patriots" who were attacking Haase from the right.

The coming of the war, therefore, far from easing the inherent dilemmas of centrism for Haase, merely aggravated them, while at the same time drastically reducing the base of support which the party chairman could count on in his struggle simultaneously to defend the traditional principles of Social Democracy and to preserve the unity of the party. It is little wonder, then, that Haase was accused by those who opposed him of duplicity, or inconsistency, or as David trenchantly expressed it, of posing a "psychological riddle."[7] The extremists could assert their points of view with far more clarity and forthrightness than Haase, for he had refused to abandon the responsibilities which by their very nature ruled out any simplistic approach to the problems faced by the party. The conciliator's role is never an easy one, but for Haase the war had magnified all of the normal difficulties associated with it. In the end it would make them insurmountable.

At the beginning of 1915, however, it was only the extremists who had given up all hope of keeping the party intact. The centrist leaders, as well as the great majority of the membership, continued to try to live with their problems as best they could, hoping that somehow, perhaps through an early end of the war and the convening of a national convention, these problems might still be satisfactorily resolved.

The executive committee remained, of course, a principal arena of the growing internal struggle during this period, and the available evidence suggests that Haase's experience in this body was particularly trying. Even disregarding entirely the strain caused by political disagreement, the executive committee members' work was both difficult and tedious. They were constantly being called upon to intervene with the government on behalf of censored Social Democratic newspapers, to arrange for governmental approval of local meetings, to come to the aid of soldiers who found themselves being unfairly dealt with by their superiors, and generally to try to ease somewhat the social and economic difficulties of the working class which naturally increased radically as the war progressed.[8] Haase, because of his part-time commitment to party work, was undoubtedly not as deeply involved in such work as the "professionals," but as the S.P.D.'s most eminent jurist, he was obliged to take on his shoulders a large share of the legal work which represented a major portion of the total burden. In any case, he found that the war significantly reduced the flow of his non-party litigation, thus freeing him for more active participation in political affairs.[9] The strain upon the party leaders was so great that even Scheidemann and Ebert, who were in essential agreement on the fundamental political questions, at times came into conflict concerning relatively trivial matters.[10] This tension was in Haase's case, of course, immensely magnified by the impassioned struggle in which he was engaged. When major policy decisions were to be made, he found himself almost inevitably in the minority, yet the constant pressure he exerted at the very center of the party organization occasionally resulted in partial victories and in the last analysis undoubtedly did much to moderate the policies actually carried out by his opponents.

The struggle in which Haase now found himself almost constantly engaged ranged over a wide variety of issues. One type of problem that repeatedly arose involved the question of how those who departed from the officially sanctioned policies should be disciplined. On December 22, for instance, a meeting of the executive committees of the party and of the Reichstag delegation was called to consider the case of Georg Weill, an Alsatian Reichstag deputy who had joined the French army. Haase regarded Weill's action as entirely understandable. After all, Ludwig Frank, another S.P.D. deputy, had been the first member of the Reichstag to be killed in action and had been much praised for his patriotism. If Weill, as an Alsatian, felt himself obligated to serve the French cause as Frank had the German, there was, for Haase, little to choose between them. The S.P.D. was more or less obliged to sever its connections with an enemy soldier, but there was no reason why this necessary separation should be accompanied by criticism of a perfectly honest and conscientious act. Such an attitude, however, was absolutely incomprehensible to those who, like David, themselves had been gripped by the patriotic enthusiasm engendered by the war. David and his friends insisted upon an explicit condemnation of Weill's deed and eventually were successful in winning their point, but only by a majority of seven to six.[11]

At the same session, Ledebour introduced a motion to call an immediate meeting of the Reichstag delegation to consider the case of David's friend, Albert Südekum, who had recently engaged in various activities at the behest of the government without first obtaining the permission of the party executive committee. This motion was defeated over the spirited objections of Ledebour and Haase, with Ebert arguing for the majority that the matter was of concern to the party executive alone.[12] This defeat in turn led to the resignation of Ledebour from the executive committee of the Reichstag delegation, an act which, for the moment at least, further aggravated Haase's difficulties.[13]

Early in January the party's executive committee was confronted with another highly divisive issue. Rosa Luxemburg, who had been sentenced during the previous spring to a year's imprisonment for her agitation against her trial her case had aroused immense sympathy among the masses of party members. Now, however, her deeds smacked of treason, and the moderates were little inclined to endanger the party for the sake of the acid-tongued

extremist who had branded them "social patriots." Nevertheless, the suggestion was made that demonstrations be organized on her behalf, and Haase
supported this proposal only to suffer another stinging defeat.[14]

Such official decisions concerning party policy were, however, not the
only matters which aroused controversy at these sessions. At the first meeting
of the party executive committee after the beginning of the new year, for
instance, Haase angrily attacked Scheidemann for having published a highly
patriotic new year's greeting to the voters in his electoral district. The message,
which praised the nation's military heroes in glowing terms and emphasized
the necessity of maintaining a determination to achieve victory, aroused
widespread misgivings among party members unaccustomed to such enthusiastically nationalistic statements on the part of their leaders.[15] When
Scheidemann sought to pacify his colleagues by arguing that anyone engaged
in a struggle wanted to achieve victory if his opponents rejected reconciliation,
Haase heatedly pointed out that however Scheidemann himself interpreted
his statement, it was bound to be misunderstood by the public. Scheidemann
conceded this point but refused to apologize for or retract any part of his
greeting.[16]

One major factor that undoubtedly tended to increase the tension among
executive committee members was Scheidemann's increasing intimacy with
the representatives of the government. Although on many occasions Haase
was of course invited to participate in meetings with government officials,
Scheidemann apparently was increasingly consulted individually, and indeed,
many of his meetings with the Chancellor were kept secret even from his
closest associates.[17] This relationship, so unlike that which had existed between
Social Democratic and government leaders before the war, could not but
make an adverse impression on Haase, who was devoting all of his energies to
directing the party back to its prewar stand of adamant and consistent opposition to the status quo.

Another scene of frequent conflict was the party council, which gained
increased importance as it became apparent that the continuation of the war
would make the calling of a regular national congress impossible in the
foreseeable future. The majority leaders quickly recognized that the constitution of this body insured their predominance, and thus repeatedly turned to it
as the best available means of obtaining sanction for their more controversial
policy decisions.

At the council's first meeting of 1915 which was held in mid-January, Haase
found himself compelled to take a defensive position on nearly every issue
discussed. The debates abounded in attacks upon the foreign socialist parties,
upon the editorial policy of the *Vorwärts* and upon Liebknecht's vote against
the war credits in the Reichstag. In his replies, Haase in each case conceded

some degree of justification to the majority spokesmen. He regretted recent statements by some French socialist leaders, but insisted that equally provocative remarks had been made by members of the S.P.D. He urged his colleagues to try to preserve international ties wherever possible and to pursue a policy of strict self-criticism while seeking to understand the problems of others. He also agreed that the *Vorwärts* left much to be desired, although he was in essential agreement with its editorial policy. He urged the council members, however, to recognize that many of the paper's problems could be traced directly to the government's censorship which was applied with special rigor to the party's central organ. He further declared that he too regretted Liebknecht's breach of discipline. He insisted, however, that Liebknecht was conscientiously trying to do what he believed to be in the best interests of the party. Obviously eager to avoid giving any further sanction to the actions of the Reichstag delegation, he urged the council to avoid any vote on the issue of war credits, maintaining that a thorough debate was necessary before any final decision could be made.[18]

Dealing briefly with the question of war credits, Haase insisted that events were simply proving the validity of the party's prewar program. The imperialistic character of the conflict was becoming increasingly clear. The guilt of the German government was well documented even by its own *White Book*. "That we must defend our country is self evident," Haase declared,

but what good will it do if after we have fought against the policies of a government and these policies have led to a catastrophe, we then support that government by voting it war credits? That is the key point in the question of war credits.

Concerning the possibility of embarking on an effective peace offensive in the near future, he expressed himself on the whole pessimistically, but he predicted that with care and tact, concerted action by the united international proletariat could before long be initiated.

In reply to those who argued that any peace offensive should be delayed until Germany's borders had been secured, he declared that when the spokesmen of the bourgeoisie talked of security, they meant to imply something very different from what Social Democrats intended when they used the term. The goals of the S.P.D. were clear. They included no annexations and no "rounding off" of border districts. "How long . . . shall we wait?" he concluded. "Between victory and defeat there is a middle way which we now see before us. We are the interpretors of the yearning for peace of the working classes and of many other groups as well."[19]

Perhaps the liveliest exchange of the session was initiated by the revisionist labor leader Carl Severing who denounced Haase for destroying the homogeneity of the party executive and thereby rendering it ineffective at the most crucial moment in the history of the movement. Backed by Scheidemann as well as by a number of those who shared his views, Haase vigorously counterattacked. Severing had no right to try to silence him, he asserted. The party did not have a "homogeneous ministry." If that were the case he would gladly return to the ranks. There might be some who wanted him to do just that, but they would have to have patience. He intended to remain at his post and continue to say openly whatever he thought it was in the interest of the party to say.[20]

The two-day meeting came to an end after the council had taken two formal actions. The agreement reached at the previous session not to discuss publicly the policy of the Reichstag delegation was abrogated, and a resolution was passed declaring that the council considered it desirable that every opportunity be utilized to bring about concerted action by the International for peace.[21] Haase's ability to serve as a moderating influence on the majority had once more been proved, but from this point forward it would clearly begin to wane.

The meeting of the Reichstag delegation which Ledebour had so vigorously demanded in December was finally convened in February. Although Ledebour had hoped it would deal with the case of Südekum, it actually centered much more on the case of Liebknecht. Haase maintained an attitude of reserve, acting simply as the spokesman of the executive committee, until the question of initiating some action for peace was raised on the final day of the three-day session. The first day's discussions, which were devoted entirely to Liebknecht, were noteworthy for the viciousness with which the motives of the left-wing radicals were impugned. Legien even went so far as to move that Liebknecht be expelled from the Social Democratic delegation. The question of discipline, however, was a difficult one, especially for many members of the revisionist wing who but a few years earlier had been engaged in a struggle to assert their independence against a radical majority. In the course of the debate, indeed, one of the revisionist leaders admitted that if the delegation had voted against the war credits on August 4, he and some thirty of his colleagues would have broken discipline and voted openly for the credits.[22] Expulsion, therefore, was a solution which at this point had little chance of receiving majority support, especially in view of the fact that the party's by-laws included no provision for such an action to be taken by the delegation. Nevertheless, the debate ended with a clear defeat for Haase and his friends. A brief and relatively moderate resolution proposed by Haase for the executive committee of the delegation was replaced by a lengthy statement drawn up in advance by David and his friends[23] which roundly condemned Liebknecht's breach of discipline, declared his attempted justification of the act irreconcilable with the interests of German Social Democracy, and further condemned the reports of S.P.D. internal affairs which Liebknecht had circulated abroad. An amendment proposed by Bernstein, which would have formally recognized that Liebknecht's political motives were not inconsistent with Social Democratic principles, was defeated by a margin of sixty-eight to twenty.[24] The delegation then went on to pass over little opposition a statement outlining a code of procedure for future Reichstag votes. Those who were in the minority would have the right to leave the chamber before a vote was taken, but they would be obligated to do so without giving their abstention a demonstrative character.[25]

On the second day of the meeting, the deputies finally grappled with the case of Südekum. The result stood in stark contrast to the action taken against Liebknecht. A resolution was passed which merely confirmed an earlier statement by the combined executive committees of the delegation and the party which rather mildly critized Südekum's activities on behalf of the government and then went on to instruct party members to obtain the permission of the executive committee of either the party or the delegation or of the delegation as a whole before undertaking similar projects in the future. Haase and his friends were also frustrated in their efforts to persuade the delegation to undertake an immediate initiative for peace.[26] The only clear victory they achieved occurred at the end of the meetings when, by a narrow margin, Gustav Hoch, one of the most articulate spokesmen of the oppositionists grouped around Haase, was elected to replace Ledebour on the executive committee of the delegation.[27]

The results of the February delegation meetings were undoubtedly depressing for Haase and his friends. In a letter addressed to Victor Adler a few days after its conclusion, Kautsky declared that a few months earlier it had appeared to him that the greatest danger to party unity came from the extreme left.

Now it comes from the right. Those around David and the trade union leaders believe the moment has come to cleanse the party of all its Marxism. It would be difficult for them to conceive of simply throwing us out, but they dominate the executive committee and occupy one position after another with their own people.

They were trying to condemn him and his friends to silence, he continued. Neither he nor his friends were working for a split. Indeed, until now, he had constantly urged the maintenance of internal peace, but the situation was becoming more bitter every day. "For the immediate future," he concluded, "my mood is therefore very pessimistic."[28]

The right-wing leaders were, however, also by no means completely satisfied with the situation. David described in his diary the "terrible effort" he had been required to make during the delegation meetings. Haase, he noted, was an "unbelievably cunning jurist, pettifogger and stage manager," and he and his associates were much more capable parliamentary tacticians than the leaders of David's own group.[29] In one of his regular reports to the ailing reformist leader of the Bavarian Social Democrats Georg von Vollmar, Heine expressed a somewhat similar view of the situation. David seemed to him to be unsuited for leadership. Scheidemann, although at times lacking in tact, was at least reliable, but Ebert remained inconsistent. The great majority of his friends still did not know precisely what they wanted, and, unfortunately, the anti-nationalistic phrases of the party's traditional propaganda had sunk firmer roots than he had thought. Nevertheless, they must try to make good use of the patriotic passions aroused by the war. Otherwise, the opportunity might be lost for good.[30]

The S.P.D. therefore approached the March session of the Reichstag under a cloud of growing mutual antagonism among its leaders and a general sense of confusion and frustration in all its parts. And the new session gave little promise of providing an opportunity for clarifying the situation. Indeed, the war credits issue was further clouded in March by the government's decision to tie the new credits to the budget. It had been possible in August and December of 1914 to argue that the voting of war credits represented a response to an exceptional situation rather than an explicit expression of confidence which, according to the program hammered out before the war, a vote for a regular budget entailed. Now it appeared that the issue would have to be more clearly faced.

Recognizing the delicacy of the situation, Ebert decided to convene the party council immediately before the March session, hoping and no doubt expecting to obtain the sanction of this body for a decision to vote for the budget.[31] Haase was prevented from attending this meeting by a prior commitment to address a local gathering in Königsberg. He clearly recognized the significance of the budget issue, however, and therefore addressed a letter to Ebert in which he detailed his views on the question at some length. He had, he wrote, carefully considered the matter and come to the conclusion that a vote for the budget was clearly irreconcilable with the decision of the 1908 party congress as Bebel and Ebert himself had interpreted it. The present situation, he wrote, could in no way be considered as fulfilling the criteria outlined for the exception which was allowed by that ruling. The question could, therefore, only be "whether the party council and the Reichstag delegation want consciously to break the resolution passed . . . by the party convention by temporarily setting aside . . . this ruling." Even if, as had apparently been suggested, a statement were to be made that the vote was only to be viewed as a response to an exceptional situation, they would still be clearly contravening the will of the party as expressed by its national conventions.[32]

When the council met on March 7, it was immediately apparent that Haase's letter had been very much to the point. In his opening speech, Ebert repeated the by now familiar argument that the situation had not fundamentally changed since August 4 and that those who had voted for war credits in the past should therefore vote for them again during the approaching Reichstag session. He admitted that the inclusion of war credits in the budget caused certain difficulties, but insisted that any contradiction between the granting of this particular budget and the resolutions passed by pre-war conventions was more apparent than real. He went on to argue somewhat lamely that the exception which had been allowed by these resolutions could in fact be applied to the present situation. Certainly, if the refusal to vote for the budget endangered the welfare of the entire Reich, such a refusal should be construed as being inimical to the interests of the working class. In any case, the actions of August and December represented in the strictest sense votes for the budget of the Reich. It was, furthermore, clear that the present budget was designed to reinforce the war effort. A decision to oppose the budget would thus represent a reversal of the policy of August and December, a reversal which would have to be viewed as a misfortune for the German people and a threat to the future of the party. The debate which followed indicated that a few, at least, of those present shared Haase's rather than Ebert's view. Nevertheless, the council voted by a margin of thirty-one to ten to recommend the granting of the budget. Indeed, the majority went so far as to include in its resolution an explicit statement that in their opinion the present case represented the kind of exception provided for by the congress's rulings.[33]

Haase was in the chair when the Reichstag delegation as a whole met on the following day. Despite their victory in the party council, several of the majority leaders approached the session with considerable misgivings. The general recognition that there was little prospect for an early peace combined with the increasing difficulty of provisioning the populace and the government's obvious reluctance to concede any meaningful reforms had led to a widespread decline in enthusiasm for the position taken by the S.P.D. on August 4.[34] Haase opened the meeting with a report on recent meetings of Social Democratic leaders with government representatives who had urged them to refrain from following their usual practice of making a general speech on the occasion of the first reading of the budget. The majority of the delegation's executive committee had voted to recommend that the delegation pass up this opportunity for a policy statement, but the growing dissatisfaction of the delegation made itself felt in the discussion which followed, and a large majority voted to override the objections of David and Scheidemann and support Haase's demand for such a speech. An attempt by the right wing to have Scheidemann give the speech instead of Haase also was defeated, although by a less substantial margin.[35]

Between the delegation meetings of March 8 and 9, Bethmann made another concerted effort to dissuade the Social Democratic leaders from their intention to speak on the first reading of the budget. If they were determined to speak, he urged, they should avoid any reference to the peace issue, inasmuch as the government was just at that time engaged in highly delicate efforts to deal with some apparent peace feelers. Bethmann's argument apparently made some impression on Haase, for in his report to the delegation, he declared that he could understand why some of those present at the discussions with the Chancellor were opposed to any attempt to raise the peace issue at the moment. He had also been impresed, however, by the Chancellor's statement that he hoped "a larger and stronger Germany would emerge from the war." Haase therefore continued to insist upon the necessity of including the question of achieving an early and just peace in his speech. The issue must be clarified, he declared. "We must demand that Germany conduct no war of aggression. The government must declare its goals."[36] After a lively debate, the delegation voted by a slim majority to authorize him to include the peace issue.[37]

Haase's speech, at least in so far as it touched upon the question of peace, was quite moderate in tone, and, as he had predicted to his colleagues, could hardly have been considered "dangerous" to the German war effort.[38] Indeed, he began his statement by frankly recognizing that the S.P.D. was moved by the conviction that the defense of one's homeland was a duty. He added, however, that the public expression of justified criticism of one's government was by no means irreconcilable with that obligation. He then launched into a telling assault upon many of the government's domestic policies since the beginning of the war. It was only toward the end of his speech that he touched briefly on the peace issue. The yearning for peace, he declared, was becoming increasingly apparent in every country. The expression of this obvious fact could not, as some maintained, be construed as a sign of weakness, especially on the part of the Gemans, whose military successes and economic strength were undeniable. On the contrary, it was the special obligation of the strongest power to first extend the hand of peace. As the most consistent supporters of international peace, both in Germany and abroad, the Social Democrats demanded a settlement which would involve the oppression of no people, for only such a settlement could become the basis of a permanent peace.[39]

Contrary to the fears of many of his moderate and right wing colleagues, Haase's speech aroused no great outcry from the other parties. A very brief reply was made by the Center Party deputy Spahn, speaking for most of the nonsocialist parties represented in the Reichstag. Interestingly enough, Spahn declared that he and his friends felt that only Haase's references to the peace issue required an immediate comment. His reply, however, simply took the form of a repetition of the ominous but quite nebulous assertion, which was fast becoming almost a cliché, that Germany must fight on until it could be assured of its future economic and military security.[40] Haase later remarked to his colleagues that in his judgment his speech had given little or no cause for offense.[41] Even Heine reported that Haase's discussion of the peace issue had not been dangerous, although he added that the speech "reads better than it actually sounded."[42]

If Haase's speech of March 10, therefore, precipitated considerable debate within the S.P.D. and may even, as Eugen Prager suggests, have been greeted by many workers as "the first proletarian trumpet blast . . . amidst the fog of chauvinism,"[43] it did not have any serious impact upon the continuing crisis within the party. Far more important in this regard were the events associated with the final three days of the Reichstag session, held after an intervening week of committee work.

The right wing leaders approached the next meeting of the delegation, scheduled for March 17, with considerable trepidation after their defeat on the issue of Haase's speech. On the evening of March 16, David met, as usual, with a number of his friends to discuss their strategy. Two of those present declared that they would vote for the budget regardless of what the delegation might decide to do. David himself solemnly wrote in his diary on the following day:

If the opposition wins, then the hour of decision will have come for me; then [we must make] a clean split for the sake of both the nation and the working class. A party based on Haase, Liebknecht, etc., would be discredited and impotent.[44]

The tensions within the party were obviously once more approaching the boiling point.

In the meantime, a new factor had been injected into the situation in the form of a frankly annexationist speech delivered by the President of the Prussian Herrenhaus on March 15.[45] This highly provocative statement obviously tended to lend added credence to Haase's argument concerning the imperialistic character of the German war effort, and as such it immediately became a major issue in the debates of the delegation. Scheidemann had been delegated to comment for the party on the Reichstag speeches of the Chancellor and Foreign Secretary scheduled for March 18, and in the delegation meeting of March 17 Josef Simon, one of the more recent recruits to the opposition forces, unleashed a major debate by proposing that Scheidemann include an attack upon the Prussian offical's speech. Scheidemann opposed the motion, arguing that such an attack would merely provide an opportunity for the annexationists to launch a full-scale campaign. Simon's motion was eventually defeated by the relatively slim margin of forty-eight to thirty-nine.[46] It had, however, provided another dramatic illustration of the potential instability of the majority forces.

It was not until the eighteenth that the issue of war credits was formally raised within the delegation. After the usual heated debate, in which Haase played no major role, the deputies defeated by a margin of sixty-four to thirty-four an opposition proposal to grant only half of the government's request[47] and then went on to vote by a margin of seventy-seven to twenty-three in favor of approving the full amount.[48] Although for the moment defeated, the opposition was continuing its slow but steady advance within the delegation on the fundamental question of voting war credits. Moreover, Haase and his friends had not yet played their trump card. On this occasion the delegation was compelled to determine whether it would break with tradition and grant the government its entire budget. When the question was raised, Ebert immediately pointed out the obvious fact that a refusal to grant the budget would nullify the decision they had just made to vote for war credits. He went on to argue for the acceptance of the budget in much the same terms he had used in the debate within the party council.[49]

The cogency of Ebert's argument, however, was not sufficient to dispel the misgivings of a number of deputies concerning this apparently blatant breach of a resolution passed by the representatives of the party as a whole. Haase now entered the debate with a major speech in which he sought to capitalize on this uneasiness. Ranging over the whole history of German Social Democracy, he insisted that it was impossible to read into the decisions of the national conventions what was not there. The S.P.D. had rejected funds for military expansion in peacetime even when the government had declared that the situation was absolutely critical. The claim that a refusal by the party to grant the present budget would strike the sword from the hand of the government was completely unfounded. The question at issue was rather whether they should rally to the support of the government or whether they should declare that they refused to condone the government's policies. It was absurd to claim at a time when all of the bourgeois parties were busying themselves with plans for annexations that the government wanted merely to defend the Reich. The government was no opponent of annexations. It merely recognized more clearly than the bourgeois politicians the difficulties of Germany's military position and therefore was more inhibited than they were about making claims it knew were impossible of achievement.[50]

The impact of the arguments presented in this vein by Haase and his friends upon party members trained to view the decisions of their national conventions as absolutely binding was obviously considerable. When the final vote was taken on the issue of the budget, the opposition had risen to thirty. Thus, within eight months, the group supporting Haase had doubled.[51] The opposition now numbered nearly a third of the entire delegation and gave every indication that its growth would continue. David noted in his diary that night that he had suffered one of the most harrowing experiences of his life. With the defeat of the opposition "an immense weight had been lifted from [his] soul."[52]

The opposition was, however, no longer willing merely to express itself within the confines of the closed party caucuses. Encouraged by their recent successes and by the growing sympathy they sensed among the masses of party members, thirty deputies demonstrated their disapproval of the majority's policy by absenting themselves when the vote on the budget was taken in the Reichstag on March 20. Liebknecht was now joined by his friend Rühle in his open vote against the government. The publication of the names of the abstainers in the *Vorwärts* gave their action a demonstrative character which insured that it would have an immense impact upon the party as a whole.[53] After months of intense struggle behind the scenes, the opposition suddenly emerged as a powerful and imposing force.

This, of course, did much to deepen the split in the ranks of German Social Democracy. The very fact that Scheidemann, an outspoken leader of the majority, rather than Haase now read the statement on war credits in the Reichstag removed one major symbol of party unity. The situation had reached the point where key centrist figures such as Ebert, who had done so much to bridge the widening gap between right and left, now found themselves drawn inexorably into one of the two camps so that their ability to perform a mediative function was in large measure impaired. On March 19, Ebert, in a conversation with David, clearly endorsed the reformist tactics so long advocated by the right wing, although he still was unwilling to abandon the formal concept of the class struggle.[54] Early in April, Ebert informed David's friend Schöpflin that he had decided to begin preparing in the local party organizations for the decisive struggle with Haase, which would inevitably erupt during the next national congress.[55]

On the other hand, there was increasing evidence that Haase, who had also done much to preserve party unity, no longer considered that the central issue. Whereas a few months earlier he had refused to participate publicly in the growing polemic within the party, he now undertook vigorously to defend his position in meetings held throughout the country. Apparently his efforts met with considerable success. In a letter of April 17, he confidently outlined to his son his plans to visit Hamburg, Lübeck, Nuremberg and Frankfurt in the near future. The correctness of his position, he commented, was becoming ever more apparent. Many of his old friends, who had earlier opposed him, now admitted that if they had known what would happen, they would have supported him from the beginning. Some did not have the strength to reverse themselves now, but those who had not yet committed themselves would not be difficult to win over.[56]

Later in April Haase delivered a speech before a large Berlin audience which David termed a "brilliant demagogical achievement." David's own efforts at the meeting were hindered by the heckling of youthful party members who had occupied the front rows, and he had to be satisfied with receiving at least some applause, which he felt indicated that he had a minority behind him which must be strengthened.[57] After Haase's Frankfurt speech had been extensively reported in the Social Democratic press, David urged Ebert to take official action against his colleague. Ebert refused, insisting that Haase had a right to express his views, and suggested instead that David and others increase their efforts as individuals to counteract his influence. He also reported that he was seriously considering the publication of a series of leaflets defending the majority position and that he would perhaps arrange for the executive committee to issue an official statement reflecting the majority's point of view.[58] In the meantime, a series of meetings in Scheidemann's electoral district had developed into something of an oratorical duel between the two co-chairmen of the Social Democratic Reichstag delegation. Significantly, the last of these meetings was reported in the *Vorwärts* and in the influential *Vossische Zeitung* under the headline "Haase Against Scheidemann." As Scheidemann later remarked, such a thing was unheard of in the history of the party.[59] When David met his friends in Berlin on May 11, the declared topic was "The Haase Scandal."[60]

The central issue of the developing polemic was no longer the acceptance or rejection of the decision of August 4. Rather, the debate turned on the various interpretations of the Social Democratic statement of that date, especially its condemnation of aggressive war. The spring of 1915 brought with it the emergence of an increasingly vocal campaign for a frankly annexationist policy. Haase eagerly seized upon this issue which seemed to confirm his own earlier analysis and also provided a welcome opportunity to circumvent the still very delicate question of national defense. The war had now clearly become a war of aggression on Germany's part, he contended, and if the S.P.D. intended to live up to its solemn declaration of August 4, it was obligated to deny the government any further support. Even the question of German expansion was, of course, far from a simple one, but whatever its theoretical merits, it provided a basis upon which large numbers of party members could join the opposition, regardless of what their position had been during the tumultuous early days of the war.

The opposition campaign had become all the more important for Haase because a long series of efforts had by this time clearly failed to bring any prospect of united action by the International. Haase himself had, of course, been directly involved in these complicated negotiations, but the net result had been limited to the partial neutralization of the International's executive committee and to the convocation of a series of separate meetings of socialist leaders from the neutral, allied and central powers. Although the statements issued by these conferences did tend to indicate general agreement on a number of abstract principles, their references to the concrete situation created by the war made it apparent that no concerted action could be expected. Taken as a whole, they accomplished little more than to illustrate vividly how deep the divisions in the International had become.[61] This failure was, of course, attributable to many factors: the mutual distrust which had developed among individual leaders since the previous August, the exigencies of the war effort in which several of the major parties were now direct participants, the general growth of nationalistic feelings in every country and the fact that at least some of the most important leaders were determined to forestall any united action for the time being.[62] In any case, by mid-April Haase had concluded that for the moment he would have to be content with, at the most, small steps forward on the stage provided by the nearly defunct International.[63] Although attempts to revive the International would continue, those who, like Haase, were committed to an active peace policy would have to direct most of their energy toward promoting some kind of unilateral action on the part of their own national parties.

The annexationist campaign reached its first peak during the May session of the Reichstag. The session began on May 18, just as the question of Italy's entry into the war hung in the balance. For a moment this new factor seemed to jeopardize Haase's leadership of the opposition. Deeply impressed by Bethmann's remonstrances against any disturbance at such a delicate moment, Haase argued in the delegation meeting of May 17 that the party spokesmen should postpone their discussion of the peace issue until after the Chancellor had delivered his major political address in the Reichstag, by which time the Italian question would be resolved one way or the other. Any earlier Social Democratic offensive, he contended, would be a major political error and was certain to be misinterpreted by the press. At this point Haase found himself in the uncomfortable position of having to defend his point of view against the vigorous protests of many of his closest associates, who urged an immediate interpellation directed toward forcing the government to clarify its position.[64]

By the time the delegation met again on May 27, however, Italy had entered the war, and the central question now became how the Social Democrats should react to the Chancellor's speech scheduled for the following day. The delegation executive committee proposed that Ebert reply for the S.P.D. to the Chancellor's speech, and Ebert sketched out what he planned to say. He proposed a short speech which would include strong criticism of the

Italian government, but would also, referring to the party's statement of August 4, restate the Social Democratic opposition to any attempt at territorial expansion. This did not, however, satisfy the leaders of the opposition, who proposed that Haase speak instead of Ebert. This suggestion was vigorously attacked on the grounds that Haase had recently, through his many speeches, made it clear to everyone that he was the leader of the minority and Ebert was thereupon chosen by a majority of sixty-one to twenty-nine. The debate then turned to the text of the speech itself. Haase opposed any statement of moral indignation over the Italian decision, though he suggested that a calm discussion of its apparent irrationality would be appropriate. Above all, he urged, the S.P.D. should make clear what separated it from the other parties, all of which supported annexations. The Social Democratic spokesman must strongly criticize the recent speeches of highly placed annexationists and "attack the government with sharp and definite words." It was naive to assume that the Chancellor was on the side of the S.P.D. There were, to be sure, various points of view represented in the government, but, he asked, "should we always go with the most stupid of these?" Finally, he insisted that the S.P.D. speak out explicitly against the recent sinking of the Lusitania.[65]

Of particular interest in this debate was Noske's declaration which shocked many, that "only an idiot" could advocate a return to the territorial *status quo ante* after the war. To Dittmann's excited protest, Noske replied that he did not support annexations; he merely wanted to prevent Belgium from becoming an "English domain." Noske then concluded his argument by insisting that it was impossible to demand that the government clearly outline its war aims.[66] It was becoming increasingly apparent that the differences within the Social Democratic leadership extended far beyond the relatively simple tactical question of how and when the party should undertake its initiatives for peace.

The Social Democratic plan to take the floor immediately after the close of the Chancellor's address on May 28 was frustrated by a parliamentary maneuver, and it was not until the following day that Ebert was allowed to speak. He began by launching a vigorous attack upon the Italian government, an attack which undoubtedly pleased the Reichstag majority, but which the Social Democratic opposition could only view as an attempt to reinforce the government's efforts to maintain German morale for the continuation of the war. He then proceeded with a very general defense of the S.P.D.'s position, urging the conclusion of peace as soon as security had been achieved and including in his remarks an explicit condemnation of those who wanted to make peace dependent upon "all sorts of conquests." He repeated the party's traditional argument that a people who had achieved so much deserved equal rights, but concluded with a patriotic declaration that the S.P.D. would continue to support the struggle for German independence.[67]

Ebert's specific references to the peace issue did not differ radically from Haase's remarks on March 10, but his speech was in general much more patriotic in tone. Moreover, the political situation had changed fundamentally since March. This was made abundantly clear by the Conservative and National Liberal spokesmen who followed Ebert to the Reichstag podium. Though differing in the extent of their criticism of Ebert's speech, both frankly declared that Germany must not shrink from territorial expansion in order to insure her future safety. The tremendous sacrifices of the German armies must not have been in vain. More important, both spokesmen interpreted Bethmann's references to the necessity of obtaining "substantial guarantees" of German security as being in fundamental agreement with the views they had just expressed, and the Chancellor made no effort publicly to dispute this interpretation. To be sure, Scheidemann then tried to "correct" the impression thus conveyed by asserting that the Social Democratic deputies continued to accept in good faith Bethmann's denial on August 4 of any aggressive intent on Germany's part,[68] but this effort could only be viewed by the opposition as new evidence of the majority's naive belief in the government's good intentions.

Thus, the May session of the Reichstag did nothing to halt the rising tide of dissatisfaction with the policies pursued by the majority leadership. Indeed, the fact that the majority leaders now asserted their right to speak for the delegation as a whole lent added credence to the increasingly voiced complaint that they were trying to silence the opposition entirely. Moreover, Ebert's obvious move to replace Haase in the leadership of the delegation, a very natural development under the circumstances, made that leadership much more vulnerable to attack. Heretofore, many members of the majority had been uneasy about the fact that the leading Social Democratic spokesman in the Reichstag belonged to the opposition, but at least they had been able largely to control what he actually said. Now, the situation was in a sense reversed. The majority leaders who spoke for the delegation obviously made some effort to express the major concerns of the opposition, but in view of the fact that the opposition was unable to exert any direct influence upon what was said, the situation was much less conducive to the preservation of unity.

Under these circumstances, the opposition began in June, 1915, to take on a much more highly organized form. The first step in this direction was undertaken not by Haase but by the extreme left wing, albeit with considerable assistance from many of Haase's friends. Moved by the increasingly widespread antagonism toward the policies of the majority leadership and by the rash of annexationist pronunciamentoes, the group around Liebknecht drafted a statement addressed to the executive committee of the party and delegation which quickly received the endorsement of more than 600 party functionaries.

Dated June 9, it declared that recent events had brought the S.P.D. to a point of no return. The policy of August 4 had inexorably led the majority of the Social Democratic leadership to a *de facto* endorsement of what had, since the Chancellor's speech of May 28, become a frankly imperialistic policy on the part of the German government. Because of its general tone and the circumstances which surrounded its delivery, Ebert's Reichstag speech of May 29 represented not a repudiation of that policy but rather a blind acceptance of it. The party's adherence to the *Burgfrieden* had resulted in a repudiation of the class struggle, the tried and tested pillar of Social Democratic political action. The statement concluded with an ominous warning against the continued adherence to the policy of August 4 and May 29 and disclaimed any responsibility for what would happen in the future if this warning were not heeded.[69]

Although drafted as a contribution to the internal debate, the declaration of June 9 was widely distributed as an illegal leaflet and thus had repercussions far beyond the party leadership. Haase himself did not sign it, but many of his closest associates did. It must therefore be considered a joint effort of the extreme left and those who fundamentally identified themselves with the party chairman's more moderate position.[70]

This left wing initiative undoubtedly contributed significantly to the decision of Haase, Bernstein, and Kautsky to publish a few days later a much more important manifesto directed against the policies of the majority. On June 19 this statement, drafted by Bernstein and endorsed after minor revisions by Haase and Kautsky, appeared in the *Leipziger Volkszeitung* setting out clearly the position of the moderate opposition and calling for a fundamental revision of Social Democratic policy.[71] Although the Leipzig paper was immediately banned for a week and the rest of the party press thereby restrained from reprinting the manifesto, it was widely criticized in both the bourgeois and right wing Social Democratic press and thus achieved a much broader dissemination than the statement of June 9.[72] The fact that it was signed by the two most prominent theoreticians of the party as well as by the party chairman also contributed substantially to its immense impact.

Like the petition of June 9, the manifesto of Haase, Bernstein and Kautsky declared that the hour of decision had come. The recent annexationist campaign which had not been disavowed by the government had made the aggressive character of the German war effort clear to all. Unlike the authors of the earlier statement, however, the three moderate leaders chose not to attack the position of August 4, but rather demanded that the party live up to the sentence in the party's Reichstag declaration of that date which condemned all wars of conquest. "That sentence will be branded a lie," they asserted, if the German Social Democrats limit themselves to the expression of academic wishes for peace in the face of such declarations by the representatives of the ruling classes. We have seen all too clearly that no attention is paid to such general statements. What several of us have feared is becoming ever more apparent: the German Social Democrats are allowed to grant the means to make war, but when the most important decisions concerning the future of our people are made, they are coolly ignored.

The manifesto went on to describe in dramatic terms the immense suffering the war had caused and the ever-growing yearning for peace among the people, a yearning which had to be expressed by the party that had historically been identified as the party of peace, the S.P.D. Now that the plans for conquest had become apparent to all, the S.P.D. had not only the opportunity but also the duty to assert its opposition to the policies of the German government. The party must take a "decisive step" toward peace; if it did not, it would destroy the trust placed in it by both the German people and the people of the whole world as the defender of international understanding. The statement concluded, again in contrast to the functionaries' petition, with an expression of confidence in the ability of the party to recognize its responsibilities.[73]

The manifesto of June 19, despite its relative moderation and generally positive tone, was immediately recognized as a more significant threat to the majority leadership than the earlier petition. The eminence of its authors alone was enough to insure that. Perhaps equally important, however, was the fact that its very moderation allowed those many thousands of restive party members who still were unable to abandon their basic commitment to national defense to endorse the kind of opposition it represented.

The reaction of the majority leaders was therefore prompt and direct. As early as June 21, David, Richard Fischer and Scheidemann drew up a counter-statement.[74] Haase's participation in the action of June 19 was specifically condemned. As party and delegation chairman, it declared, he had neither proposed such a manifesto to the executive committees nor communicated his intentions to those bodies. The party leaders had, in keeping with the declaration of August 4, continually opposed the annexationist propaganda and had sought to promote peace. There existed therefore not the slightest justification for such a pronunciamento. Nothing could endanger the unity of the party more than such an act. Signed by most of the members of the executive committees of the party and the delegation, this statement was published on the following day in the *Vorwärts*.[75]

Haase dramatically confronted his accusers at a combined meeting of the two executive committees on June 26. He was, of course, vigorously attacked by a number of his colleagues. Scheidemann noted in his diary that night that Ebert treated Haase "brutally."[76] Defending himself, Haase repeatedly became flushed, struck the table with his fist and, contrary to the hopes of the majority, refused to resign.[77]

Another statement was drafted, apparently at the same meeting, which was directed primarily against the petition of June 9. This counter-manifesto questioned the accuracy of certain statements in the petition and insisted that any successful prosecution of the class struggle required the maintenance of German economic and political independence. It concluded by roundly condemning the functionaries' implied threat to split the party.[78] To David's great surprise, Haase voted with the other members of the committees for the draft as finally formulated.[79]

Just three days earlier the executive committee had finally published a manifesto which, after vigorously criticizing the socialist parties of western Europe, urged that Germany formally declare its willingness to enter into peace negotiations.[80] David had heatedly demanded that its final and decisive sentence be radically modified, but without success. Despite the fact that Haase had voted against the text as it stood, the majority leaders argued that they could not revise it according to David's suggestion out of consideration for Haase and his supporters.[81] Apparently the pressure exerted by the opposition was beginning to bear substantial fruit.

The crisis came to a new head at a meeting the party council held on June 30 to deal with the recent assaults upon the majority leadership. Hermann Müller opened the meeting with a report for the executive committee which quickly degenerated into a tirade against Haase. The petition of June 9, he declared, indicated that the opposition had established its organization throughout the Reich. The manifesto of June 19, however, represented a still greater threat to the unity of the party. It could not be considered, as Haase had claimed, just a newspaper article. Rather, in form and tone it was a manifesto. The executive committees' criticism of it, therefore, had nothing to do with the question of free speech. If Haase felt that "the hour of decision had come," he should have informed his colleagues of this fact and certainly should have told them of his plans to publish such a proclamation. The executive committees had been forced to react immediately in order to dispel the impression that anarchy reigned in the party leadership. Haase's criticism of previous policies had been unjustified, and the only result of his action had been to create confusion. It was now apparent, he concluded, that the opposition was so thoroughly organized that the party leadership would have to begin the systematic publication of materials designed to counteract the opposition's propaganda against the majority.[82] Obviously, Müller and his colleagues had decided to use the June actions as justification for a major campaign aimed at restoring confidence in the majority leadership.

Haase defended himself in two major speeches during the meeting. He considered it his duty, he declared in his reply to Müller's charges, to express his point of view. His article had been designed "to describe the political situation accurately" and to stimulate among party members discussion of the important points at issue. The S.P.D. now stood with the other parties on the war issue. This was a situation which, especially in view of recent events, he considered extremely dangerous. The party's expressions of its yearning for peace would remain academic until they were backed up by a refusal to vote for war credits. Furthermore, the recent annexationist campaign had been dangerously underestimated by the majority. He too regretted the manner in which the petition of June 9 had been organized, but the appropriate remedy was not indignation, but rather a serious examination of the causes of the dissatisfaction which had spawned it.[83]

Haase's second speech, delivered at the end of a long and heated debate in which he had been repeatedly and severely criticized, was much sharper in tone and perhaps more revealing. He had been accused, he declared, of believing himself to stand above the other party leaders. This he denied. But he did insist upon being given the same rights as all other party members. He noted that other executive committee members had done essentially what he had done without having been subjected to the slightest criticism. Why then did such a storm develop now? It had become increasingly clear that the attacks upon him stemmed from the fact that he did not agree with the majority. In fact, these attacks represented an effort to restrict his freedom of speech. Whatever the party council should decide, he added, he wanted to make it completely clear that he would not resign his chairmanship of the party. That would constitute an evasion of his duty toward the party as a whole. He declared again, however, that the Reichstag delegation had the right at any time to ask him to resign from its chairmanship.[84]

The result of the long debate was, of course, never in doubt. The council voted, against a minority of twelve, to declare that Haase's endorsement of the manifesto of June 19 was "not in keeping with the duties of a party chairman."[85]

The impact upon Haase of the bitter campaign against him during the summer of 1915 must have been considerable. He was a man who had always valued personal integrity very highly, and it was upon his reputed disloyalty and duplicity that his critics now concentrated. Yet he was seemingly not as upset by the barrage of criticism as might have been expected. In a letter to friends written in mid-July, he admitted that he had endured a few sleepless nights, but insisted that the flurry of attacks upon him had not caused him much discomfort, inasmuch as he was confident that he had done his duty. Undoubtedly the fact that he had already experienced nearly a year of similar, if somewhat less virulent, criticism within the confines of the party's central leadership had helped to prepare him for the struggle which now erupted on a more public stage. A still more significant factor in his continuing self-confidence was his consciousness that his plunge into a public polemic was bearing substantial fruit. The very furor of the majority reaction provided confirmation of this fact. More tangible, however, were the many expressions of support which he now received from every part of the Reich, his continuing success in speaking to local membership meetings, and the private admission by still more Reichstag deputies that they were now inclined to change their positions on the issue of war credits.[86]

A year after the beginning of the war, Haase's strength thus seemed to be clearly in the ascendant. He had consistently refused to relent in his opposition to the Social Democratic support of the German war effort, and, in contrast to August 1914, he now enjoyed the open support of a large part, in his opinion, perhaps even a majority of the party.[87] He continued to insist that the preservation of party unity was a matter of utmost importance for him, but he was no longer willing to pay the price of silence for a superficial conformity which played into the hands of those who, he was convinced, were subverting the principles of Social Democracy.

As yet, however, he had refrained from carrying his opposition to the point of committing a formal breach of discipline. Indeed, his vote in favor of the resolution denouncing the petition of June 9 indicated that he still was convinced that threats to the unity of the party could not be condoned. This attitude undoubtedly contributed substantially to Haase's continuing problems with his allies on the left, but it should not be understood simply as a reflection of his reluctance to break with the traditions of the S.P.D. During the summer of 1915 there still seemed to be good reason to believe that the opposition could win over a majority of the Reichstag delegation to its point of view. At that point the continued existence of a unified and disciplined party would become a factor of crucial importance to Haase and his associates.

But if one result of the June crisis was to demonstrate the strength of the opposition, another was to convince the majority leaders that an active campaign against Haase and his friends could no longer be postponed. The disintegration of the centrist group, which hitherto had provided at least a modicum of stability for the party, would now of necessity be accelerated. Like Haase, Ebert and his associates felt themselves driven to undertake increasingly determined action in defense of their position. A further result was, of course, the strengthening of the alliance between these men and the right wing, many of whose leaders had long since become convinced that a split in the party was inevitable.

CHAPTER VII

THE GAUNTLET THROWN DOWN

It was during the autumn of 1915 that Haase finally began seriously to consider the possibility of breaking openly with the majority of the Reichstag delegation. Although the steady if unspectacular growth of the opposition, reflected by the abstention of thirty-six deputies from the August vote on war credits,[1] tended to militate against such a step, the increasing aggressiveness of the majority gradually convinced Haase that only an open breach of discipline would enable the minority to avoid being effectively silenced. Undoubtedly one of the most important factors that finally led him to make this decision was the emergence of Eduard David as a major spokesman for the party on foreign policy.

David first assumed this role at a combined meeting of the party council and the delegation which was convened immediately prior to the August session of the Reichstag.[2] His increasing importance was then underscored by his selection to speak for the delegation on the peace issue at the ensuing Reichstag session. The choice of an acknowledged leader of the nationalists within the party could hardly be viewed with equanimity by the opposition. Moreover, the speech itself only confirmed the fears of Haase and his friends. Although David included the usual Social Democratic plea for an early peace and declared that the war should not be prolonged by any hope of conquest, he sandwiched these remarks between such vigorous denunciations of Germany's enemies and enthusiastic praise of German military valor that the overall impact of the speech was anything but pacifistic. The spokesmen of the other parties were so pleased that they refrained from expressing their customary objections and, indeed, in some cases went so far as to compliment the S.P.D. on its recently discovered patriotism.[3]

A few days later, Haase commented in a letter to his son that he had listened to David with deep misgivings. The best that could be said was that the situation had been somewhat clarified. "Whoever still allowed himself to be deluded by the August phrases," he wrote, "must now recognize where that path leads." Under the circumstances he had only refrained from resigning from the delegation chairmanship because of the express wishes of his colleagues in the opposition, who felt that he could still play a useful role in that capacity. He had, of course, given the majority ample opportunity to remove him, but they had been afraid to take up this challenge. Now that the selection of David as the Social Democratic spokesman in the Reichstag had closed the most effective forum for the propagation of the minority point of view, he continued, he and his friends must be prepared to expand their efforts outside of that body. He personally was determined to embark again on a speaking tour, despite the many difficulties created by the government's increasingly vigorous political persecution.[4]

This persecution, however, made it increasingly difficult to simply dispense with the forum provided by the Reichstag. Particularly frustrating for the opposition spokesmen were the problems they faced in trying to express themselves through the party press. They found themselves at a decided disadvantage in the lively polemic that had raged among the various Social Democratic papers since the collapse of the internal truce early in the year. In the first place, it soon became apparent that about two-thirds of the papers generally supported the majority point of view.[5] Still more galling, however, was the fact that although all of the party's papers suffered to some degree under the rigors of censorship, the opposition, with its anti-government and anti-war position, was by its very nature condemned to incur the censor's wrath to a disproportionate degree. It was hardly surprising that this apparent favoritism led to a widespread belief that the majority leaders were at least tacitly accepting the aid of the government in their efforts to silence their rivals in the party.[6]

Under these circumstances even many of those who, like Haase, continued to hope that the unity of the party could still be preserved gradually came to the conclusion that the enforced silence of the minority was generating such intense antagonism that a breach of discipline by the parliamentary opposition would have, on the whole, a salutary effect. This point of view was most effectively expressed by Kautsky in a series of articles appearing in *Die Neue Zeit* during the fall of 1915. It was not the expression of the deep seated differences of opinion within the S.P.D. which endangered the party's unity, he wrote, but rather the existence of these differences. In fact, open discussion, even if conducted during plenary sessions of the Reichstag, would tend to keep them within reasonable limits. Any continued effort to suppress such discussion would simply encourage the extremists of both sides who were least interested in holding the party together.[7]

These articles stirred considerable controversy and, by daring to question the aura of unassailable dogma which surrounded the traditional discipline of the Reichstag delegation, undoubtedly helped to clear the way for a new escalation of the internal conflict. Kautsky's arguments gained further weight when they were endorsed late in November by the *Leipziger Volkszeitung*, a paper particularly influential among representatives of the moderate opposition.[8] Perhaps the most important unofficial reply to Kautsky and his friends was published by Otto Braun in *Die Neue Zeit* late in November. Braun, an increasingly influential figure in the party leadership, asserted categorically that an independent action by the opposition in the Reichstag would necessarily result in a rupture of the party as a whole.[9] The majority's public efforts to head off or at least to lessen the impact of the proposed action culminated in the publication on December 18 of a long manifesto, endorsed by the party executive committee, which dramatically declared that the S.P.D. faced the greatest crisis of its history and sought to invoke its long tradition of discipline against those who would at such a moment place the party in jeopardy.[10]

As the December Reichstag session approached, however, it was not at all certain that such an outright clash would actually materialize. By that time there was general agreement within the delegation that Germany's military position was secure enough to permit some kind of a peace offensive by the S.P.D.[11] The principal question, therefore, was what form such an offensive should take. The opposition again urged an interpellation of the Chancellor in an effort to obtain a clarification of the government's position. The majority leaders, hoping to forestall any really radical action along these lines and recognizing that some initiative had to be taken, decided at a meeting on November 27 to propose their own interpellation.[12]

On the same day that the majority leaders were thus planning how best to control the situation, Haase was writing optimistically to a friend that he had already won almost half of the delegation to his point of view on the proposed interpellation. He had resolved, he added, to remain absolutely calm during the debates on the issue and hoped that by doing so he might draw the majority over to his side. He admitted, however, that the government's plan to request further war credits could very well complicate the situation.[13] The issue of war credits thus continued to hang like an ominous cloud over the delegation.

The first four meetings of the delegation were largely devoted to a discussion of domestic issues about which there continued to be general agreement and to a new effort by Liebknecht to question the Chancellor on his own.[14] When formal debate concerning the delegation's interpellation opened on November 29, however, the hitherto latent conflict once more quickly came to a head. Both the opposition and the majority leaders had prepared drafts for the interpellation, which by now nearly everyone agreed had to be undertaken. The majority text was limited to a simple inquiry whether the Chancellor was prepared to explain under what conditions he would be prepared to enter peace negotiations. The opposition draft, which bore the signatures of forty-eight deputies, was more specific, asking Bethmann whether he was prepared to initiate immediate peace negotiations on the basis of a mutual renunciation of conquests of any kind. It also asked whether the government was willing to lift the state of siege in order to permit the free discussion of the peace issue.[15]

The ensuing debate was dominated by the speeches of Haase and Scheidemann. Haase, seeking to follow the tactical course he had outlined two days earlier, stressed the general agreement which now reigned in the delegation concerning the necessity of working actively for peace. He even asserted that the delegation appeared united in its opposition to annexations. It was not enough, however, to express a humanitarian desire for an end to hostilities. The S.P.D. must demand a concrete initiative on the part of the government, an initiative which would include a clear renunciation of all annexations. Scheidemann conceded that the delegation had come to Berlin determined to intervene in the cause of peace, but insisted that it was politically impossible for Bethmann to publicly declare that he would abandon all of Germany's conquests in order to obtain a cessation of hostilities.[16]

The strategy of the majority proved for the moment successful. When a vote was taken on November 30, the opposition draft was defeated by a margin of fifty-eight to forty-three. The alternative text was then accepted by a vote of ninety-three to five.[17] The minority was, however, in no mood to accept such a defeat passively. A motion was immediately introduced to allow them freedom of action on the issue. Haase sought to postpone any decision for the time being, but the situation was then further complicated by the selection of Scheidemann and Landsberg to speak about the interpellation on the Reichstag floor. Two leaders of the majority had thus again been chosen as spokesmen on an issue which the opposition considered to be within its own special province. This decision caused Haase to lose some of his reserve. It had always been an accepted practice, he declared, to consider both the minority and the majority when choosing the delegation's spokesmen. Indeed, when the majority and minority were almost equal, it was the duty of the delegation to do so. Soon the delegation would be divided exactly in half. What would happen then? The speeches supporting the interpellation could be delivered in a completely objective manner, he asserted. All polemics could be avoided. But despite Ebert's intervention in favor of giving the minority a speaker, Haase was supported by only forty-seven deputies when a new vote was taken, and Landsberg and Scheidemann were again selected. Moreover, a resolution was passed which expressly denied the opposition the right to undertake any independent action.[18]

The atmosphere of relative amity in which the delegation meetings had begun had thus very largely dissolved even before the issue of war credits had been raised. The situation was then further exacerbated by the course of events on the Reichstag floor when the interpellation was actually presented on December 9.

Scheidemann's speech in support of the interpellation provided no unusual grounds for criticism on the part of the opposition. He expressed the party's firm opposition to all dreams of conquest and declared that it was the obligation of Germany as the stronger power to take the first step toward initiating negotiations. He included, to be sure, lengthy attacks upon the intentions of the Entente and fulsome praise of German military might, but such expressions had become part of the usual parlance of the majority leaders, intent as they were upon dispelling the last traces of the party's reputation for lack of patriotism.[19]

Bethmann's reply to the interpellation, however, could not but be viewed as a staggering embarrassment to the Social Democratic majority. He utilized the occasion to denounce the Entente powers and asserted that as long as they refused to recognize the fact of German military power, any peace offer would be foolish. Although he declared himself prepared to enter into negotiations for an honorable peace at any time, he refused to discuss the German war aims in specific terms. Moreover, he ominously added that the longer the war continued, the greater would be the "guarantees" upon which the German government would have to insist. The character of these guarantees was suggested by his insistence that the Reich could not permit the continued existence of "invasion gates" in the east or west and that Germany must be assured opportunities for future economic development. The aggressive tone of the Chancellor's speech was further accentuated by a statement read in the name of the non-socialist parties immediately afterwards which explicitly declared that Germany's demands must include the territorial additions necessary to her security.[20] The excitement generated among the Social Democrats by this open attack upon their declared principles was then brought to a peak by the introduction of a motion to close debate.

At this point Haase's firm resolution to remain calm under all circumstances was completely forgotten. He indignantly demanded at least a dozen times to be recognized by the president, but he did not receive permission to speak until the motion to close debate had been passed. In a voice made hoarse by excitement and strain, Haase then expressed both his indignation at the "terrorist methods" of the Reichstag majority and his personal rejection of the views expressed by the Chancellor and the representative of the bourgeois parties. In this, he added, he knew that he was supported by the overwhelming majority of the German people. "We demand," he concluded amidst stormy applause from the Social Democratic deputies, "the renunciation of all plans for conquest by any side and in any form. We want peace!"[21]

After further excited wrangling, the Reichstag finally agreed to allow Landsberg to make a formal reply for the S.P.D., but his speech turned out to be a terrible disappointment to most of the Social Democratic deputies. He began by urging the house to forget as soon as possible the unruly scene which had just transpired. He went on to interpret Bethmann's remarks in such a way as to remove every trace of annexationist sentiment from them. The declaration of the majority parties he dismissed as a gross misrepresentation of the government's position.[22] The opportunity for a decisive defense of the Social Democratic position was thereby totally wasted, and the bitterness within the delegation reached new heights.

There is little reason to doubt that the events which took place in the Reichstag on December 9 did much to clear the way for decisive action by the opposition later in the session. David noted that day in his diary that the affair represented a triumph for Haase and his friends. Although Landsberg's speech had helped to restore the party's public image, he wrote, it had brought on a crisis within the delegation. A number of those who hitherto had remained on the fence now declared that they would have to vote against new war credits. Even Ebert had shown signs of weakening. If the opposition now achieved a majority, he declared, the government must bear the primary responsibility.[23]

Thirty-six deputies immediately published a statement dissociating themselves from the annexationist views expressed by the Chancellor and the bourgeois parties which could only serve to lengthen the war. In this rejection, they declared, they knew themselves to be united with the overwhelming majority of the working population.[24] Haase's personal reaction, however, was hardly one of triumph. Writing to a friend a few days later, he explained that he felt that his own intervention had, momentarily at least, partially saved the situation, but Landsberg had thereupon succeeded in undoing what he had accomplished. The Chancellor's provocative speech had destroyed any possible seeds of peace.[25]

The delegation meetings of December 13 and 14 turned directly to the question of voting new war credits. The antagonism stirred by the events of December 9, however, added a tone of increased bitterness to the now standard debate on the issue. Landsberg's explanation that although he had recognized the annexationist implications of Bethmann's remarks, he had decided to avoid any attack on them for fear that such criticism would have been used by Germany's enemies only exacerbated the situation. Contrary to David's fears, however, the majority retained its hold over the delegation. Haase was unsuccessful in his efforts to get the party to speak on the first reading of the credits bill, and a motion to vote again for credits was passed by a majority of sixty-two to forty-one. A motion introduced by Ledebour to condemn Landsberg's failure to react effectively to the statements of the Chancellor and the bourgeois party spokesman was defeated by a still larger margin.[26]

Convinced by these developments that the majority had capitulated to the annexationists, a considerable number of the most convinced members of the opposition now decided to break discipline, vote against the credits and present a separate statement in the Reichstag.[27] At first Haase was undecided as to what role he should play. As late as December 18, he informed his colleagues on the delegation executive committee that he would not participate in this revolt, but also warned that he could not cooperate in any effort to condemn the action of his friends.[28] Two days later, however, he declared in a delegation meeting that he intended to join the projected demonstration. He justified his decision by declaring that the minority had been deprived of any other opportunity to express its point of view. Furthermore, if no such action were undertaken, part of the active party membership would leave the S.P.D. It was therefore not the minority but the majority who endangered party unity. The majority had not only joined the party's traditional enemy; it had sought to prevent the opposition from fighting against that enemy. The majority had refused to grant the minority any tolerance. It was therefore the duty of the opposition to do alone what the entire delegation was in fact obligated to do. He promised, however, that he and his friends would engage in no polemic against the majority. They would simply state the facts. Later in the debate, Haase formally declared that he would now resign from the chairmanship of the Reichstag delegation. He would, however, continue to serve as party chairman until the next congress.[29]

The revolt, so long discussed, yet until now surrounded by an aura of unreality, struck the deputies with an immense and confusing impact. More than half of the opposition, including some of its staunchest leaders, could not bring themselves to break the discipline which had so long been the special pride of the Geman party. Gustav Hoch, a close friend of Haase and one of the most articulate and forthright spokesmen of the minority, urged a return to the policy of abstention.[30] He himself refused to join the demonstration, yet he insisted on joining Haase in his resignation from the delegation executive committee.[31] Josef Simon, another persistent critic of the majority position, declared that a few days earlier he had endorsed the plan for a separate vote, but now had changed his mind and felt himself incapable of participating in it.[32]

On the other hand, the reaction of many of the majority leaders was much more conciliatory than might have been expected. Richard Fischer, usually one of the most outspoken of these, counseled patience, predicting that the opposition might soon become the majority. Several concentrated their attacks upon Haase rather than upon the dissident group as a whole. Most, of course, emphasized the dire consequences for the unity of the party. When the delegation met after the decisive Reichstag session of December 21, however, it proved reluctant to take any drastic action against the rebels. Legien's motion to expel them received only eighteen votes, and a much more moderate resolution was passed in its stead which merely condemned their action in vigorous terms.[33] David's reaction to his colleagues' moderation was predictably strong. He called the twenty-first "a day of triumph for the minority." "Haase knows what he wants," he added. "[He] is smart and audacious and will continue to disrupt the majority from within and win it for himself."[34]

Haase himself, once the decision had been made, appeared much more relieved than troubled by the course events had taken. Writing to friends on December 21, he declared,

Finally I am free of my position as chairman of the Reichstag delegation, and I am breathing more freely than I have in a very long time. I am no longer in conflict with myself and believe that, through what I have accomplished in the Reichstag, I have done a service for the great cause on which my heart is bent.[35]

The actual events in the Reichstag on December 21 must have appeared anticlimatic to those who had experienced the tense struggle which led up to them. The minority statement, drafted by Haase but read by Fritz Geyer as the oldest of the dissidents, received the applause of many of the Social Democrats who did not belong to the group which presented it and was greeted by none of the catcalls which Liebknecht's attempted interventions usually evoked.[36] Speaking simply "for myself and nineteen of my colleagues," Geyer explained that they had been compelled to speak in the Reichstag by the "military dictatorship" which prevented them from expressing their views elsewhere. He did not merely echo the statement read by Ebert for the majority, which condemned annexations in general terms, but rather explicitly declared that the Chancellor himself had on December 9 encouraged dreams of conquest and had, furthermore, rudely rejected the S.P.D.'s plea for a German peace initiative. The only realistic basis for successful peace negotiations must be the complete renunciation of all attempts to destroy the political or economic independence of any other people, and Germany, because of her preeminent military position, was obligated to take the first step in this direction. As long as the German government refused to undertake any such initiative, its policy stood in "crying opposition" to the interests of the masses and therefore must be opposed by a rejection of war credits.[37] As Haase had promised, Geyer's statement contained not a single phrase which could have been considered an attack upon the majority. This fact undoubtedly had much to do with the relatively mild treatment Haase and his friends received at the hands of their colleagues following the Reichstag session. Apparently, despite the growing mass of evidence to the contrary, the moderates on both sides continued to hope that some form of unity could continue to be maintained.

For the moment at least, David's assessment of the December events appeared to be correct. Haase and his friends had gained a forum for the public propagation of their ideas without being cut off from the party organization which, of course, remained their chief point of contact with the membership. In the process, however, the opposition had itself been painfully split. It is true, of course, that strong ties continued to bind together the two major groups which disagreed primarily on the issue of party discipline. But as the artificial unity imposed by that discipline was partially disrupted, the very real and fundamental differences within a group which stretched from revisionists such as Bernstein to the revolutionary Marxist Liebknecht of necessity emerged with increasingly embarrassing poignancy.

The earliest and ultimately most significant dissident group to arise within the opposition was, of course, the small but extremely active band of agitators who gathered around Karl Liebknecht and Rosa Luxemburg. Although they at first devoted their very considerable polemical talents almost entirely to attacking the "social patriot" leaders of the majority, it was not long before they turned much of their attention to the less intransigent members of the opposition who eventually came to be known in radical parlance as "social pacifists." Although the Luxemburg-Liebknecht group did not become numerically significant until after the war, it included in its ranks such dedicated organizers and propagandists that it could at least occasionally exert considerable influence far beyond its own immediate membership. This fact had been amply demonstrated by the petition of June 9 which, although initiated by Liebknecht and his associates, obtained the support of large numbers of party functionaries who normally looked to Haase and his more moderate friends for political guidance.

To the outsider it must have appeared that the vote of December 1915 against the war credits would serve to attenuate the differences which had developed between Haase and this left wing group. In fact, however, it was at just this point that their differences began to come clearly into the open. According to Liebknecht, he had at first agreed to join the action of December 21, but sharply disagreed with the mild tone of the statement prepared for presentation in the Reichstag and was included among the twenty deputies represented by Geyer against his wishes and without his foreknowledge. Moreover, again according to Liebknecht, the moderate opposition group had on December 19 forced him to endure a veritable "inquisition" in an attempt to force him to abandon any plans for an independent initiative which might have detracted from the impact of their own demonstration.[38] In any case, after that date Liebknecht no longer attended the meetings of the opposition, and a few weeks later he and his friends launched the polemic against "the December men" which would continue throughout the war and into the revolutionary period.

In one of the illegal *Spartacus Letters*, published in January 1916, Haase and his associates were accused of lacking the agreement on fundamental principles which was a prerequisite for any serious action. Most members of the opposition, it declared, were affraid to go beyond their parliamentary demonstration on the issue of war credits and, indeed, even claimed that their recently discovered radicalism constituted the most effective means of pacifying the unruly masses. Geyer's statement reflected the "distressing superficiality of their achievement." It avoided taking any clear position against the S.P.D. majority or even against the government and the bourgeois parties. It was marked by the moderate tone of "prudent statesmanship." It lacked any historical analysis of the war, avoided even the word imperialism, mentioned the government's aggressive intentions as if they had just recently become apparent, and, most important, it contained an implied acceptance of the principles of national defense. The action of the "December men" would therefore remain little more than a "pretty gesture" unless it was followed up by a decisive resumption of the class struggle and the initiation of a full-fledged offensive against the S.P.D. majority, both within and outside the Reichstag. Failing this,

the twenty will condemn themselves to impotence, their impotence will become obvious, their growing influence on the masses will go to the devil, and both the S.P.D. Reichstag majority and the government will in the future be in a stronger parliamentary position than they were before December 21, 1915.[39]

At a meeting of leaders of the *Gruppe International*, later known as the Spartacists, which was held in Liebknecht's office on January 1, a series of theses were adopted which added further to the growing polemic within the opposition.[40] Georg Ledebour and Adolf Hoffmann soon thereafter published a leaflet attacking the theses, despite the fact that Ledebour himself had on December 21 circulated a letter criticising the Geyer statement as lacking the necessary "aggressive sharpness and clarity of principle."[41] The Spartacist theses, the two left centrists insisted, placed too much emphasis upon the creation of a new centralized International whose constitution would contradict the traditional socialist adherence to democratic principles. Moreover, the tactics of the Spartacists simply tended to play into the hands of the Reichstag majority. The opposition should rather establish a relationship of mutual trust and cooperation within its ranks.[42]

Haase's point of view on this quarrel within the opposition is difficult to establish in any detail. It is clear that he did not share the views of the Spartacists, and one must assume that he resented their attacks upon himself and his friends. Nevertheless, he apparently did not fully share the feelings of complete distrust and bitter antagonism which so strongly moved many of his associates. Kautsky's only major criticism of his friend's leadership during the war was that he refused to recognize the danger inherent in the Spartacist position and therefore continually tried to bridge the deepening divisions which the Spartacists so avidly tried to promote between themselves and the "social pacifists."[43]

Haase was later to write that the events of December 1915 finally made it possible for the opposition "to explain to the systematically misled German people the facts about the causes and the impact of the war,"[44] and the hard-pressed party chairman who had so long borne the brunt of the political infighting in the S.P.D. must indeed have experienced an enormous sense of relief at being free to express frankly and publicly his own views regarding the issue which had become the central concern of his life. It was also undoubtedly true that the December demonstration allowed the opposition to make a much more profound impression on the public than had hitherto been possible.

This increased freedom of expression, however, had been purchased at an enormous price. The opposition, which had steadily grown since the beginning of the war, was now split as it had never been before. On the one hand, the opposition within the Reichstag delegation was divided between those who had decided to break discipline and those who could not bring themselves to take this decisive step. On the other hand, those who actually had voted against the war credits were divided between the overwhelming majority who generally followed Haase's leadership and the Spartacists, represented in the Reichstag only by Liebknecht and Rühle, but numbering among their adherents some of the most effective and dedicated polemicists within the S.P.D.

At the same time, the majority delegates now tended to draw increasingly together. David and the other right wing leaders no longer played such a divisive role within the majority once Haase and his friends had set themselves outside the pale of traditional party discipline. Moreover, the majority itself had been given new freedom to attack the opposition now that the latter had come more fully into the open. Haase still hoped that he would be able to continue to function within the party and eventually bring the majority around to his point of view, but with the ranks of his supporters so badly divided, the advantage, at least within the party leadership, had passed to the majority.

CHAPTER VIII

THE DELEGATION DIVIDED

The new mood of the majority became clearly apparent during a meeting of the party council early in January 1916. Acting as prosecuting attorney for the executive committee, Scheidemann directed his attacks almost exclusively against Haase, verging at times upon outright accusations of dishonesty. Haase was, however, obviously prepared for such an assault. He calmly recited the by now familiar arguments which had led him and his supporters to take the step they had so long avoided and vigorously insisted that they had no intention of splitting either the party or the Reichstag delegation. Indeed, those who hoped to achieve such an end, he declared, would find in him their most determined opponent. He confidently described the progress the opposition had made since August 1914 and urged the council members to keep in mind the possibility that the present minority might soon become the majority. As was to be expected, however, the meeting resulted in an official condemnation of the breach of discipline. In accordance with the view so strongly expressed by Scheidemann, the committee's resolution singled out Haase, who had "again . . . failed to fulfill the duty imposed upon him by his position as party chairman," for special criticism.[1]

The opposition suffered another defeat a few days later when the Reichstag delegation voted in effect to expel Liebknecht for his persistent refusal to be muzzled by its discipline.[2] Despite their own differences with the fiery Spartacist, the "December men" immediately issued a public statement denying the delegation's right to expel duly elected members.[3] During the same series of meetings, Ebert was elected to replace Haase as co-chairman of the delegation, thus placing one more of the key reins of power in the hands of the former saddler who was rapidly assuming a dominant position within the majority.[4]

Despite these setbacks, Haase remained optimistic. He was encouraged by the messages of support he received from party organizations throughout the Reich and above all by the very positive reaction he evoked whenever he was able to defend his position before local Social Democratic audiences.[5] When the Reichstag reconvened in March, therefore, he was hardly in a mood to forgo his newly gained freedom.

Not even a series of defeats during the preliminary delegation meetings could dampen his enthusiasm. He took a new refusal to permit him to speak for the delegation in stride[6] and argued vigorously, if unsuccessfully, for a rejection of the temporary budget submitted by the government,[7] adding that he would not cooperate if the majority decided to support it.[8] This was not an idle threat. The "December men" had already decided to vote against the budget and had assigned to Haase the task of delivering a major speech in support of their position. Moreover, they had determined not to inform the majority of their intentions for fear that Haase's speech might be prevented by parliamentary maneuvers, a fear that seemed well justified in view of Liebknecht's recent experiences.[9]

On March 24, the temporary budget was brought in for debate and passage by the Reichstag. As he entered the chamber, Haase informed Scheidemann of his intention to speak,[10] and even before the session began, many of the Social Democrats began to gather in small excited groups. Despite Haase's warning, Scheidemann merely delivered his short prepared statement that the S.P.D. would vote to grant the government's request. Shortly thereafter Haase rose to discuss the opposition's stand. From their point of view, he asserted, even a vote for the temporary budget would constitute a vote of confidence in the government which they were not prepared to give. The proposed new tax program proved conclusively that the state had lost none of its class character. The government's ineffectual efforts to control the distribution of food had been criticized by almost every party. Freedom of speech had been restricted as never before. The trade unions, despite their contribution to the war effort, were prevented from properly defending the interests of the workers. The majority of the troops risking their lives at the front would return as second-class citizens.

As long as Haase limited his remarks to an appraisal of domestic policy that was shared by most of his Social Democratic colleagues, he was disturbed only by the repeated insistence of the president that he speak to the point. As he moved on to foreign affairs, however, he was repeatedly interrupted by heckling, much of which came from his own delegation. Striving desperately to speak over the mounting din, Haase predicted that neither side would emerge victorious from the war. More and more people were beginning to realize that if the government had been willing to be satisfied with the successful defense of the Reich, peace might well have already been achieved. The feeling was rapidly growing among the proletariat that they were being made to fight for the interests of others. Even many capitalists, at least in so far as they were not war profiteers, had come to the conclusion that the war had been a miscalculation. Unfortunately, at the same time the demands of the annexationists were becoming more strident.[11]

At this point Haase was completely drowned out by outraged cries of indignation from every side of the house. A number of majority socialists served as the focus of the tumult as they formed a gesticulating mass around their chairman.[12] The president seized the opportunity to call for a vote as to whether Haase should be allowed to continue speaking. The motion to silence him was easily passed, with a number of Social Democrats joining the majority. Karl Helfferich, who represented the government in the debate, then sought to increase the embarrassment of the Social Democrats by formally expressing his indignation at Haase's remarks, which, he insisted, were designed to strengthen the will of the enemy and thus prolong the war. "Thank God!" he added, addressing Haase directly, "love of the fatherland is still strong enough in your party as well."[13]

Even Scheidemann could not resist the temptation to exploit the situation. The S.P.D. delegation had had no intention of speaking out on the issue, he declared, but now that they had been surprised by Haase's speech, he found it necessary to explain their position. After briefly summarizing the majority point of view, he ironically concluded his remarks by paraphrasing Haase's statement of August 4, 1914: "We confirm what we have always said: in the hour of need, we will not abandon the fatherland."[14]

The scandalous scene in the Reichstag drove the tensions within the S.P.D. to new heights. The stage was set for a decisive break. When the delegation gathered immediately after the plenary session, Ebert made a short but abusive speech in which, as usual, he focused his ire upon Haase, whom he accused of committing not only a breach of discipline but an act of "unheard of treachery." He then read a resolution prepared by the delegation executive committee which explicitly condemned Haase for his "disloyalty" and deprived him and his seventeen colleagues of the rights which they enjoyed as delegation members. Although one of the rebels read a formal declaration drafted by the opposition deputies stating that Haase had acted with their full support, a motion to moderate the executive's personal attack upon Haase was defeated. The resolution was then passed in its original form by a majority of fifty-eight to thirty-three with four opposition deputies, including Haase, abstaining.[15]

Those who had thus been expelled from the delegation met immediately thereafter to organize a new delegation, which they called the "Social Democratic Working Group" (*Sozialdemokratische Arbeitsgemeinschaft*, hereafter referred to as the *S.A.G.*), in an obvious attempt to avoid giving the impression that a new party was being formed. Haase and Ledebour were elected co-chairmen of the new parliamentary group, and Dittmann was named secretary. A public statement was formulated explaining that they had been expelled from the S.P.D. delegation, that they continued to believe that they had acted in complete accordance with the principles of the S.P.D. and the resolutions of the party conventions, and that they had formed a new delegation simply in order to be able effectively to fulfill their obligations to their constituents. They dismissed the accusations of disloyalty and breach of discipline as completely unfounded.[16]

The situation within the party had thus taken a decisive and highly unexpected turn within the course of a few hours. To David, the events of March 24 appeared to constitute an immense victory for his point of view. That evening he described in his diary his feeling of "liberation." A division along these lines had long been his objective. Haase had acted very ineptly. "I have won!" he triumphantly concluded.[17] This interpretation seemed further confirmed during the next day's meeting of the party executive committee. Scheidemann informed David beforehand that the majority had decided to force Haase out of his last post. When confronted by the demand of the majority leaders that he resign his position as party chairman, Haase at first requested time to consider his decision, but when this was denied, he finally took the step that he had so often rejected in the past. His friends, Zietz and Wengels, then tendered their resignations from the executive committee.[18]

Despite David's enthusiasm, Haase does not seem to have been very seriously disturbed by the course events had taken. Writing to a friend on March 25, he described the accusations levelled against him as simply an attempt to deceive the public. The rage of the majority had been aroused by the refusal of the opposition to sink with them into the swamp of impotence into which they had wandered. His colleagues in the executive committee had made any further cooperative effort impossible. He therefore found it necessary to abandon his earlier determination to retain the party chairmanship and in fact was happy to be rid of the office which was now only a fetter on his freedom to fight for his point of view.[19]

A few days after the formation of the S.A.G., the majority leaders published a manifesto attacking the "separatists." The question of who was responsible for the crisis was an important one, for the party's traditional commitment to unity and discipline was still a force to be reckoned with among the membership at large. For their part, the members of the S.A.G. soon issued a pamphlet designed to counteract the impression conveyed by the majority that their action constituted a premeditated effort to dismember the party. They argued that, however deplorable, the formation of a new delegation had become unavoidable because of the fundamental differences of opinion that had developed among the deputies concerning the questions which were most important for the life and future development of the S.P.D. Moreover, the formation of the S.A.G. did not, they maintained, have to lead to a formal division in the party as a whole if the majority did not willfully strive to bring this about. Supporters of the new delegation were urged to refuse to allow themselves to be provoked into breaking with their local organizations. They should continue to fulfill their obligations within the existing framework of the S.P.D.[21]

Kautsky later argued that the formation of the S.A.G. effectively thwarted the effort to gain a majority for the opposition in the Social Democratic delegation and relegated the opposition deputies who remained in the old delegation to political impotence.[22] It is a fact that the S.A.G. (and its successor, the Independent Social Democratic Party delegation) was unable to increase its membership significantly during the remainder of the war.[23] On the other hand, the creation of a separate delegation did provide a focus for the rapidly mounting opposition sentiment within the party. A large number of the more important local organizations declared their support for the S.A.G. during the weeks following the split,[24] and the strength of this movement presumably contributed significantly to the old delegation's decision to vote against the budget in June.[25] Kautsky himself, analysing the situation early in August, insisted that the split had been unavoidable and maintained furthermore that the S.A.G. really represented the one remaining bond that held the S.P.D. together. The formation of the new delegation, he wrote, had sharply limited the growth of the extremist groups on both the right and the left whose principal goal was manifestly the dissolution of the party. If it had not been created, Berlin would have been won over to the cause of the Spartacists, and the majority of the Reichstag delegation would have been driven much further to the right than had actually been the case.[26]

In any event, it is apparent that after the stormy scene in the Reichstag on the twenty-fourth, a split could hardly have been avoided. It is equally clear that Haase and his friends both gained and lost as a result of the split. As in December, their newly won freedom of movement and expression had been purchased at a not inconsiderable price in terms of their position within the now badly weakened party structure.

Regardless of any misgivings he may have had concerning the new situation in the party, Haase did not hesitate to make immediate and effective use of the opportunities it provided. In his letter of March 25, he had already voiced his eagerness to speak openly and without danger of being cut off in response to the Chancellor's major political address expected in the near future.[27] Bethmann's speech, delivered on April 5, certainly provided ample grounds for criticism. Filled with new confidence inspired by Germany's recent military successes, the Chancellor explicitly declared that there could be no return to the *status quo ante* in either East or West. The Reich had not entered the war for any purpose other than to defend itself, but the course of the struggle itself had raised the question of what should be done to insure Germany's borders against future attack, and the government now could hardly be expected to accept a peace which did not include fundamental political, military and

economic changes in Belgium, Poland and northeastern Europe.[28] The implications of the Chancellor's remarks were unmistakable. He had virtually
capitulated to the mounting pressures of the military leaders and their
annexationist allies.

Ebert, who commented on Bethmann's speech for the majority socialists,
refused to recognize this now obvious fact. He again attempted to explain
away the Chancellor's all too clear remarks and directed his attacks instead
against the spokesmen of the non-socialist parties who accepted them at face
value.[29] Haase was thus provided with an excellent opportunity to draw a clear
line between his policy and that of the majority delegation. Avoiding any
direct reference to the position of his former colleagues, he vigorously attacked
the Chancellor himself for having espoused a point of view which would make
the achievement of peace in the foreseeable future impossible. He thus
underscored what had come to be the fundamental difference between the
two delegations. Haase and his friends fully accepted the role of an opposition
party, while the leaders of the old delegation continued to conceive of themselves as the supporters of the Chancellor against his critics from both the
right and the left.

This relationship was made still more apparent by the majority's position
on the question of submarine warfare which was being widely debated at the
time. The Chancellor had insisted in his speech that the submarine was a
weapon which the Reich was fully justified in using to combat the English
blockade. Rather than question this argument with all of its possible implications, the S.P.D. delegation had agreed to join the other parties in supporting
a resolution which endorsed the full employment of this relatively new weapon
with the proviso that "the justified interests of neutral countries will be
respected."[30] Haase, on the other hand, pointed out that the proviso was
phrased in such general terms that even the Conservatives could support it
and thus was worse than useless. In effect, what it did was to provide the
government with parliamentary support for whatever policy it should decide
to pursue.

Throughout his speech, Haase emphasized that the statesmen of every
country had blundered into a dead-end street. They all favored peace, but
only on their own terms, terms which were completely unacceptable to the
other side. Under these circumstances, it was up to the masses to deliver the
statesmen from their own blindness.[31]

After Haase had completed his remarks, which had been interrupted by
some heckling from the right, but had provoked nothing approaching the
general tumult of March 24, a second round of speeches was initiated by
Scheidemann, who went to still greater lengths than Ebert to prove that
Bethmann was in essential agreement with the S.P.D. on the peace issue. In

the course of his speech, he vigorously censured various foreign socialist parties, coupled his criticism of the annexationists with complaints against those on the left who encouraged the enemy by giving the impression that the German people did not stand united behind its government,[32] and generally left such a bad taste in the mouths of the opposition that Haase's friend Heinrich Ströbel maintained afterwards that if a split had not come in March, Scheidemann's speech would have made it inevitable.[33] The debate was then terminated despite the indignant protests of Ledebour, who had been scheduled to deliver a second speech for the S.A.G.

Haase was well satisfied with the results of this April speech. Writing to a friend in May, he described the U-boat resolution which Ebert and Scheidemann had endorsed as an "ineradicable stain." If he and his friends had not left the delegation, they would have had to share the responsibility for it, his speech would not have been delivered, and the S.P.D. would have seconded Bethmann's "war fanfares" without contradiction. A large number of letters, he reported, had indicated how necessary the speech had been. Tens of thousands of copies had even been ordered by members of the majority delegation for distribution.[34] To be sure, Ströbel criticized Haase in the new opposition journal, *Sozialistische Auslandspolitik*, for not having made his remarks still stronger, but even he admitted that the contrast between his and Scheidemann's speech served to draw a clear line between the policies of the S.A.G. and those of the old delegation.[35] For his part, Haase noted that he could have given his speech a more agitational tone, but he preferred to be able to conclude it without having to face the kind of tumult he had experienced in March.[36]

While Haase and his associates had thus gained a relatively open forum for the propagation of their ideas, Liebknecht and Rühle, who remained outside the new delegation, continued to find themselves condemned to silence. For months Liebknecht had not been allowed to complete a speech on the Reichstag floor. No longer members of a recognized delegation, he and Rühle also were prevented from participating in commission meetings. They had in effect become pariah figures.

The public persecution of the two radicals reached new heights on April 8, when in the course of a wholly innocuous speech and after having been repeatedly interrupted by cries of "He must not speak!" Liebknecht was physically assaulted. A Progressive deputy first tore his notes from his hands. Then, when he left the podium to retrieve them with the aid of several members of the S.A.G., the President declared that he had given up the floor. When Liebknecht nevertheless tried to resume his speech, another Progressive leaped at him and attempted to drag him from the rostrum and was only prevented from doing so by the physical intervention of Haase and some of his friends.[37] The attempts of the S.A.G. to obtain an immediate formal condemnation of this harassment was frustrated, at least in part, by the majority delegation's refusal on technical grounds to support it, a refusal that was coupled with a new attempt by Scheidemann to discredit Haase.[38] The rapid growth of personal antagonism between the leaders of the various factions in the S.P.D. had obviously reached the point where the issues themselves were often treated as matters of only secondary importance.

Before the affair of April 8 could be brought to the floor of the Reichstag again, Liebknecht had been arrested for his participation in a May Day demonstration protesting Germany's participation in the war. This act deeply moved Haase as it did the thousands of socialist workers who first demonstrated, then went out on strike in protest against Liebknecht's sentence to two and one-half years' imprisonment. In spite of the vigorous and at times vicious attacks which the Spartacists mounted against him and his friends, Haase continued to manifest a deep respect for their bravery and consistency, if not for the soundness of their tactical judgment. When the two Social Democratic delegations unsuccessfully sought to persuade the Reichstag to uphold Liebknecht's parliamentary immunity, Haase's speech for the S.A.G. was markedly warmer than that of Landsberg, who, speaking for the old delegation, simply sought to defend the principle of immunity while explicitly deriding the "grotesque" character of Liebknecht's demonstration.[39] The government's charge of treason, Haase insisted, was completely absurd. Liebknecht had acted in complete accordance with what he considered to be the best interests of Germany. In the past a similar line of reasoning had been expressed by nearly every member of the S.P.D. delegation. Public demonstrations had always been an integral part of popular movements, and even the police admitted that the May Day demonstration had been peaceful. The case against Liebknecht, he concluded, was politically motivated and had to be opposed if the Reichstag intended to uphold its traditional principles and rights against the dangers of arbitrary government.[40]

Haase's letters at this time included many expressions of praise for the honesty and bravery of Liebknecht, of sympathy for his wife, and of frustration owing to his inability to do more to help his former colleague.[41] Undoubtedly much of this feeling can be traced to his general sympathy for the persecuted, developed over long years of defending political dissenters and the poor against a system characterized by class justice. In reading these letters, however, it is difficult to escape the impression that Haase continued to feel a genuine respect for the man himself. There is little question but that this feeling of personal sympathy and respect contributed significantly to Haase's continuing efforts, so vigorously criticized by Kautsky, to bridge the growing gap between himself and the extreme left.

Moreover, Haase was deeply impressed by the reaction of the workers to Liebknecht's imprisonment. As one of the lawyers most often called upon to defend those arrested for their participation in the demonstrations and strikes organized in support of the Spartacist leader, he was both surprised and encouraged by the fact that the working class had apparently begun to emerge from its apathy.[42]

Despite his evident feelings of sympathy and respect for some of the Spartacist leaders, however, Haase was engaged during much of the summer in a struggle with them for control of the opposition. The crucial issue in 1916 was not, as much of the radical propaganda tended to suggest, that the S.A.G. was opposed on principle to direct action. Undoubtedly Haase and his friends did tend to question the effectiveness of the Spartacists' constant appeals for revolutionary action by the proletariat,[43] but when this approach did seem to have borne fruit, Haase, at least, gave no indication that he was reluctant to endorse it. Of much greater immediate importance were the differing attitudes of the S.A.G. and the Spartacists regarding what tactic should be followed *vis-à-vis* the S.P.D. Convinced that the old party had completely discredited itself, the Spartacists mounted an increasingly vocal campaign to bring about a formal split and the formation of a new party in a new International. They therefore tried to initiate a movement to withhold dues from the S.P.D. and advocated the creation of separate opposition organizations wherever feasible.[44] Haase and his associates, however, still maintained at least a slight hope that the old party structure could be preserved. Moreover, they were convinced that the opposition point of view could best be propagated within the existing framework. Most important, they realized that the vast majority of even the most radical workers were still so psychologically attached to the S.P.D. that they would hesitate to follow leaders who took upon themselves the full responsibility for its dissolution.

This analysis of the mood of the party membership was confirmed by the course of a struggle within the Berlin party organization which reached its climax in June. Berlin, always a principal center of radicalism in the S.P.D., was in 1916 still dominated by an executive committee which endorsed the views of the majority of the Reichstag delegation. Late in June a general meeting was called to elect new local leaders who would more adequately reflect the view of the Berlin party membership which by that time was clearly in the opposition camp. At this meeting, in which Haase played an active and effective role, the old executive committee members were defeated by a majority of better than five to one.[45]

Moreover, the attempts of the Spartacists to capitalize on their energetic agitation in Berlin and on the widespread sympathy for Liebknecht were turned back by a similar margin. A decisive test of the relative strength of the two opposition groups developed when Rosa Luxemburg, temporarily released from prison, introduced a motion to direct the new executive committee to establish contact with the leaders of other electoral districts dominated by the opposition in order to initiate "organizational measures" designed to strengthen the position of the opposition in the Reich as a whole. At this point, Haase intervened energetically, pointing out that such a step would provide just the opportunity the majority leaders had been looking for to castigate the entire opposition as the deliberate destroyers of the party, since the proposed resolution could easily be interpreted as a call for the creation of an independent organization operating outside the existing party structure. The delegates, who at first appeared to be wavering, recognized the cogency of this argument and defeated the Luxemburg proposal by a large majority.[46] Haase and his friends had thus won a decisive battle against both the right and the left. The S.A.G. had established itself beyond any doubt as the spokesman of the overwhelming majority of the opposition party members.

Although the struggle with the Spartacists was certainly a matter of considerable moment during the summer of 1916, Haase's attention continued to be focused primarily upon the activities of the national party leadership. Many of the majority spokesmen undoubtedly shared his vague hopes that at least the formal unity of the party might still be preserved, and some even tried to work toward a reunification of the Reichstag delegation.[47] But it was becoming increasingly apparent to most of the leaders on both sides that under the circumstances the wisest course would be to prepare for the worst.

Thus, while Haase successfully fought off the attempts of the Spartacists to create a formal organizational structure for the opposition, he simultaneously advocated the establishment on an informal basis of more effective communication and cooperation among the various opposition groups.[48] He continued to speak at local party meetings whenever possible and achieved a striking success when in June Ebert's own electoral district organization went over to the opposition after Haase had addressed it.[49] When the party executive committee sought to assert its control over the *Vorwärts*, he enthusiastically supported the steps taken by the Berlin organization to ward off this attack upon the integrity of its local organ.[50] He also undoubtedly welcomed the publication of a series of pamphlets during the spring and summer of 1916 designed to defend the position of the S.A.G. against attacks from both the right and the left.[51]

Many of Haase's former colleagues in the executive committee obviously found themselves in a similar position. Although it is difficult to determine whether Ebert, for instance, had by this time become convinced that a final split was inevitable,[52] it is clear that he and the other majority leaders had decided to initiate a vigorous campaign to assert their control over the party's organization and press. Like Haase, however, they recognized the danger of appearing in the role of the aggressor in this struggle and therefore continued to resist right wing pressures to expel the opposition formally. What emerged during the summer and fall of 1916, therefore, was an energetically conducted campaign on both sides to secure positions of strength before the final split should occur.

Despite the rapid growth of opposition sentiment at this time, the majority leaders still controlled most of the S.P.D.'s imposing organizational structure, and it was undoubtedly with the intention of making maximum use of this advantage that they decided to convene a "national conference" in September.[53] Although the declared aim of the conference was to provide an opportunity for a thorough discussion of differences which would, hopefully, bring about a general reduction of internal strife,[54] the opposition remained justifiably suspicious and only reluctantly agreed to participate. They made their preparations for the conference with few illusions about the possibility of achieving a real rapprochement, but with a determination to make effective use of the forum it provided to defend themselves against the increasingly bitter attacks of the majority and, if possible, to make further inroads into the support the majority still enjoyed in the party bureaucracy.[55]

When the conference opened on September 21, it was immediately apparent that those who hoped that it would lay the foundations for the restoration of unity would be disappointed. It was only with difficulty that the opposition was able to persuade the majority to confirm Haase's right to speak on equal terms with the two major speakers chosen by the executive committee.[56] The participants thereupon also agreed to give a Spartacist spokesman a half hour in which to reply to both the majority and the chief opposition speakers. Before the formal debate could begin, Ledebour dramatically revealed the opposition's distrust of the majority's intentions by reading a declaration signed by more than one hundred of the delegates which argued that inasmuch as the conference was not a democratically elected body, no resolutions of any kind should be passed. In the event that the majority should decide, nevertheless, to pass resolutions, the signers of the declaration would abstain from voting.[57]

The remainder of the first day's session was devoted to the speeches of Ebert and Scheidemann, who energetically defended the policy of the party leadership and attacked the machinations of the opposition. The first part of Scheidemann's speech did, to be sure, seem to reflect a conciliatory attitude. Areas of agreement were emphasized, and, on the peace issue, the majority spokesman seemed to some observers to have moved perceptibly closer to the opposition point of view.[58] Toward the end of his remarks, however, he returned to the familiar argument that the division within the party was directly ascribable to the "well prepared" attacks of the minority upon the party leadership, an argument which was then taken up and developed with considerable vehemence by Ebert.[59]

Much of Haase's long and frequently interrupted reply on September 22 took the form of a counterattack against the party leadership. The majority spokesmen were fond of pointing out that the opposition was not united, he declared, but the differences that existed within the majority were at least as profound. Indeed, if one were to exclude those who no longer espoused a socialist position on the most important contemporary issues, the so-called majority would find itself in the minority even within the Reichstag delegation. The utter bankruptcy of the leadership's policies had become ever more obvious as the government continued to refuse to give in to any of the significant demands made by the S.P.D. It was the obligation of a party claiming to represent an oppressed class to make effective use of any difficulties the government might get itself into, but the majority leaders had relied instead upon the good will of the ruling class. They refused to recognize that the class struggle was not eliminated by war, but rather drastically accentuated. Now the old delegation found itself with absolutely no ability to influence the representatives of the ruling class, for they were confident that they would receive Social Democratic support under practically any circumstances. The results of this policy were manifest. The tax structure had been revised in such a way that the burdens borne by the working class were even heavier than before. Limitations upon civil liberties had been extended rather than reduced. The distribution of food and other necessities had been regulated in such a way as to benefit the profiteers rather than the proletariat.

Moving on to the war credits issue, Haase no longer stressed as he had in earlier speeches that circumstances had changed since August 4, 1914, but rather argued explicitly that the Social Democratic delegation had made a grievous error in the policy it had chosen to follow at that time. The vote for war credits was a political act, and, whatever phraseology accompanied it, it in fact represented a vote of confidence in the government. Haase went on to emphasize, however, that it would be a mistake to suggest that the credits issue was the only matter which divided the party. In fact, the whole policy of the majority leadership represented a departure from the fundamental principles of Social Democracy.

The opposition, he insisted, continued to hope that the unity of the party could be preserved, but any such possibility was being rapidly undermined by the majority which refused to exercise the kind of tolerance which alone could prevent a final and complete split.

Haase himself, however, then concluded his remarks with a ringing statement which could easily be interpreted as lacking the spirit of tolerance he had demanded of the majority. "We want unity in the party," he declared,

> but not in a party which makes open or concealed concessions to imperialism. We want unity in the party, but not in a party which supports colonialism. . . . We are opposed to a party which promotes protective tariffs that enrich the propertied classes. We do not want a party which attenuates the class struggle. We want unity in the party, but on the granite-hard basis of the Social Democratic program. We want it as international socialists.[60]

Characteristically, Käthe Duncker, who spoke for the Spartacists, devoted the largest part of her speech to defining the differences within the opposition camp. The most important of these, she asserted, concerned the future character of the International and the issue of national defense. The Spartacists insisted that a new, more centralized international organization be constructed which would prevent any recurrence of the debacle of August 1914. A simple resurrection of the old International, which the S.A.G. advocated, would be wholly inadequate for this purpose. Furthermore, they absolutely condemned the acceptance of the principle of national defense in any form as long as the major states were controlled by imperialistic governments. A socialist's position regarding any and every war was therefore absolutely clear as long as the era of imperialism persisted. It did not, as the members of the S.A.G. maintained, in any way depend upon the circumstances surrounding the outbreak of any specific conflict or upon the fortunes of war in any given situation.[61]

It was thus again apparent that the left radicals, like the extremists of the right, were convinced that the war had created a fundamentally new situation which required an open breach with the past, while Haase and his friends continued to advocate a return to the forms and principles of the prewar era. The Spartacists continued as in the past to concentrate much of their formidable verbal fire upon the leaders of the main body of the opposition, for it was from among their adherents that the extreme left could best hope to gain converts to its own position. Yet these attacks did not rule out cooperation between the two opposition groups. As the Spartacist spokesman at the conference pointed out, they planned to continue to march separately, but would fight together against the common enemy.

The debate that followed these major addresses was characterized by the exchange of recriminations rather than by efforts to achieve a rapprochement. Toward the end of the conference, the suspicions of the opposition were confirmed when the majority rejected by a margin of 276 to 169 a motion made by Haase and two of his associates declaring that the conference was incompetent to pass resolutions.[62] Having been outvoted on this crucial procedural issue, the opposition left the meeting.

Despite their formal defeat, however, the opposition leaders were convinced that they had achieved an important success. Hans Block, writing in

Sozialistische Auslandspolitik, commented that those members of the majority who had insisted on holding such a meeting must now feel that they had committed a gross error. The opposition could hardly have been provided with a better opportunity to express its point of view. The attempts of the majority spokesmen to force the minority onto the defendant's bench had backfired. The reverse had in fact occurred. The enthusiasm with which Haase's remarks had been received by the opposition indicated that they had made an unusually strong impression. Furthermore, it appeared that the conference had drawn the various groups within the opposition closer together.[63]

This analysis was undoubtedly somewhat overly optimistic. It is significant that David was also generally satisfied with the results of the conference. Writing in his diary immediately after its conclusion, he commented that although the number of delegates supporting the leadership should have been greater, the majority had emerged as a somewhat more unified bloc.[64]

On balance, it appears that the conference, heralded by its conveners as a sincere attempt to initiate a process of reconciliation, in fact did little more than provide an opportunity for the frank expression of contrasting points of view. As such, it was probably of greater value to the opposition, which felt itself completely stifled by censorship, than to the majority, which had only succeeded in proving that substantial opposition sentiment did indeed exist even at the lower levels of the party organization. The resolutions passed by the majority, condemned in advance as they had been by 169 delegates, could hardly be considered an overwhelming endorsement of the policies of the established leadership.

In any case, the leaders of every faction now appeared to have moved much closer to an acceptance of the fact that a split in the party organization had become unavoidable. Haase, speaking for the main body of the opposition, had clearly indicated that he and his followers were separated from the party leadership by much more than the issue of war credits alone. They had reached the point where they rejected the entire policy of the majority, with its deemphasis of the class struggle, its concessions to the government on nearly every significant issue and its refusal to exploit the war situation in the interests of the proletariat. It could now be only a question of time before these differences, coupled with Haase's own increasingly outspoken intransigence, would lead to the debacle he had so long struggled to prevent, the disintegration of the German Social Democratic movement.

CHAPTER IX

THE FINAL BREACH

If it appeared to some members of the opposition that the majority leaders left the party conference in a somewhat chastened mood, it soon became apparent that they were by no means inclined to capitulate. A few weeks after the conclusion of the conference, the executive committee carried out, with the aid of the military establishment, the most provocative of its coups against the foci of opposition sentiment within the party structure.

Since early in 1916 the executive committee had sought with increasing persistence to impose its will upon the *Vorwärts*, which as the months passed had allowed its sympathy for the opposition to become more and more evident.[1] These efforts met only very limited success. In the fall, however, the military authorities provided the majority leaders with an opportunity to gain full and complete control of the party's central organ, an opportunity which they seized with surprising alacrity considering the many vigorous protests they had previously registered against the activities of these same authorities. On October 8 the paper was ordered to cease publication until such time as the national party leaders should agree to assume responsibility for its political content. Armed with this ultimatum, the executive committee within the next few weeks successfully imposed its own censorship upon the paper, forced the resignation of the six opposition editors and installed the majority journalist, Friedrich Stampfer, as editor-in-chief.[2]

The *Vorwärts*, which had been built up largely through decades of effort by the Berlin party organization, had thus been completely removed from the control of that organization. When Haase and two of his colleagues applied to the military authorities early in November for permission to publish a new daily paper, their request was bluntly rejected.[3] The Berlin organization, the most important center of opposition activity, was left without any means of communicating regularly with its membership.[4]

The reaction to this blow was, of course, intense. Haase, like many members of the moderate opposition, regarded the "theft" of the *Vorwärts* as final and irrefutable proof that all their hopes for an eventual reconciliation had been illusory. Writing to Kurt Eisner early in November, he described the coup as "the most shabby" act he had ever witnessed in political life. He added that he had now ceased to be surprised by "any level of vulgarity."[5] He expressed his indignation still more pungently a few days later in a long letter to his old friend Gustaw Hoch who, although sympathetic to the opposition, had decided to remain in the old delegation. The majority leaders, he wrote, were intent upon imposing their policy by brute force even at the expense of breaking the party statutes and ignoring every principle of democracy and propriety. They now had advanced to the point of openly seeking to split the party. Under these circumstances the opposition had to face the urgent question of whether it should undertake organizational measures to defend itself against these "power politicians."[6]

Hoch's response to this letter provides further insight both into the dilemma which confronted many of Haase's friends when faced with the alternatives of following him into the S.A.G. or remaining in the old delegation and into the magnitude of the problems Haase now faced in his efforts to generate broader public support. While expressing sympathy for his friend's criticisms of the executive committee, Hoch was himself sharply critical of the S.A.G. He agreed with Haase that the opposition within the old delegation was weak, but insisted that those who had joined the S.A.G. were, "unfortunately," completely incapable of advancing the peace movement and that, indeed, their secession had weakened that movement. Moreover, he charged Haase and his colleagues with having "poisoned" the debate within Social Democracy. What had begun as a disagreement about the right course to pursue toward a common end had necessarily become a "struggle for power" once they had left the delegation.[7]

Haase had undoubtedly heard these and similar arguments from many of his friends since the previous spring, but events continued to drive him inexorably toward a final break with the party whose unity had meant so much to him. When the Reichstag reconvened late in November, the Social Democrats confronted an issue that could not but add further fuel to the flame of internal discord. Faced by growing economic problems caused in large part by the English blockade, the government brought in its so-called "Fatherland's Service Law," which was designed to mobilize the entire German labor force for the war effort. Haase's reaction was sharp and immediate. While the proposed legislation was still being discussed in the budget commission, he wrote to his son that he considered it "a monstrosity beyond anything yet known in the history of the world." The old delegation had, to be sure, attacked the law in the budget commission, but he judged this to be merely "theatrical thunder." The government would make superficial concessions, and then the delegation, pointing to this "great achievement," would give its support to the law as a whole.[8]

Haase's cynicism concerning his former colleagues was undoubtedly not fully justified. With the assistance of Center and Progressive Party deputies, they obtained what from their point of view were very significant changes in the bill.[9] Nevertheless, in the last analysis they did, indeed, agree to support it, and the announcement of their intention to do so brought a heated rejoinder from Haase. In effect, he declared, the bill constituted an exceptional law directed specifically against the working class. The proletarian's only possession, his labor, would be commandeered while capital remained untouched. The effect of the law would be to "place the fate of the entire male population between the ages of seventeen and sixty in the hard, ruthless fist of militarism." The measure was clearly politically motivated, and it was obvious from past experience that the law would be used to persecute dissenters. It would significantly sharpen class differences and would thus have a revolutionary impact. The concentration of capital would be accelerated, the understanding of the causes of the war and its prolongation would spread, indignation would grow, and the socialist point of view would gain in strength "With your law," he concluded ominously,

you show us that the difficulty of expropriating the expropriators is not too great. You believe that you have strengthened the dominion of capital . . ., but in fact you will yourselves prepare the way for us, for socialism.[10]

This was the strongest statement Haase had yet made in the Reichstag, and it could not fail to call forth heated rejoinders. One of the most bitter of these came from a Social Democratic spokesman who accused Haase of being a doctrinaire "who fails completely to understand the difficult situation in which our country finds itself."[11] The new law was, of course, shortly thereafter easily passed with only the S.A.G. and Rühle voting against it, but in the process the differences between the two Social Democratic factions had become clearer and broader than ever.[12] Writing to his son a few days later, Haase commented sadly that the dissolution of the party was taking place under extremely painful circumstances. He "had not thought it possible that the old delegation would vote for a law . . . that will fetter the workers."[13]

On December 12 the Reichstag was again summoned under extraordinary circumstances to consider a matter of considerable importance for the conflict within the S.P.D. During the latter part of the autumn Germany's military position had improved substantially. Romania had been defeated, the allies had been unable to force a breakthrough on the Somme, and the German armies elsewhere had either hell their own or been able to advance still further into enemy territory. Under these circumstances, Bethmann decided that the time had come for a formal peace offensive by his government.[14] The Chancellor prefaced his reading of the Kaiser's peace note in the Reichstag with a lengthy enumeration of the recent military successes of Germany and her allies. The note itself was dominated by an emphasis upon the strength of Germany's position and her ability and willingness to carry the struggle to a victorious conclusion if the Entente should reject her peace overtures. It proposed the immediate initiation of peace negotiations "in order to prevent further bloodshed," but said nothing about the nature of the terms Germany was prepared to offer other than to declare that her representatives would bring proposals to the negotiating table which would serve as the basis for the establishment of an enduring peace. The session was then immediately terminated by a motion which was supported by the majority socialists, but energetically opposed by the S.A.G. as well as the Conservatives and National Liberals.[15] The Reichstag did not meet again until late in February.

The situation created by this move was an extremely difficult one for the Social Democratic opposition. Bethmann's action undoubtedly appeared to many party members to be just what the S.A.G. had been demanding. The successful parliamentary maneuver of the majority socialists and their allies had effectively prevented the opposition spokesmen from utilizing their most effective forum to clarify their objections to the government's offensive.[16] Writing to his son two days after the Chancellor's speech, Haase complained that even his wife could not understand his skepticism. It seemed to him that the peace initiative gave scant grounds for hope. After her victory over Romania, Germany appeared once again to be the victor, and at such a moment the Entente would be little inclined to enter negotiations. The Entente leaders did not by any means view themselves as the vanquished party, and their warmongers, like those in Germany, believed now as before in the eventual triumph of their cause. They would view the note simply as a German maneuver, undertaken with the expectation that it would fail, but with the intention of casting the Reich in the role of "the true friend of peace." The rejection of the note would certainly increase the intensity of the conflict. The initiation of unrestricted submarine warfare would then be imminent, and the peace enthusiasts would suffer a severe disappointment. Haase did hope, however, that the Entente leaders would at least ask the German government to outline its proposals in specific terms, since this would force Bethmann to clarify his position.[17] He also explained that, despite his pessimism, he felt that the note did had some positive significance inasmuch as it was the first official expression of an interest in negotiations. As for the action of the majority socialists in helping to cut off debate, it did not surprise him, for these "official apologists" had lost "every trace of democratic sensitivity."[18]

Far from reducing tensions within the S.P.D. as might have been expected, the peace initiative in fact helped to set the stage for the final rupture. Many members of the majority felt that the Kaiser's note and its rejection by the Entente completely justified the policy of the established leadership.[19] From this point of view, the continued skepticism of the opposition leaders seemed to indicate that any further attempts at reconciliation would be useless.

Moreover, it was just at this point that the opposition made a decisive move to establish a firmer organizational basis within the party and thus gave further credence to this view. Faced with the offensive of the executive committee against its positions of strength within the party organization and press, the S.A.G. leaders called a meeting of the combined opposition for January 7, 1917, in Berlin. The meeting was held in the Reichstag building to avoid police surveillance and was officially described as a regular gathering of the S.A.G. There were, however, more than 150 participants, elected as far as possible according to the stipulations of the S.P.D.'s statutes for party conventions. Seventy-two electoral districts were represented. Outside of Berlin, Spartacists were elected only in the few areas where they dominated the opposition. In Berlin itself a separate Spartacist slate was elected along with the delegation of the principal opposition group.

The conference opened with speeches by Haase and Richard Lipinski representing the S.A.G. and by Ernst Meyer of the Spartacists. Haase devoted the major portion of his remarks to an attack upon the members of the majority whom he characterized as "tools of Bethmann-Hollweg." Their recent support of the "Fatherland's Service Law," their refusal to permit a debate on the Chancellor's speech, and their eager acceptance of the government's peace proposal at face value had made their subservience even more apparent than before. Toward the end of his speech he touched upon the central issue of the conference, the future tactics of the opposition. It was time for the opposition to unite, he declared. It was their right, indeed their duty to do so. This did not mean, however, that he wanted to destroy the party:

We want to remain in the party because we know with certainty that we will get the masses to support us. We would be fools if we wanted to remain a mere sect, for the workers' movement can only exist as a mass movement. But we also do not want to become a party of reformism. . . . We want to be a party of democracy and of socialism.[20]

The first Spartacist spokesman, however, quickly dispelled any hopes the delegates may have had that agreement upon a plan for united action would come easily. He roundly attacked the members of the S.A.G. for having failed to speak out loudly and often enough concerning the questions Haase had raised. The opposition delegation, he declared, should in the future use the Reichstag as a tribune from which to galvanize the masses into action rather than persist in the vain hope that something solid might be achieved through parliamentary action. The only way to prevent a dissolution of the party, he concluded, was to conduct an energetic struggle, and the organizational proposals that had been presented by the S.A.G. were far too weak for this purpose.[21]

During the debates which followed, Haase responded to a bitter personal attack upon him by another Spartacist by emphasizing once again that the members of the S.A.G. were perfectly willing to be criticized. He added, however, that it was apparently necessary to explain that the S.A.G. was merely a Reichstag delegation and could only act within the Reichstag. It was absurd to ask indignantly what the S.A.G. had done. He and his colleagues had even gone so far as to attack the executive committee on the Reichstag floor. His Spartacist critic had also asked about the program of the S.A.G. That question was not difficult to answer. Its members wanted simply to carry out the established program of German Social Democracy and the International. He recognized that the lines already laid down would not be sufficient for the future, but the task of developing a new program would have to be undertaken later.

In keeping with the organizational resolution which had been presented by the S.A.G., Haase went on to urge the establishment of regular contact between organizations in which the opposition had already gained a majority. Where the opposition was in the minority, it must create organizations within the established framework of the party and then work to bring the majority over to its point of view. Eventually they could hope to establish a central press bureau which would facilitate the dissemination of information. All of these measures, he declared, would be meaningful, far more so than fanatically calling for "deeds" to end the war. If the opposition proceeded realistically while simultaneously striving to maintain the unity of the party, significant progress could be made; otherwise not.[22]

The tone of Haase's remarks is suggestive of the mood that pervaded the entire conference. There obviously existed a strong mutual interest in cooperation, but the situation was not yet desperate enough for the theoretical, tactical and personal differences which rankled within the opposition to recede into the background. Toward the end of the meeting Dittmann, as chairman, formally recognized that no amalgamation of the various groups was for the moment possible.[23]

In spite of their failure to forge an effective organizational alliance, however, the delegates did unanimously endorse a manifesto drafted by Kautsky which expressed the opposition's reservations about the Kaiser's peace note and called for united action by the international proletariat to end the war.[24] As Hans Block noted in *Sozialistische Auslandspolitick*, the conference had provided an opportunity for a clarification of the situation within the opposition and, more importantly, had given dramatic proof, just when the majority was pointing to the German peace offensive as conclusive evidence of the success of its policy, that fundamental differences continued to exist between the two major groups within the S.P.D.[25]

The conference was thus productive in that it prepared the ground for more effective cooperation between the opposition groups. Within the context of the party struggle as a whole, however, it could well be viewed as a major tactical blunder, for it provided the majority with an ideal excuse for initiating still more aggressive measures to strengthen and extend its position. Haase and his friends, despite their often expressed forebodings about the imminent dissolution of the party, continued to emphasize the necessity of maintaining their organizational ties with the S.P.D. Where earlier simple feelings of loyalty to the party and aversion to sectarianism had played a major role in preventing any break with the majority-dominated organization, tactical considerations now had come to predominate in the debates on the unity issue. As the struggle within the S.P.D. took on increasingly concrete forms, it had become ever more apparent to the opposition leaders that they desperately needed the party's organizational structure if they were to gain and maintain loyal and effective mass support.

Unfortunately, the majority leaders also recognized the tactical advantages which the party organization provided for the opposition. The January conference provided them with the opportunity, which they were undoubtedly by this time seeking, to deprive the minority of these advantages. Their answer to this "provocation" was, as usual, to call a meeting of the party council. As early as January 11, David could gleefully note in his diary that the executive committee had decided to carry out the division of the party.[26] When the council met on January 18, a resolution was easily passed which, in effect, did just that. The convening of the opposition conference, it declared, represented

the creation of a separate organization directed against the party, and the members of the S.A.G. as well as their followers have thereby separated themselves from the party. The creation of this separate organization and membership in it is irreconcilable with membership in the party as a whole. It is therefore now the task of all the organizations that remain loyal to the party to put an end to the dishonest duplicity of those intent on destroying the party and to take the organizational measures made necessary by the splitting off of the separate organizations.[27]

It is surprising that Haase and his friends apparently did not forsee the reaction of the executive committee. Now that the majority had seized the initiative, they were, in effect, forced to reverse the policy they had so recently outlined. As the majority leaders began to carry out the program of expulsion enunciated by the party council, the opposition was thrown into apparent confusion. A manifesto was immediately published calling upon opposition members to close ranks "to preserve our rights in the party organizations." Exactly how this was to be accomplished, however, would have to await "later decisions."[28] Heinrich Ströbel, writing in *Socialistische Auslandspolitik* a few days later, was able to shed little light on the situation. It was now the duty of the minority, he declared, to break away "from the ruthless clique of bureaucrats . . . not from the party."[29]

It was not until February 9 that the opposition's policy received some degree of clarification in a manisfesto signed by Haase, Ledebour and Vogtherr for the S.A.G. After detailing the measures undertaken by the majority to expel the opposition, it outlined a program designed to achieve the earliest possible organizational consolidation. In agreement with a large number of party members from all parts of the Reich, the manifesto declared, the S.A.G. leaders had decided to call a conference of all those interested in working with the opposition Reichstag delegation. The purpose of the conference would be to determine what measures should be taken to unify the opposition. Those electoral districts which already supported the opposition were directed to register with the S.A.G. leaders. In electoral districts where opposition members had been "robbed of their party rights," they were to form their own organizations and then inform the S.A.G. leaders of their commitment to join the movement. All preparatory organizational work was to be completed by mid-March.[30]

This call to action was answered immediately. On February 11, Haase addressed a meeting of the electoral district leaders of metropolitan Berlin. A resolution endorsing the action taken by the S.A.G. leaders and directing the individual district organizations to carry out the proposals made in their manifesto of February 9 was passed unanimously.[31] Similar resolutions were soon passed by a considerable number of organizations throughout the Reich. Haase was, of course, frequently called upon to address these meetings. Writing to a friend in March, he reported that the opposition was rapidly gaining strength in many places. He wished that he could be even more active in encouraging this movement outside of Berlin, but he simply did not have enough time or energy.[32]

The struggle was no longer confined to the party organization itself. During the previous autumn, Liebknecht had been deprived of his seat in both the Prussian Landtag and the Reichstag when his original sentence was raised by a higher court to four years at hard labor, and in the elections which now were called to choose successors, both Social Democratic factions nominated candidates. Franz Mehring, the opposition candidate, who was like Liebknecht a Spartacist, easily won the seat in the Landtag, since the district lay in the heart of opposition territory in Berlin. Liebknecht's Reichstag mandate, however, came from a district which had only been very tenuously held by the S.P.D., and the majority candidate now had the support of the bourgeois parties. Nevertheless, the opposition conducted a spirited campaign in which Haase played an active role. Although Mehring's defeat was under the circumstances quite understandable, it nevertheless represented a distinct setback for the S.A.G., particularly inasmuch as he received only 5,000 votes as compared to the nearly 22,000 votes garnered by Liebknecht in 1912.

Haase commented somewhat lamely afterwards that the opposition could be well satisfied with the number of votes Mehring had received, especially since they had come largely from convinced socialists.[33]

Before the new opposition conference could convene, a number of momentous events had occurred which helped to determine its course. Early in February, 1917, unrestricted submarine warfare was initiated, and as Haase had feared,[34] the result was a break in relations between the United States and Germany. War was actually declared on April 6, the day the conference opened at Gotha.

Of greater immediate importance was the outbreak in March of the Russian Revolution. Although Haase scarcely felt that a German revolution was now an immediate possibility, he was clearly encouraged by the Russian upheaval[35] and did not scruple to use the threat which the Russian events implied. Thus, in a major Reichstag speech on March 30 in which he attacked Bethmann's recent refusal to support an immediate reform of the Prussian electoral system,[36] he declared that the government was playing "a dangerous game" and asked whether the Chancellor planned to wait until the German masses learned to "speak Russian." He quickly added that this rhetorical question should not be construed as a threat, for revolutions were not made but grew out of existing conditions.[37] Nevertheless, the implication was clear, and as the months passed, such warnings would not be without effect, both upon the government and upon the increasingly restless German workers.

The explicit refusal of the government to initiate domestic reforms as well as its colossal blunder in provoking war with the United States considerably strengthened the position of Haase and his friends which had been not a little shaken by the December peace offensive. Their consistent opposition to the Chancellor and his policies now regained its popularity among the workers who were facing increasing scarcity, inflation, political oppression and the prospect of an indefinitely prolonged war.

It was therefore with renewed confidence and enthusiasm that the opposition delegates gathered at Gotha on April 6. The 143 participants included elected representatives from ninety-one electoral districts as well as the opposition Reichstag deputies and a few other members of the S.P.D. national hierarchy.[38] The revolutionary fervor aroused by recent events did not, however, engender a consensus concerning the tactics to be followed by the opposition. On the one hand, several of the most highly respected delegates such as Kautsky and Bernstein still hoped that any new organization created by the conference would be able to preserve at least the appearance of remaining within the S.P.D. At the other end of the spectrum, a small number of extremist representatives came to the conference determined to reject any proposal which would involve formal organizational ties to the S.A.G.[39]

Haase's postion, as usual, lay somewhere in the middle. He was far more willing than Kautsky to work with the Spartacists, hoping thereby to establish the broadest possible popular base for the new organization. He was also finally prepared to recognize that the opposition could no longer function within the old party. He was, however, by no means willing meekly to accept the dictation of the relatively small Spartacist group. Much of his energy during the three-day meeting was devoted to an effort to impose at least a modicum of organizational discipline upon his unrully allies.

The actual course of the debate was very similar to that of January 7. Yet the impact of events in Russia, the increasingly restive mood of the German workers and the rising tide of opposition sentiment produced a new confidence and a belief in the possibility of initiating an effective program of action for peace and socialism. This optimism was reflected in the obvious conviction of the overwhelming majority of the delegates that, despite their deep and continuing disagreements, every effort should be made to create an organizational framework within which the entire opposition could be united.

In his welcoming speech, Haase made it clear that from his point of view there was little sense in continuing to discuss the possibility of achieving a compromise with the "government socialists." "Social Democracy is now divided," he declared,

but the hope exists that today's conference will allow the party to awake to a new life. . . . The conference should prepare the way for a truly socialist policy, sharply differentiated from that of the government socialists who have made their peace with the bourgeois parties.

The meeting "had become a historical necessity," and there was good reason for optimism. "The storms of March bluster through the world," he concluded. "The dawn of freedom shines across Russia's borders into this very conference hall."[40]

As the delegates actually got down to business, it quickly became apparent that the general enthusiasm had not by any means erased the feelings of antagonism and distrust that had so clearly manifested themselves in January. Haase devoted a considerable portion of his major address on "The Situation in the Party" to a detailed criticism of the Spartacist position. He began by pointedly stressing the necessity of dealing with practical matters rather than wasting valuable time on purely theoretical disputes. The question of national defense, for instance, should not be considered in the abstract, but rather in relation to the conflict in which Germany was engaged. Such an approach, he predicted, would soon lead to agreement. The important thing was to create an organization. If the various factions were interested in serving the common cause by practical work and not just words, then the basis for common action already existed. If any of the left wing groups were merely trying to obtain protection from government persecution,[41] then he would actively oppose their participation. But he hoped that such was not their intent and that all would unite in the common effort to lead German Social Democracy back to a principled policy.

He complained that the Spartacists appeared to be fighting not so much against the government socialists as against the so-called "centrists." In any case, this term could not be justifiably applied to himself and his friends. "We stand firmly on the left in the party," he declared. Addressing the radicals directly, he asserted that he could not accept their argument that the opposition should have split off from the old party earlier. It was far better that they had waited while the majority "heaped misdeed upon misdeed" until the opposition had no alternative but to act independently.

Haase then launched a long and extremely bitter attack upon the policies and practices of the majority leaders who had "systematically" sought to split the party. He emphasized that the disagreements which had torn the party apart antedated 1914. "It would be superficial," he declared, "to maintain that these differences . . . were created by the war." The war had only revealed their full intensity.[42] Haase was here expressing, at the very birth of the new party, a point of view that would separate him from more moderate colleagues such as Bernstein and Kautsky who insisted that the war alone was responsible for its creation and who would therefore agitate for immediate reunification as soon as the war was over.

During the discussion of the new party's organizational framework, Haase again emphasized the importance of achieving unity, although he did not hesitate to reiterate his criticism of the Spartacists for their constant search for phrases that they might attack. He also insisted that they must consent to a reasonable degree of discipline, thereby provoking a stormy debate which only subsided when his Königsberg friend Gottschalk proposed a compromise resolution stipulating that there would be united action on every project planned by one of the party organizations and that only one organization would exist in each district.[43]

The structure that emerged from this debate was patterned after that of the S.P.D., but it also took into account many of the left wing criticisms of the old party that had been put forward during the previous decade and a half. A concerted effort was made to prevent it from falling into the hands of paid bureaucrats, and provision was made for a greater degree of independence on the part of local organizations. The programmatic introduction to the basic statute largely reflected the point of view of Haase and his colleagues in the S.A.G. The new party would be "led by the principles and demands of the party program (i.e., the Erfurt Program), the decisions of the party conventions and of the international congresses." It would stand

in fundamental opposition to the ruling governmental system, to the war policies of the Reich government and to the policies of the nominal party which has been led by the executive committee into the wake of the government.[44]

At Haase's suggestion, the delegates decided to call the new party the Independent Social Democratic Party of Germany (U.S.P.D.).[45] Its central committee, to which Haase was easily elected, was made up largely of his friends and consistent supporters.[46]

Now that the primary objective of the conference had been achieved, the participants moved on to a general discussion of the "tasks" of the new party, in the course of which the Spartacists indicated that they had lost none of their penchant for sharp criticism of their colleagues. To be sure, Ledebour, who delivered the major speech on this subject for the S.A.G., waved the red flag in front of their faces by strongly attacking their "defense nihilism" and by pointedly asserting that mass actions could not be artifically produced.[47] Hecker, replying for the Spartacists, reiterated the usual radical criticisms of the "bourgeois pacifist" proclivities of the center. He particularly condemned the work of Kautsky, who as an "impractical theoretician" had done much to confuse the masses. He also developed the argument, which would become central to much of the radical polemic, that the German party must look to the Russians as the great teachers of revolutionary theory and strategy.[48]

This speech evoked a spirited response from Haase, who defended his friend Kautsky against "those who were not worthy of untying his shoes."[49] This constant wrangling must have made Haase not a little uneasy about the future of the new party. Writing to a friend on the final afternoon of the conference, he noted that he was in a depressed mood, a mood which was deepened by the news he had just received that his son was being sent to the front for political reasons. Nevertheless, in the same letter he praised Hecker, whose genuine "thirst for freedom" had been justly recognized by Ledebour and whose concluding speech had been far better than his earlier remarks which had included the attack upon Kautsky.[50] Whatever misgivings he may have had about the continuing conflict within the opposition, he still was able to sympathize with those who were led to criticize him out of deep personal conviction. He must have been further encouraged by the fact that at the end of the day a manifesto drafted by Kautsky, which in all essentials expressed his own point of view, was adopted almost unanimously.[51]

The major objectives which Haase had sketched out for the Gotha conference had thus been achieved. Almost the entire opposition had been united in a single organization and had officially endorsed a program which reflected both his theoretical principles and his analysis of the political situation. To be sure, the differences within the opposition had not by any means been resolved, but agreement had been reached on common goals, and a structure had been created which would permit Haase and his friends to pursue these goals with renewed vigor and, hopefully, with increased effectiveness.

Some of Haase's closest friends, however, were not at all satisfied with the results of the meeting. Kautsky in particular had from the beginning been uneasy about Haase's efforts to include the Spartacists in the new organization, and the conference at Gotha strengthened his misgivings. Furthermore, many of those who attended it were still not convinced that the formation of a new and completely separate party would be necessary. When the conference took this course, Kautsky, Bernstein, Emanuel Wurm and undoubtedly many others as well had to go through a period of serious soul-searching before they agreed to join the new organization, and when they did so their decision was based largely on the realization that if they remained independent, they would be totally ineffective in the all-important struggle for peace.[52]

Kautsky later argued with considerable cogency that the formation of the U.S.P.D. in effect completed the disruption of the opposition begun the year before with the creation of the S.A.G. The U.S.P.D.'s power of attraction was severely circumscribed by this fact, while its effectiveness was further limited by the dissension within its own ranks.[53]

Although events were to prove the validity of many of Kautsky's reservations, it must be remembered that these arguments were developed with the benefit of hindsight. It is highly probable that in the spring of 1917 Kautsky himself was by no means as clairvoyant as his later statements would suggest. In a letter to Victor Adler, written late in February, he vigorously rejected his Austrian friend's accusation that the opposition had provoked the break in the party. He forcefully argued at that time that the majority had actually done the provoking and that, in any event, if the opposition had not decided to undertake independent action, the masses of workers sympathetic to its position would have been driven into the arms of the Spartacists. He concluded by declaring that he was not conscious of any error on his part except that of failing to follow Haase's leadership in August 1914.[54]

In any case, it is difficult to imagine what practical alternative was available to the opposition at the time. They might, of course, have tried at Gotha to maintain the appearance of remaining within the S.P.D. as Kautsky seemingly desired, thus forcing the S.P.D. executive committee to take further aggressive steps against them. Such a stratagem, however, would only have added further confusion to a situation that urgently required clarification. It would also have provided further ammunition for the Spartacist critics of the moderates' "half measures." The S.A.G. leaders might also have refused to cooperate with the Spartacists, but in the context of the situation that existed in the spring of 1917, it is not difficult to perceive why Haase decided to reject such a policy: It would have met with little understanding among the increasingly radical workers who identified themselves with the S.A.G. Kautsky himself had declared a few months earlier that Liebknecht was the "most popular man in the trenches."[55] A formal rejection of the Spartacists would have been viewed by many as a betrayal of Liebknecht, Luxemburg and others who had come to be known as the most active and dedicated of those opposing the war. It would also have represented another break with the well established Social Democratic principle of "unity above all." It appears, therefore, that whatever its long-range disadvantages, the policy followed by Haase and the majority at Gotha was the most reasonable and practical of the possibilities available to them.

CHAPTER X

LEADER OF A NEW PARTY

With the foundation of the U.S.P.D. at Gotha, Haase found himself faced with the formidable task of creating under wartime conditions a new and viable instrument for the propagation of his increasingly radical views. The period between the Gotha Conference and the end of the war was marked, to be sure, by a perceptible shift in the orientation of the old party in the direction of Haase's own position as of August 1914. Any serious possibility of achieving a rapprochement, however, was ruled out, on the one hand, by the personal antagonisms generated by years of fratricidal strife and, on the other, by the rapid movement of Haase and most of his secessionist colleagues toward a more aggressive attitude, a movement which culminated in 1918 in the active preparation of revolution.

In his efforts to build up the new party Haase confronted an incredible web of wartime restrictions which were frequently manipulated by government agencies in such a way as to work to the advantage of the S.P.D. The Independents' inability to publish a daily paper in cities such as Berlin where the S.P.D. had been successful in maintaining or regaining control of the existing organ constituted an immense obstacle to the new party's growth. Moreover, in some cases where the U.S.P.D. did control the local paper, the S.P.D. was permitted by the authorities to publish a new daily of their own.[1] Furthermore, the formation of a separate party made it possible for the S.P.D. executive committee to act with still greater aggressiveness against the opposition press. In May *Gleichheit*, the party's publication for women, was taken out of the hands of the radical Klara Zetkin,[2] and, more important, at the end of September *Die Neue Zeit* returned to majority socialist control when its founder Karl Kautsky was unceremoniously fired.[3]

The persecution of the new party was, however, by no means limited to its press. As Germany's military situation deteriorated and the ideas fomented by the Russian Revolution began to arouse growing sympathy among the German workers, the government reacted with increasing severity against the one party which consistently opposed its policies. Ever larger numbers of the U.S.P.D.'s most effective spokesmen were silenced. Even its membership meetings were often forbidden, and during crises like the mass strikes of April 1917 and January 1918, many of its most active agitators were either imprisoned or summarily inducted into the armed forces.[4]

In spite of these difficulties, the U.S.P.D. was able at first to make impressive progress. A considerable number of electoral district organizations, particularly in industrial centers with a long tradition of radicalism such as Berlin and Leipzig, went over to the new party within the first few months of its existence.[5] The core of a mass party had thus been created. It was after this consolidation of already existing opposition sentiment had been completed, however, that the fundamental weakness of the Independents' position became fully apparent.

The old party reacted by forming its own organizations wherever it had been unable to maintain control, and because of the general confusion surrounding the political situation and the restrictions placed upon the Independents, they were often able to quickly stem the flow of members into the new party. The continuing dissension within the opposition only served to exacerbate the difficulties imposed from without. Under these circumstances it required considerable effort even to maintain the strength of the new party, and it was only very slowly that, after the first rush, new local organizations could be developed and the overall membership increased.[6] The U.S.P.D. was thus doomed from its inception to achieve only limited success in its efforts to win over the overwhelming majority of the old Social Democratic constituency, at least as long as the war continued.

The success of the S.P.D. in promoting the widely heralded Reichstag peace resolution of July 19, 1917 served to further complicate matters for the Independents.[7] Returning to Berlin shortly before its passage, Haase wrote to his son that the intentions of the majority block were clear. The Reichstag would pass a resolution which would be worded in such a way that even the Chancellor could accept it. A representative of the Progressives had approached him to inquire whether he would support the resolution inasmuch as in their opinion the parties which had formulated it had now arrived at a position which closely approximated his own. It was indeed correct, Haase commented, that the Reichstag majority had finally come to the realization that a victory of conquest had become impossible. He quickly added, however, that he and the majority parties were still separated by "a gaping chasm."[8]

On July 19 Haase outlined in detail the nature and extent of these differences in one of his most important Reichstag speeches. He spoke after the new Chancellor, Georg Michaelis, a career bureaucrat and political novice who enjoyed the patronage of the high command, had, as Haase had predicted, expressed his agreement with the resolution, adding, however, the qualifying phrase, "as I understand it."[9] He had also listened while Scheidemann, although obviously uneasy about Michaelis' remarks, sought to interpret them in such a way as to indicate a clear endorsement of the majority's position and then committed the S.P.D. to vote again for war credits.[10]

In his long and sharply worded statement for the Independents, Haase strongly criticized both the policy outlined by the new Chancellor and the text of the peace resolution. During the political crisis from which the resolution had emerged, he reminded his colleagues, cries had been heard from all sides demanding an end to ambiguity. Michaelis' reply, however, had completely failed to fulfill this demand. Yet, despite their numerous threats, the members of the left-center majority block had immediately capitulated and expressed their general satisfaction with the government's response. Furthermore, he pointed out, in order to assess correctly the Chancellor's remarks, it was necessary to take into consideration the fact that Michaelis had in effect been appointed as the representative of Hindenburg and Ludendorff, men whom no one could seriously accuse of favoring a peace of understanding.

Turning to the text of the peace resolution, Haase declared that it did indeed represent a progressive step for those who until recently had enthusiastically demanded annexations. For the U.S.P.D., however, it was unacceptable on a number of counts. In the first place, its depiction of the genesis of the war was historically indefensible. Furthermore, it did not reject the aims of the annexationists clearly and decisively enough. Most important, it said nothing about the right of all peoples to self-determination. Moreover, it failed to oppose explicitly all demands for reparations and neglected to assert the necessity of providing for general disarmament as a prerequisite for the establishment of a lasting peace.

The resolution could have had a salutary effect, he admitted, if the majority bloc had chosen to make the recently proclaimed peace program of the Russian Soviet its own.[11] In that case it would have strengthened the provisional government and thus enabled it to put greater pressure for peace on the Entente. As presented to the Reichstag, however, the resolution fell far short of that program, and its impact could be expected to be virtually nullified by the mistrust which had developed everywhere toward both the German government and the parties, including the S.P.D., which had hitherto been the prisoners of Bethmann-Hollweg and which now had indicated their willingness to become prisoners of Michaelis.

In order to demonstrate how completely the program outlined in the resolution differed from that of the U.S.P.D., Haase read in its entirety the manifesto recently prepared by the Independents for the Stockholm conference of socialist party representatives, a manifesto which had characteristically been suppressed in Germany. Then, summarizing the essential points in this document, he declared that any effective peace program would have to include an explicit renunciation off all annexations and reparations, a commitment to the right of self-determination for all peoples and an expressed determination to initiate a vigorous struggle against any government which refused fully and forthrightly to accept these principles.

Toward the end of his remarks, Haase returned to a theme which had become increasingly fundamental to his position, the necessity of generating a mass movement for peace. Amid the growing restlessness of the Reichstag deputies, he asserted that the workers everywhere were becoming aware of the fact that they must themselves take action to achieve their goals of peace and freedom. He described a recent demonstration in Russia in the course of which a banner had been raised over the heads of the crowd showing a Russian and a German worker joining hands and bearing the inscription, "Comrade, make haste!" "Yes," he declared dramatically, "make haste! That is the call which goes out from Russia to the masses in Germany and Austria, to the masses in France, England and Italy, and only if the masses make haste will we reach the object of our yearning, the end of this gruesome war."[12]

Despite Haase's passionate speech, the passage of the peace resolution over the opposition of the U.S.P.D. and the Conservatives could not but add further confusion to the political situation at a time when the Independents could ill afford it. It was only many months later, after the conclusion of the Treaty of Brest Litovsk, that the accuracy of Haase's analysis became fully apparent. In the meantime, it must have seemed inexplicable to many a sympathetic German worker that the Independents had chosen to oppose what appeared to be the first genuine peace action taken by the German parliament.

The position outlined by Haase on July 19, however, reflected his firm determination to reject any compromise with the old party as it gradually moved toward a point of view on the peace issue which appeared at least superficially similar to that long advocated by Haase himself. The peace issue remained, to be sure, at the center of Haase's concern, but as the war progressed and the party conflict increased in intensity, the question of consistent unqualified opposition to the existing regime, always extremely important to him, moved into the forefront among the issues separating him from his former colleagues. And, of course, with the formation of the majority bloc in the Reichstag during the summer of 1917, this was an issue about which the S.P.D. was little inclined to compromise.

Haase's consistency in this matter was clearly demonstrated by his attitude toward the efforts to convene a conference of representatives from the socialist parties of the belligerent countries in Stockholm during the summer and fall of 1917. Repeated efforts had been made almost since the beginning of the war to bring about such a meeting. All of these attempts had shattered against the innumerable obstacles erected both by the various governments and the parties themselves. The only important exceptions had been the Zimmerwald and Kienthal conferences of 1915 and 1916, but on these occasions only opposition groups had been represented.[13] Most of the leaders of the established parties, who still represented the overwhelming majority of the members of the International, remained so estranged from one another that every attempt to move toward a reconciliation had failed.

To many observers, however, the situation in 1917 appeared much more promising than heretofore. As the war approached its fourth year, peace sentiment was growing more intense everywhere. More important, the Russian Revolution appeared to have created a fundamentally new situation. The resulting optimism led to a number of initiatives which gradually evolved into a major effort to convene a truly representative conference in Stockholm.[14] Throughout the summer socialists throughout the world focused their attention on that neutral city where it was hoped some kind of decisive international action for peace would be formulated.

Haase, however, had from the beginning few illusions concerning the possibility of success at Stockholm. Writing to his son early in May, he predicted that little could be expected from the conference projected by the neutral organizing committee. He and his political associates would refuse to participate in the fabrication of a resolution which merely served to cover up differences. The conference would only make sense if the socialists of every country would resolve to engage in a policy of determined resistance to their governments' war policies. "But," he asked, "who can place such hopes in the *Scheidemänner?*"[15] Nevertheless, his pessimism was not such as to cause him to consider a trip to Stockholm totally useless. In any case, even before the first invitations had gone out, he had applied for permission to visit Stockholm, hoping to obtain there a more accurate view of the Russian situation which consumed much of his attention during these months. Moreover, in May and June it appeared possible that a conference might be successfully convened under the leadership of the Russian Soviets, a prospect which Haase greeted with considerable enthusiasm.[16]

Haase's mood was thus not wholly negative as he left on his journey late in June. His letters from Stockholm reflect the immensely refreshing impact of intercourse with his old associates from the International under conditions of relative freedom and prosperity.[17] There is no indication, however, that his experiences caused him to modify his pessimism concerning the possibility of effective international action for peace at that time. Indeed, the manifesto which he and his colleagues drafted for the Stockholm committee reflected an obvious intention to draw still more clearly the line which separated the Independents from the S.P.D.[18]

Returning to Berlin in the midst of the crisis surrounding the Reichstag peace resolution, Haase spent the rest of the summer watching, undoubtedly with some misgivings, but without surprise, as attempt after attempt to convene a general conference was frustrated, first by the stubbornness and hostility of the various parties and finally by the refusal of the Entente powers to issue passes to their parties' prospective delegates.[19] The only concrete achievement of the summer's feverish activity was the calling in September of a third and final "Zimmerwald" Conference. This conference, which Haase attended as a member of the U.S.P.D. delegation, met under the shadow of the rapidly growing crisis in Russia and was dominated by the conviction that everything possible must be done to "save" the revolution. The mood of the delegates was, moreover, colored by a sense of impotence stemming from the fact that the meeting was even less well attended than the earlier Zimmerwald Conferences, and also from the painful impression produced by the representatives of the various Russian factions who made little effort to conceal their mounting differences in the course of the debates.[20]

Nevertheless, the participants decided to issue a call for an international mass strike, the goal of which would be simultaneously to rescue the Russian Revolution and to compel the belligerents to end the war.[21]

It was characteristic of Haase that at this point he permitted his inherent prudence to overcome his eagerness for immediate action,[22] and he was one of the few delegates to question the wisdom of issuing such an appeal. Without questioning in principle the desirability of initiating revolutionary action, he declared that he was reluctant to make commitments which he knew it might well be impossible to fulfill.[23] It was also typical of Haase, however, that once the overwhelming majority of the delegates endorsed the proposal, he agreed to cooperate and was appointed to the commission assigned the task of determining its text.[24] In actuality, the manifesto proved to be of little significance. The conferees agreed to keep it secret until support could be secured from the Zimmerwald elements not represented at Stockholm, and by the time it actually was published in November, it was overshadowed by the Bolshevik revolution and had little impact.[25]

Nevertheless, by the autumn of 1917 it was becoming increasingly apparent that Haase's traditional centrist rhetoric of eventual but still distant revolution would no longer suffice. Soon after his return from the September meeting in Stockholm, the revolutionary zeal of others within his party once again compelled him to confront, if not to solve, some of the problems that this development entailed. On October 9 Michaelis dramatically declared in the Reichstag that the U.S.P.D. did not deserve to enjoy the same rights as the other parties, since it pursued ends which endangered the very existence of the Reich. He then turned the floor over to his naval secretary, Eduard von Capelle, who announced that plans for a naval mutiny had been discovered and that its principal fomenter had implicated Haase, Dittmann and Vogtherr.[26]

Haase reacted immediately to this dangerous attack. He frankly admitted that he had spoken with the accused sailor, but emphatically denied that he

had anything to hide. Like many other members of the armed forces who had
visited him, the sailor had complained of conditions and had requested
political literature which he and his comrades could read and discuss. Haase
added that the accused had made a very favorable impression on him and that
he had personally been deeply shaken by the news of his execution merely for
having sought to pursue actively his high political ideals.[27]

As the ensuing debate unfolded, it became increasingly apparent that
Michaelis had committed a major political blunder. The government was
compelled to reveal that it in fact possessed no evidence that the Independent
leaders had done anything illegal. The U.S.P.D. delegation found itself in the
unusual position of being strongly defended by spokesmen of the S.P.D. and
the Progressives.[28] The other parties contributed to the government's
embarrassment by demanding the initiation of legal proceedings against the
three if they had indeed been guilty of crimes against the state.

Under these circumstances, Haase had little difficulty during his second
speech of the day in turning the whole affair into a sharp indictment of the
government. He pointed out that Capelle had been able to present no proof of
illegal activity on the part of himself or his colleagues and that if, indeed, such
proof existed, the government would long ago have instituted charges against
them. He furthermore accused the government of committing a terrible
injustice in not calling him and his colleagues as witnesses in the case. The
condemned man might well have been saved if they had been allowed to tell
the truth about the case. He concluded by declaring, amidst the stormy
applause of his colleagues, that it was obvious that the issue had been raised in
the Reichstag only in order to distract its members from the government's
efforts to propagandize the army in a sense directly contrary to that expressed
by the Reichstag majority in its peace resolution.[29]

The Independents thus emerged from the crisis essentially unscathed.
They had turned the accusations made against them into a disastrous defeat for
the government and had succeeded to some degree in exposing the extent of
the government's discrimination against their party.[30] Indeed, the government's embarrassment was so extreme that the increasingly unpopular
Michaelis was forced to resign late in October and was replaced by the aging
Center Party leader and Prime Minister of Bavaria Count Georg von Hertling.
Nevertheless, the experience could not but serve as a dramatic reminder of
the dangers involved in engaging in or even in encouraging revolutionary
activity and undoubtedly served to reinforce Haase's cautious attitude in this
regard.

This is, again, not to suggest that Haase opposed radical direct action in
principle. Indeed, he assumed an increasingly active role in the strikes that
shook Germany during 1917 and 1918. When the first massive work stoppages

of the war occurred in April 1917, Haase, along with other Independent leaders, addressed mass gatherings of the strikers, trying to put political content into a movement which had flared up largely as a result of food shortages.[31] On the third day of strike he and two of his Independent colleagues were appointed by the strikers to negotiate with the government, albeit with little success.[32]

It may well be that Haase joined this movement with some trepidation. His very cautious letters of this period give no clear indication of his response to it. Moreover, Wilhelm Groener, at the time head of the war office and primarily responsible for controlling such disturbances, claims that he sought out Haase late in April and after informing him that any new strikes would be put down by force of arms, secured from him a promise that he would use his influence to dissuade his followers from unleashing a new wave of work stoppages on May 1.[33] Although it is impossible to ascertain just how much of a commitment Haase made to Groener, he may well have expressed his intention to try to discourage his comrades from pursuing tactics which, for the time being at least, would inevitably lead to increased suffering without any reasonable prospect of success.[34]

Whereas the April movement had burst forth spontaneously largely as a result of antagonism aroused by difficulties in food procurement,[35] the strikes of January 1918 were organized by the Independent Socialist leadership for specifically political ends. At a meeting of the U.S.P.D. executive committee and advisory council shortly after the first of the year, some of the militants suggested that a strike be organized in connection with the negotiations currently going on at Brest Litovsk. The party leaders were at first uncertain as to whether sufficient numbers of workers would support such an action, but a rapid survey indicated that sentiment for a strike was already strong. At a second meeting, therefore, they decided to publish a strike call signed by the entire Reichstag delegation.[36] When the delegation convened two days later, however, the majority decided against issuing such an appeal, arguing that in all probability it would lead to the effective decapitation of the movement. They revised the proposed manifesto in such a way as to eliminate any specific reference to a strike and directed that the necessary agitation be conducted by word of mouth and unsigned leaflets.[37]

The movement gained further impetus as news filtered through of the highly successful Austrian work stoppages of mid-January. The strikes broke out in Berlin on January 28 with surprising intensity. Several hundred thousand workers left the factories in Berlin alone, and the movement rapidly spread to other industrial centers.[38] Following the Russian precedent, a "workers' council" was quickly elected which agreed on a series of political demands obviously patterned after the U.S.P.D. program.[39] The council also elected an action committee made up of eleven workers, all of whom were Independents and most of whom were associated with Haase's wing of the party. The council, however, rejected the plan of the Independent leaders for a limited three-day demonstration strike, giving instead the power to decide when and how the movement should be terminated to the action committee. As in April, the strikers voted to invite three Independent deputies, Haase, Ledebour and Dittmann to join the action committee. A motion to request similar representation from the S.P.D. was at first narrowly defeated, but when a delegation of workers from S.P.D. headquarters appeared with a message to the effect that the majority leaders had decided to participate if invited, this motion was reconsidered and passed.[40] The tradition of proletarian solidarity had proved once again its durability among the German workers.

It is clear, however, that the Independent and majority socialist representatives entered the strike leadership for very different reasons. The S.P.D. executive committee decided to participate only reluctantly and with the explicit intention of limiting the strike as effectively as possible.[41] The Independent leaders, on the other hand, had from the beginning played an important, if cautious role in organizing the strike, and although they too may have been at least partly motivated by a desire to prevent its falling into the hands of the extremists,[42] they obviously were eager to have the strike achieve the greatest possible impact. They also insisted successfully on the maintenance of the political demands originally accepted by the workers' council.[43]

The government's reaction to the strike was immediate and determined. The right of assembly was abrogated, thus neutralizing the potentially dangerous workers' council. Even the action committee was explicitly forbidden to meet. As in April, members of the action committee made repeated efforts to obtain permission for representatives of the striking workers to gather, but their pleas were again rejected. It was not until February 2 that Haase, Ledebour, Scheidemann and Otto Braun were even able to arrange a meeting with the Chancellor, and on that occasion the government merely made a totally unacceptable offer to permit a meeting of strike representatives on the condition that it would be devoted entirely to bringing the strike to an immediate end.[44]

Contrary to the government's expectations, however, its repressive measures at first only served to aggravate the workers who streamed out of the factories in increasing numbers and with growing militancy. By January 31 the situation had become so threatening that a more severe state of siege was imposed, and courts martial were established.[45] Under these circumstances the majority socialist leaders had no opportunity to mediate and found themselves in the embarrassing position of officially supporting a movement with which they fundamentally disagreed and which they could not control.[46]

The ultimate result was that the S.P.D. suffered a significant loss of prestige at least among the more radical segments of the working class while the Independents reaped a substantial moral victory.[47] The increased popularity of the U.S.P.D. in these circles was reinforced by the persecution of one of its best known leaders, Dittmann, who was arrested while speaking to demonstrators on January 31 and quickly sentenced to five years imprisonment.[48]

Despite the enthusiasm and militancy of the strikers, the government was ultimately successful in disorganizing their leadership, and the movement gradually dissipated. In any case, it is apparent that the U.S.P.D. leaders who directed the strike were incapable of breaking out of their original conception of it as a limited demonstration. They were thus in no position to provide effective leadership once their immediate goal had been achieved.

To many, perhaps most, observers, therefore, the strike movement must have been judged a total failure. It had achieved none of its stated objectives. Far from acceding to the demands of the workers, the government had refused even to negotiate with their leaders. Moreover, it had used the opportunity provided by the strike to imprison or induct into the armed forces thousands of the most militant oppositionists.[49] It may come as some surprise, therefore, that Haase considered it "the greatest event in the history of the German working class." Writing to a friend early in February, he declared that he had just experienced "the most difficult and most exciting time of my life." The significance of the strike, he continued, was not diminished by the fact that it had ended without any concrete achievement. Such idealism and willingness to sacrifice had not been seen for a long time. A mass movement had never had to overcome such obstacles in Germany before, and yet they had been overcome. He went on to describe in indignant terms the extreme character of the government's repressive measures and his own efforts to ameliorate them whenever possible.[50] For Haase, therefore, the January strikes represented a great moral victory and a massive demonstration of support for the point of view he had so long espoused.

The question as to whether he at any point considered the possibility that the movement might be used as a possible springboard for actual revolution cannot be answered with certainty. His apparent early caution concerning the strikes, his deeply felt sympathy with the victims of even this limited action, and his consistently realistic and perhaps overly prudent attitude concerning projects such as the Stockholm manifesto suggest that he did not.

His remarks in the Reichstag concerning the strikes do not shed much light on this matter. In a major address delivered on February 27, he strongly expressed the complete solidarity of his party with the strikers. He decried the repressive measures of the government, but predicted that the workers would immediately seek out new leaders to replace those who had been taken

from them. He emphasized the political character of the strikes and criticized
the half-hearted support offered by the S.P.D. and the unions. The closest he
came to attributing explicitly revolutionary implications to the movement,
however, was when he declared that the entire Independent delegation
endorsed the view expressed earlier by Ledebour that an international mass
strike would be the most effective means to end the war.[51]

Although Haase could not express himself freely in either the Reichstag or
his private correspondence at the time, the evidence thus suggests that he had
not yet come to the point where revolution appeared to him to represent a
realistic immediate objective. He continued to use it in the traditional Social
Democratic fashion as a specter with which to threaten the supporters of the
government, but his fundamental caution and detestation of violence prevented
him from coming to grips with the practical problems which the preparation of
a revolution would of necessity entail.

The January strike movement was intimately related to the Bolshevik
Revolution and the ensuing peace negotiations at Brest Litovsk. The reaction
of the two Social Democratic parties to these events reveals once again the
depth of the chasm which continued to separate them despite their temporary
and extremely superficial alliance at the time of the strikes.

Although the Independents apparently were never in doubt concerning
their opposition to the Treaty of Brest Litovsk, the task of explaining this
rejection of the first peace treaty of the war was by no means an easy one. The
efforts of the U.S.P.D. Reichstag deputies to interpret this apparently para-
doxical stand occupied much of their attention during the winter and early
spring of 1918.

Haase's speech of February 27 in which he dealt at length with the strike
movement also provided him with an opportunity to unleash one of the
strongest Independent attacks upon the negotiations going on with the
Russians. Haase, who had never been optimistic about the value of a limited
peace, declared that the recent German ultimatum had revealed the full
extent of the German objectives in the East.[52] The ultimatum, he predicted,
would "go down in history as a document of exorbitant power politics and
annexationism." No one, he added, could now honestly maintain that the
government sought a peace of understanding.[53]

At the time of the final vote on the treaty in March, Haase repeated his
ringing denunciation of German policy, but in more specific terms and with
greater attention to its political consequences. Unlike the S.P.D. which
greeted the peace with "mixed feelings,"[54] he declared, the U.S.P.D. reacted
"with just one feeling, the feeling of shame." Focusing his attack upon his
former colleagues as well as upon the government, Haase condemned the
decision of the S.P.D. to abstain on the decisive vote. The majority socialists

had explicitly recognized that the treaty could not be reconciled with the Reichstag peace resolution, yet they refused to draw the necessary conclusions, preferring to maintain their rapprochement with the bourgeois parties and thus remaining firmly entangled in the train of the government. The end result of the treaty, he insisted, would not be, as had been claimed, an early end to the war. Henceforth Germany's word would be believed nowhere in the world. The war would thus be lengthened rather than shortened. Turning finally to the implications of the treaty for the fate of the Russian Revolution which had come to mean so much to him and his colleagues, he declared that the counter-revolutionary intent of German policy was fully apparent. The revolutionary movement could not, however, be halted whatever the German government might do. He concluded with a warning that they were simply sowing the wind, and, he declared prophetically, "Whoever sows the wind will reap the storm."[55]

For Haase, therefore, the Peace of Brest Litovsk both confirmed once again the legitimacy of the policy he and his friends had long been pursuing and served as another indication of the fundamental bankruptcy of that followed by the majority socialists. The Bolshevik revolution which brought the issue of a separate peace to a head, however, also created a number of very real problems for his party.

The simple fact of its success insured that the impact of the second Russian upheaval upon opposition socialists throughout the world would be immense. The implications of this success for the western parties, however, were so variously interpreted that its ultimate effect was of necessity divisive as well as enormously stimulating and encouraging. In Germany, where the opposition was already severely rent on a number of issues, this divisiveness was to prove especially ominous. The Spartacists were, at least at first, unreserved in their enthusiasm for the Russian achievement. Among the non-Spartacist majority of the U.S.P.D, however, the reaction was by no means unanimous. There were, it is true, relatively few important figures who from the beginning took an essentially negative attitude toward the October Revolution. Nevertheless, those who did found a highly articulate and influential spokesman in Kautsky, who considered it his most important task to oppose what he felt to be the pernicious influence of the Bolsheviks.[56] As the nature of the new Russian regime became more apparent, the number of those who shared at least some of Kautsky's reservations concerning its essentially non-Marxist and undemocratic character grew rapidly.[57]

As on so many other occasions, Haase took a view essentially midway between the extremes within his party. He repeatedly stressed the difficulty of properly evaluating the situation in Russia. At first he hoped that the Bolshevik coup would lead to a coalition of all the socialist parties and the early convening of a constituent assembly which would make possible the effective consolidation of the revolutionary regime. Although the conclusion of a separate peace could not be satisfactory from his point of view, he recognized that in order to maintain their position, the Bolsheviks would have to avoid disappointing the masses on this issue. He feared, however, that a break with the Entente would be extremely dangerous, given the fact that, as he believed, the Russian economy and social structure completely lacked the necessary prerequisites for an immediate conversion to socialism.[58]

Even later, however, after it had become apparent that the Bolsheviks were determined to maintain their power, and many of the characteristics discerned by Kautsky had begun to manifest themselves more clearly, Haase remained fundamentally sympathetic. Writing to his son in May, he enthusiastically praised Lenin's most recent speech before the Moscow soviet, parts of which he hoped to publish in the *Sozialistische Auslandspolitik.* The speech, he commented, indicated that Lenin confronted his immense task without a trace of utopianism. The Soviet leader apparently recognized the necessity of compromise and was fully aware of the tremendous educational work yet to be accomplished. "In Lenin," he wrote, "there exists a gigantic will, and whatever happens, his efforts will be of world-historical significance." Furthermore, this pessimistic experience made it clearer than ever that socialism could be immediately achieved in England and Germany despite the many difficulties which, admittedly, would have to be overcome. He added, however, that the existence of such favorable economic preconditions could not be expected to operate automatically.[59]

Undoubtedly, Haase did share at least some of Kautsky's reservations concerning both the undemocratic methods of the new Russian regime and its apparent contradiction of traditional Marxist theory. It is significant that, in a letter to Kautsky which was written in August, he made no attempt to defend the Bolsheviks *per se.* He did, however, vigorously oppose the plans of his friend to launch a new polemic against the Russian leaders.[60] Such attacks, he insisted, constituted a "grave error" at a time when the Bolsheviks were beset by aggressors from every side. Moreover, in Germany they would undoubtedly unleash a bitter struggle within the opposition just when unity was of the greatest importance. Any polemic should therefore be postponed until some later and more appropriate occasion.[61]

By the summer of 1918, therefore, Haase found himself once more playing the traditional role of the centrist. Although united in common opposition to the war, the U.S.P.D. proved to be almost as divided on questions of both theory and tactics as the old party had been. Haase, to whom the preservation of unity had again become the central issue, had been forced to take up once again the mantle of the mediator, striving to maintain the tenuous ties which held his party together. Moreover, his position on the most important divisive issues consistently tended toward the centrist's rejection of extremes of right or left. In matters of theory he was clearly in Kautsky's camp, looking back to the Erfurt Program rather than forward toward the formulation of a new revolutionary program based largely on the Russian experience as the Spartacists urged. Yet he was at the same time sympathetic enough to the Russian experiment and to the revolutionary idealism of the Spartacists to refuse to follow Kautsky in rejecting them out of hand. On questions of day-to-day tactics, he sympathized with the left-wing's strident calls for action, and indeed, participated with some enthusiasm in strikes and demonstrations when they did erupt. Yet his natural prudence and caution and his reluctance to attempt anything which might add to the mounting toll of human suffering caused him most often to act the part of the follower rather than the leader on such occasions and thus created the impression that he had aligned himself with the right wing with its emphasis upon parliamentary rather than direct action.

For the moment, Haase could effectively gather the various opposition elements about him in a loose alliance. His position, however, continued to suffer from the fundamental weaknesses of centrism at a time of crisis and rapid change. In 1914 the coming of world war had dramatically revealed the full extent of these weaknesses. In November 1918 it would be the cessation of hostilities and the eruption of revolution which would perform a similar function.

CHAPTER XI

THE COMING OF THE REVOLUTION

As the summer of 1918 progressed, it became more and more apparent that the final German offensive which had aroused such enthusiasm in the spring had utterly failed in achieving its objective. To the alert observer, the implications of this failure were clear. Henceforth, the German armies would be pressed increasingly onto the defensive, and as the fresh American troops now in France were thrown into the struggle, the German position would continue to deteriorate. Yet the German high command refused to prepare the public for the disappointment and disillusionment which would inevitably come when the truth became known. It was symptomatic of this attitude that when, late in June, the Foreign Secretary, Richard von Kühlmann, declared in the Reichstag that peace could only be achieved through negotiations, the high command reacted with indignation and forced his resignation.[1] The public, however, could not be prevented from at least sensing the gravity of the situation. Their growing war weariness and pessimism found expression as the summer progressed in increasing restiveness among the workers and a dangerous demoralization in certain elements of the armed forces.[2]

By early September Haase had concluded that the time for decisive action was rapidly approaching. Yet in a letter to his son on September 9, he counselled continued caution. "Just because the deep yearning for peace makes it certain that any action will receive widespread support," he wrote, "it is all important that only such actions be undertaken which promise success, for the resulting disappointment will otherwise bring a severe setback."[3] The uneasiness of the government was reflected in its treatment of opposition spokesmen. Late in September, Haase reported to a friend that a secret prohibition had obviously been issued against his speaking in public. He described a recent meeting which was brutally broken up by the police just as he was given the floor. In the chaos which ensued, he and his wife had fallen beneath the chairs and had only been rescued from possible injury by the alertness and discipline of a group of workers who had contrived to shield them from the saber-swinging gendarmes. He predicted that the persecution would increase as the rulers began to feel more clearly "the knife at their throats." He added, however, that he remained "inwardly calm."[4] A few days later he wrote again, describing in vivid terms the atmosphere of tension which had developed. "The ruling system," he declared, "is creaking in all its joints."[5]

Finally sensing the magnitude of the danger confronting the Reich, the German rulers began in September to move toward thorough-going political reforms which, it was hoped, would both restore confidence in the regime and placate the Entente. Preliminary negotiations among the parties that had passed the peace resolution of the previous summer were initiated in mid-September.[6] The Social Democratic Reichstag delegation and party council agreed on September 23 that if certain conditions were met, the party would participate in a new government under someone other than Hertling.[7]

The decisive blow to the old regime, however, was delivered by the military leaders themselves, for on September 28 Hindenburg and Ludendorff concluded that Germany required an immediate armistice. They immediately requested that Hertling join them at Spa on the following day and urged him to invite influential members of the Reichstag majority to enter his government. Recognizing that he was in no position to initiate a parliamentarization of the regime, Hertling submitted his resignation. His recommendation that the relatively liberal Prince Max of Baden be chosen as his successor was followed.

Max summoned Ebert early on October 2 and informed him that he would form no government which did not include representatives of the S.P.D. Ebert emphasized the sacrifice which his party would be making by supporting him, but left him with the clear impression that it would nevertheless do so.[8] Shortly thereafter, the leaders of all of the parties represented in the Reichstag met to hear a report on the military situation from a representative of the high command. The party leaders had, of course, been well aware of the fact that Germany's position had deteriorated, but most of them were severely shocked at what they now were told. Even Haase was surprised by the degree of pessimism reflected in the report of the high command.[9]

Later that day, the Social Democratic delegation met to consider whether it was prepared to join the new government. With Max's invitation, the reformist wing had apparently achieved its primary goal, yet it had done so under the most unfavorable circumstances imaginable, and it was not without difficulty that Ebert was able to persuade the majority of his colleagues to agree to accept the offer. The union leader and later Chancellor of the Weimar Republic Gustav Bauer was chosen along with Scheidemann to represent the party in Max's government despite Scheidemann's personal opposition to the party's participation.[10] Assured of Social Democratic support, Max agreed on October 3 to form what by the end of the month was to become Germany's first truly parliamentary government.[11]

The first and perhaps most fundamental stage of the German Revolution had thus been consummated at the behest of the hitherto most effective opponents of democracy, with only the extremely reluctant participation of its traditional exponents and under conditions which insured that the new government's first tasks would be so onerous as to try the strength and endurance of even the most stable of regimes. Under these circumstances, it was obviously a matter of the greatest importance that the democratic forces should be united. Unfortunately, just as the new regime was initiated, the last feeble efforts to achieve a reconciliation between the two Social Democratic parties failed.[12] The next attempt would be made under the still more trying circumstances of violent revolution and military and economic collapse.

The depth of the differences which still separated the two parties was clearly revealed in a manifesto published by the Independent leadership on October 5, the day on which Max presented his government to the Reichstag. The manifesto, which Haase obviously helped to draft,[13] declared triumphantly that militarism had received a blow from which it would not recover, that German imperialism had collapsed and that "the idea of democracy and socialism is victoriously on the march." It proudly went on to describe the party's consistent opposition both to the war and to every effort to oppress another people. Much of the manifesto was devoted to severe criticism of the S.P.D., whose policy had, it claimed, collapsed as completely as that of the ruling classes. It condemned the S.P.D. for making no effort to use the present crisis to replace capitalism with socialism as so many resolutions of the International had urged. The conditions laid down by the S.P.D. for participation in the new government were so modest that they had even been criticized by a number of bourgeois liberal newspapers. Nothing had been said about a political amnesty, no demand had been made for the elimination of the state of siege, no effort had been made to insure that the existing peace treaties would be immediately altered, and social and economic reforms had been completely ignored. There followed a long list of measures of this sort which "even a progressive bourgeois government" should immediately enact. The manifesto went on to declare that "as international socialists" the Independents demanded much more. Their goal was a socialist republic. The document concluded with the assertion that the international proletariat would be called upon to play a leading role in the revolutionary era which was just beginning. The methods of the "government socialists," however, would only cripple the independent activity of the working class. Unity was therefore required, but unity only "under the unblemished banner" of the U.S.P.D.[14]

The manifesto of October 5 reflected the confidence of the Independent leaders that their time had come. Any possibility of cooperating with the S.P.D. appeared to be ruled out. The old party had shown its true colors by entering a bourgeois government just at the time when capitalism seemed on the verge of complete and utter collpase. This move constituted another breach of a revered socialist principle which had been hammered out before the war. Even Kautsky declared in an article published on October 10 that only the U.S.P.D. could now take up the task of defending the interests of the proletariat and the International.[15]

That Haase completely agreed with this insistence upon continued staunch opposition both to the new government and to the Social Democrats who had joined it, is apparent both from his letters and from his very important Reichstag speech of October 23. In his correspondence he never even mentioned the possibility of achieving a rapprochement with his former colleagues now that both representative government and peace seemed about to be achieved. Rather, he castigated the government for its indecisiveness, characterized the impression it made as "miserable," and predicted that it would not last long. Characteristic of his attitude was his remark in a letter of October 1, written as the government was in the process of formation, that he and his friends "could wish for nothing better than a coalition government in order to clarify the situation."[16]

His speech in the Reichstag on October 23 was among the most dramatic of his career. Standing before an assembly which had often received with derision his pessimistic predictions concerning the consequences of German policy, he must have felt a certain grim satisfaction now that he had in so many ways been proven correct.[17] Exuding, therefore, the confidence of one whom history has vindicated, he described in poignant terms the world revolution which was unfolding. German imperialism, he declared, had completely lost its "bloody game." The Independents, however, would not be satisfied with a peace which merely set limits to German capitalism while opening up new opportunities for exploitation by the members of the Entente. They were and would remain opponents of every form of capitalism.

Turning to an issue which had become central since the initiation of negotiations with President Wilson, he pointed to the many crowns which had fallen throughout Europe and asked dramatically whether Germany should retain a monarch while everywhere around her republics had been established. The proposed constitutional changes were completely insufficient. A republic must come, he declared, but a capitalist republic was by no means the ideal of the U.S.P.D. The German nation would not be destroyed, but rescue from the present misery could not be achieved within the context of the existing social system. Just as militarism had collapsed, capitalism too would soon die. The dawn of a new era could already be seen. The speed with which the revolution came would depend upon the audacity and decisiveness of the German workers as well as upon the workers of other countries. He and his friends, he concluded, trusted the workers. "We are convinced that out of all this misery there will finally emerge the complete emancipation of humanity."[18]

These were brave words. They reflected both Haase's continuing bound-less confidence in the workers and his prophetic vision of a new, rational and ethical world order which owed at least as much to his interest in Kant as it did to his commitment to Marx. According to Dittmann, Haase's speech had the effect of "a call for action" throughout the Reich.[19] But exactly how these resounding phrases were to be transformed into actual deeds was, as usual, something about which the Independents were anything but clear. To be sure, the party executive committee, meeting on October 11 with representa-tives from the provinces, committed itself to call a nationwide strike at the appropriate moment.[20] But that moment had quite obviously not yet arrived, and for the time being, Haase appears to have been content to pursue a policy of watchful waiting combined with vigorous criticism of the government and the majority socialists.

The left wing of the party, however, was by no means satisfied with such an approach. On October 7 a conference of Spartacist and other left wing elements took place which boded ill for the continued cooperation of the Spartacists with Haase and his friends. To be sure, the resolutions passed by the participants included only oblique attacks upon the Independents, but their tone was considerably more radical than that of the U.S.P.D. manifesto of October 5. Toward the end of the meeting the participants took practical steps toward organizing an uprising by resolving to form workers' and soldiers' councils "where they do not already exist" and by outlining various measures to be undertaken in order to intensify their agitation in the armed forces.[21] It was obvious that the moment was fast approaching when the Spartacists would break loose from the largely opportunistic ties which bound them to the U.S.P.D., thus splitting the proletarian forces into three rather than just two major groups.

The Spartacists were, however, not the only group which was preparing for revolutionary action. An organization known as the "Revolutionary Shop Stewards" had been formed more than a year before with that specific end in mind.[22] The group, not very large but extremely well positioned for effective action, had played an important role in the January strikes and had maintained a close working relationship with certain of the Independent leaders.[23] Some-time in October the Shop Stewards determined that the time had come to establish a more direct relationship with the U.S.P.D., and the entire party leadership was subsequently invited to attend their meetings. After Lieb-knecht's release from prison on October 21, the Spartacists also gained entry into these gatherings.[24]

Despite their similar emphasis upon the necessity of initiating revolution-ary action, the Spartacists were divided from the Shop Stewards by deep-seated differences. The most fundamental of these undoubtedly derived from the fact that the Shop Stewards were in constant contact with the workers in the factories and thus tended to be far more pragmatic than the Spartacists, whose eyes were directed toward the distant and romanticized Russian experience. The Shop Stewards unanimously rejected Liebknecht's program of constant revolutionary actions designed to build the *élan* of the workers until the final struggle should begin. They insisted rather on carefully preparing their forces for a single successful thrust, and it was this policy which received the support of the moderate leaders around Haase.[25]

As tension mounted within the Reich during the last days of October the Shop Stewards and their associatates moved from such general questions to the practical problem of deciding exactly when and how the revolution should be initiated in Berlin. The decisive meeting took place on the evening of November 2. That morning Ledebour met with a number of his friends. This smaller group agreed that the uprising should begin on November 4.[26] The final decision, however, could not be made until the evening meeting at which both the Independent Reichstag delegation and the Shop Stewards would be fully represented.

As the conspirators gathered, they had no idea that the government would collapse without a struggle. They had no knowledge of the rapidly developing events in Kiel and could only assume that the rest of the Reich would lag behind Berlin in revolutionary enthusiasm. Emil Barth had, to be sure, acquired a supply of light weapons, but they would be useless if the military remained loyal to the government. It was, therefore, in an atmosphere of great earnestness that this rather disparate group debated the fate of Germany. The Spartacists were, as usual, extremely impatient. A number of them supported Ledebour's proposal that November 4 be chosen. This suggestion, however, met strong opposition from Haase and most of the Independent deputies,[27] and the final decision was left to the actual workers' representatives present. By a narrow margin, they fatefully voted to postpone the revolution until November 11.[28]

According to Richard Müller, they were influenced in this decision not only by their fear that the necessary mass support could not be mobilized by the earlier date, but also the fact that Haase and most of the other leaders had no idea what should happen after the government had fallen. Repeated attempts to obtain a clear answer to this terribly important question never got beyond meaningless generalities and admonitions to deal with the problem when it actually arose. It appeared to Müller that they were frightened by the immensity and difficulty of the task and thus sought to avoid facing it as long as possible.[29] Müller's description may well be essentially correct; at least as far as Haase is concerned. He had long argued as a good orthodox Marxist that revolutions could not be made; but rather had to be brought to fruition by the forces of history. Haase was undoubtedly convinced at this point that the moment for such action was imminent, but for such a man the burden of having to decide exactly when it had arrived must have been heavy indeed. Above all, he had to assess the potential response of the masses of workers and soldiers who still were loyal to the S.P.D. Their participation appeared to be a prerequisite for a successful uprising, particularly beyond the confines of the capital. Yet it was all but impossible to discover with any degree of certainty how they would react to a unilateral revolutionary initiative by the Independents. Moreover, although Haase had long talked of revolution and certainly accepted it on a theoretical level, he had, in practice, spent his life attempting to achieve his goals through peaceful agitation and parliamentary action. The abrupt transition to discussions of weapons procurement and military tactics cannot have been an easy one. Finally, although Haase had often uttered fine-sounding phrases about the character of the new society which would be ushered in by the triumph of socialism, he had never before been placed in a position in which he had to spell out in detail how a revolutionary government should function.

The Spartacists had at least the Russian experience to turn to, but even they were apparently unable to go beyond vague references to workers' and soldiers' councils.[30] It must have been, therefore, with very mixed feelings that Haase returned home in the early morning hours of November 3 knowing that within the next few days, if all went well, he would no longer be able to enjoy the luxury of simple opposition to the status quo, but would have the responsibility thrust upon him to take the lead in creating the new society to which he had so often, but so vaguely, referred.[31]

In fact, of course, the German Revolution was not made, but rather broke out spontaneously in conformity with good orthodox principles. The careful plans of Haase and his fellow revolutionaries were thrust aside by events and in fact were of little consequence except insofar as they shed light on the Independents' attitude toward this fundamental issue. On November 3 the uprising in Kiel reached revolutionary proportions. The spark for a general uprising had thus been applied far from Berlin and without the slightest fore-knowledge of the Independent leaders. On November 4, Gustav Noske, Haase's old Königsberg associate, was sent to Kiel to represent the S.P.D. The leaders of the uprising, some of whom distrusted Noske, also phoned Haase and urgently requested that one or more Independent leaders also be sent. They urged Haase himself to come if at all possible.[32] Apparently, Haase's friend, Oscar Cohn, was at first assigned this task, but when he failed to appear at the Berlin railroad station at the appointed time early on November 6, Haase decided to undertake the trip himself.[33]

This was a fateful decsion on Haase's part, for it removed him from Berlin at the decisive moment when his advice and leadership might have been most useful. He was well aware of the potential difficulties that his departure at such a time might entail, but he was also convinced that the developments in Kiel were of the utmost political significance.[34] The predicament in which he found himself reflected to some extent the paucity of reliable and capable first rank leaders that was to continue to trouble the U.S.P.D. In any case, he apparently assumed that the revolution would occur more or less according to its prescribed schedule and therefore expected to be back in the capital before anything of importance occurred there.[35]

Haase's journey was also of considerable importance because of the deep impressions made upon him by his experiences *en route* and in Kiel. By the time he finally decided to leave Berlin, he was unable to board a train which travelled directly to Kiel. He therefore determined to travel to Hamburg by rail and then complete his trip by automobile. Arriving in Hamburg, he experienced his first taste of revolution. The movement had already reached that city, which he found to be securely in the hands of the revolutionaries. When Haase was recognized, he was of course much in demand, and he interrupted his journey for a time to consult with the revolutionary leaders. He was astonished by the ease with which the seizure of power had been accomplished and especially by the fact that the officials capitulated to the workers' and soldiers' council as if the success of the revolution had been a foregone conclusion.[36]

Arriving in Kiel on November 7, he immediately met with Noske, who described in detail what had occurred there. According to Hermann Müller, who spoke at length with Haase soon thereafter, the latter was now convinced of the necessity of establishing a cooperative relationship between the two socialist parties in order to carry the revolution to a successful conclusion. The masses of the workers and soldiers were demanding such an alliance and indeed were following this course on the local level wherever they had taken control.[37] By this time Haase had also become painfully aware of his error in deciding to leave Berlin when he did. The revolutionary movement had accelerated so rapidly that he now feared that it would would reach Berlin before he could return.[38]

The return trip to the capital must therefore have been a very tense and frustrating experience for Haase, especially inasmuch as the distruption of transportation was so extensive that the journey required the better part of two days. As Müller and Haase gradually drew closer to their destination, they found signs of the revolution almost everywhere. Finally, during the afternoon of November 9 they discovered in Rathenow a local paper with news of the events in Berlin. Haase was astonished at what he read. The Chancellor had ordered the troops not to fire. The government's most reliable forces had gone over to the people. Neither Müller nor Haase had expected the revolution to take such a course. But, of course, they had no notion of what had happened since they had left. Recognized by partly members in Rathenow, they were urgently entreated to work for a unification of the Social Democratic forces in Berlin.[39]

Haase's absence had been sorely felt by the Independents. As he had feared, their plans had been completely disrupted by the rapidity with which the revolutionary movement swept toward the capital. Clearly sensing the danger, the government had on November 7 prohibited a number of U.S.P.D. meetings scheduled for that evening.[40] Also aware of the increasingly radical temper of the workers and afraid of forfeiting their position of leadership to the Independents, the majority socialist leaders had put increasing pressure on the government, issuing an ultimatum on the seventh which demanded *inter alia* the abdication of the Kaiser and Crown Prince by the following day at noon. Failure to concede this and other demands, the ultimatum declared, would lead to the resignation of the Social Democratic representatives from the government.[41] Although the majority leaders extended the term of the ultimatum and repeatedly urged their followers in Berlin to remain calm,[42] they were finally compelled to act by the procrastination of the Kaiser and the increasingly successful agitation of the Independents.[43]

When the Independent leader Däumig was arrested on November 8, his colleagues decided that they could wait no longer. A leaflet was drafted that same afternoon calling for a general strike on the following morning.[44] Among the signatures appended to the leaflet was that of Haase.[45] The majority socialists, however, continued to hesitate, hoping against hope that word of the Kaiser's abdication, which was expected momentarily, might still prevent a general uprising in the capital.[46] When no word had been received from Spa on the morning of the ninth and it was apparent that the workers would wait no longer, the majority leaders finally issued their own call for a general strike. Perhaps more important, they also decided to seek an immediate alliance with the Independents.[47]

This astute political maneuver, combined with the unexpectedly peaceful character of the revolution, caught the Independents completely off guard. They had conceived of their movement as being directed against both the government and the majority socialists. Now they were suddenly confronted with the choice of either uniting with their former enemies or being decried as the primary obstacle to the reestablishment of working-class solidarity.[48] Shortly after noon the proposal was put into concrete terms after Max had bestowed his own powers as Imperial Chancellor upon Ebert.[49] Meeting with several of the Independent leaders, Ebert suggested that the U.S.P.D. join his party in establishing a revolutionary government. He proposed that the new regime should be based on the principle of complete parity between the two socialist parties. Furthermore, no limitations would be placed upon the choice of personnel. Even Liebknecht would be acceptable to the majority socialists.[50]

It was at this point that the lack of unity within the U.S.P.D. began to make itself felt with devastating effect. Ledebour rejected out of hand any possibility of cooperating with the "government socialists." Other left Independents were at first willing to consider Ebert's proposal if certain stringent conditions were imposed, but most of them soon moved toward Ledebour's strict abstentionist policy. Most of the moderates, on the other hand, felt that a coalition should be very seriously considered, especially in view of the evident popular demand for socialist unity.[51] They were aware that the S.P.D.'s rather tardy, but effective support of the revolutionary movement had enabled the old party to maintain its influence over the masses. By the afternoon of November 9, it was apparent to them that the U.S.P.D. was in no position to take over the government on its own, and they were willing to make concessions in order to prevent the eruption of a new struggle on the left which might place the entire revolution in jeopardy.[52] Undoubtedly, too, the generosity of Ebert's terms rekindled in many of them their old yearning for unity and discipline despite their continuing distrust of many of the majority leaders.

When Haase arrived shortly after 9:00 P.M., he was quickly informed of what had occurred since he had left and then eagerly asked for his opinion as to what the party should do. Obviously impressed by his experiences of the past few days, he answered that, although he had serious reservations about the wisdom of entering a coalition government with the S.P.D., the party was obligated to follow the clearly expressed will of the masses which was for the reestablishment of proletarian solidarity.[54] With that, the final decision for participation was made,[55] and the party leaders were able to turn their full attention to the conditions under which the U.S.P.D. would be willing to enter the government.

Prior to Haase's arrival, a tentative list of demands had been drawn up and communicated to the majority socialists. Bearing the clear imprint of Liebknecht's hand, they included the placing of all power in the hands of the workers' and soldiers' councils, the exclusion of non-socialists from the new government, and an explicit declaration of intent to constitute a "social republic." The commitment of the Independents was to be limited to the three days it was thought would be necessary to conclude an armistice.[56] The S.P.D. sent a formal reply to this first list of conditions that same evening. Significant modifications were demanded of the most important points, and not until the following morning was a compromise worked out under Haase's leadership which was immediately accepted by the majority socialists.[57]

In the agreement which was thereby established, the Independents abandoned the three-day limitation on their commitment. They further agreed to permit non-socialist specialists to participate in the government, but only as technical advisors to the Cabinet which was to be made up of three representatives of each socialist party. Each of the specialists was to be controlled and assisted by two socialists, one appointed from each party. The Independents continued to insist that political power should rest fundamentally in the hands of the workers' and soldiers' councils, but added a proviso that a meeting of representatives of the councils throughout the Reich should be convened as soon as possible. The convening of a constituent assembly, one of the principal concerns of the S.P.D., was declared to be a question which would be dealt with after the revolution had been consolidated.[58]

During the same meeting at which this agreement was drawn up, word was received that Liebknecht had decided against participating in such a government. Dittmann was therefore chosen to replace him.[59] The other two Independent Cabinet members, selected the previous evening, were to be Emil Barth and Haase. The majority socialists for their part appointed Ebert, Scheidemann and Otto Landsberg as their representatives in the new Cabinet. The group met briefly that afternoon and elected Haase and Ebert co-chairmen.[60]

Before the new Cabinet could begin to function effectively, however, it had to obtain the formal sanction of the workers' and soldiers' councils, or at least of some group which could reasonably claim to represent these as yet highly irregular and amorphous bodies. Elections to a Berlin workers' and soldiers' council had been held on the morning of the tenth in factories and military compounds through the metropolitan area. The delegates thus elected had been instructed to meet late that afternoon in a large hall, the Zirkus Busch. Under the circumstances, this was the only body available which could give the new government at least the semblance of a serious claim to legitimacy. The elections and the Zirkus Busch meeting had been organized at the behest of an unruly group of several hundred workers and soldiers who had gathered in the Reichstag late on the ninth and had acted on a proposal formulated by Richard Müller and some of his radical friends undoubtedly with the intention of frustrating the rapidly developing movement toward a coalition government.[61] Indeed, a Spartacist leaflet of November 10 went so far as to urge the workers and soldiers to support no one who would agree to cooperate with the detested majority socialists, thus in effect ruling out even the large majority of Independents.[62]

Events, however, were to prove how completely the Spartacists and their left-Independent allies had misjudged the situation. This was especially true of the Spartacists, who, blinded by their veneration for the Bolsheviks, failed to realize that the German workers and soldiers might honestly choose to follow a path different from that charted by their Russian counterparts. And the majority socialists made doubly sure that the radical maneuver would prove ineffective. Perceiving the danger, they instructed Otto Wels, a Reichstag deputy and experienced party functionary, to organize a campaign for socialist unity particularly among the politically inexperienced soldiers.[63] The course of the Zirkus Busch meeting indicated dramatically that the old party leaders had lost little of their organizing ability despite their recent embarrassments.

Even before the three thousand excited delegates gathered, Müller and his shop Stewards realized that the overwhelming majority would favor a coalition. They had experienced little success in their efforts to convince the workers of the majority socialists' fundamental dishonesty. Conferring during the afternoon before the meeting, they therefore concluded that they would have to agree to the establishment of a coalition government. They were not, however, prepared simply to abandon their efforts to secure a dominant position for the radicals in the new regime. Rather than try to block the sanctioning of a coalition government, therefore, they decided to propose the establishment of an "action committee," based directly on the council, which would be empowered to exercise a continuing control over the Cabinet.[64]

Even this plan, however, was largely frustrated by the well-organized moderates at the Zirkus Busch. The meeting opened with speeches by Ebert, Haase and Liebknecht. Both Ebert and Haase emphasized the difficulty of the tasks to be faced by the revolutionary government and the necessity of maintaining proletarian unity. Liebknecht, on the other hand, launched an attack upon Ebert and his majority socialist associates. All of the speeches were received with stormy applause, but it was symptomatic of the mood of the delegates that Liebknecht's denunciations of the S.P.D. were greeted with cries of indignation and that the loudest cheers were evoked by Ebert's announcement that an agreement had been reached between the S.P.D. and the Independents.[65]

It was Barth who formally proposed the establishment of an action committee as projected by the Shop Stewards. The proposal itself aroused little opposition, but when he read off a suggested list of members, all of whom were either Spartacists or left Independents, the majority of the delegates reacted with violent indignation. Ebert declared that, although he considered such a committee to be superfluous, if it were created, it would have to have an equal number of majority socialists. The efforts of Müller and Liebknecht to persuade the assembly to accept Barth's slate were drowned out in the general tumult. The soldiers were particularly adamant, at one point declaring that if the radicals did not concede, they would establish a military dictatorship. The end result was that an action committee (later entitled the Executive Council [*Vollzugsrat*]) was established, but its membership was selected on the basis of equal representation of the S.P.D., U.S.P.D. and the supposedly non-partisan soldiers.[66]

Finally recovering from the confusion and tumult provoked by the attempted radical coup, the council voted to sanction the Cabinet as constituted by the Independent and majority socialist leaders. Characteristically, it was formally designated the "Council of Peoples' Representatives."[67] The meeting was then concluded with the adoption of a radically worded manifesto which Haase had helped draft.[68] It declared, among other things, that Germany had become a "socialist republic" and expressed the council's "admiration" for the achievements of the Russian workers and soldiers.[69] The majority socialists were clearly willing to offer this verbal concession to the radicals now that they had achieved their immediate goal of establishing a coalition government.

The members of the new Cabinet retired immediately after the Zirkus Busch meeting to discuss the immense tasks which they now faced. Their first official act was to authorize the German delegation to accept the armistice terms which had been offered by the Entente.[70] On the morning after they assumed power, therefore, the most immediate goal of the revolution, the cessation of hostilities, had been achieved.

What had apparently been one of the most effective regimes of modern times had thus collapsed without a struggle. Almost as remarkable was the fact that the new government was headed by the leaders of two parties which but a few days earlier had been at each others' throats. Superficially, of course, the new Cabinet appeared to represent a reconstitution of German Social democracy's pre-war leadership. Undoubtedly it was partly for this reason that it was greeted with such enthusiasm by the majority of the members of both factions. Now that the war issue had been resolved, it appeared that the old traditions of discipline and solidarity would reassert themselves. Unfortunately, the divisions between the two Social Democratic parties had deepened as the war progressed. This was nowhere more clearly illustrated than in their contrasting attitudes toward the revolution itself. Actually, as Arthur Rosenberg suggests, the majority socialists had in effect been compelled to make a revolution against themselves.[71] They had, after all, achieved the most important of their immediate goals weeks earlier by peaceful means. They had, therefore, joined the revolutionary movement only reluctantly and were from the beginning concerned above all to keep it on an orderly path.

Haase and most of his colleagues, on the other hand, were sincere and committed revolutionaries. While the majority socialists had been striving to prevent an uprising in the capital, they had taken concerted action to foment one. Ideologically, their weakness lay not in their lack of determination to bring about fundamental change, but rather in their adherence to democratic values which made them hesitate to make full use of their suddenly acquired power as long as they were not absolutely certain that they represented the majority of the population, in their commitment to libertarian principles which made them reluctant to restrict the civil rights of their opponents even though those opponents were quite clearly doing everything in their power to destroy the revolution, and in their humanitarian concern for human life which made them eager to avoid bloodshed if at all possible.

Moreover, the course of events on November 9 had utterly confused them. The revolution had come too easily. The majority socialists had successfully reversed themselves and joined in the leadership of the movement. The Independents, therefore, viewed the course the revolution had taken with considerable misgivings and joined the new government only reluctantly and over the opposition of an important part of their constituency. In so doing, they were not only giving up their familiar opposition role with all the advantages conferred by freedom from responsibility. They were also joining a coalition in which they would from the start be the weaker party. Not only did the S.P.D. possess a much more extensive organizational apparatus and press. It could also count on the support of the anti-socialist elements in the population, at least in its dealings with the Independents. And as a result of their strategic retreat before the advance of the revolutionaries, these elements remained essentially intact and potentially very powerful. Perhaps most important, the Independents suffered from such dissension within their own ranks that they would be severely hampered at every step in their relations with the much more unified majority socialists. It was the left wing of the U.S.P.D. which would now enjoy the advantages of opposition.

Haase was undoubtedly well aware of the many difficulties he would face in his new role. He had clearly expressed his reservations about joining a coalition government. Yet, convinced as he was that if the two great socialist parties failed to cooperate all hope of a successful revolution would be lost, he had chosen to heed the call of the overwhelming majority of the workers and soldiers for socialist solidarity rather than follow the much easier path of continued principled opposition. It must, however, have been much more with feelings of trepidation than of exaltation and optimism that he assumed his new position at the head of the Council of Peoples' Representatives.

CHAPTER XII

THE CRITIC IN POWER

The Cabinet which took over the government of Germany on November 10 appeared to represent a reconstitution of the old Social Democratic leadership, and it was to this fact that it owed much of the broad support it enjoyed among the workers and soldiers during the first weeks of its existence. Haase, Ebert, Scheidemann and even Dittmann deserve to be ranked among the foremost spokesmen of pre-war Social Democracy. Although a figure of somewhat lesser prominence, Otto Landsberg had, since his election to the Reichstag in 1912, established a firm reputation in party circles as a first-rate jurist and competent parliamentarian.[1] Emil Barth, to be sure, must be considered an exception. He had risen from obscurity to leadership among the Revolutionary Shop Stewards after the collapse of the January strikes, but was as yet little known in the movement at large. In spite of his status as an outsider, however, he soon established himself as an important link between the Cabinet and more radical elements both in the Berlin Executive Council, of which he was also a member, and in the population as a whole.[2]

Moreover, despite the deep political and personal differences that continued to divide the partners in the coalition, the Cabinet functioned with surprising efficiency. Political polemics and personal squabbles were kept to a minimum, and Cabinet debates were on the whole remarkably dispassionate.[3] The first acts of the new government reflected this apparently genuine desire on the part of its members to work effectively together. On November 11 a directive was published which instructed the former government's highest administrative officials to remain at their posts.[4]

On the following day, with only Barth dissenting, the Cabinet sent a telegram to the supreme command which directed that discipline be maintained in the armed forces. Although they ordered the military leaders to see that a relationship of mutual trust was established between officers and men, they left the power of command in the hands of the officers. The soldiers' councils were to serve in an "advisory" capacity.[5]

On November 12 the Cabinet also published a proclamation drafted by Haase which Dittmann later called "the Magna Charta of the revolution."[6] It began with a formal declaration that the political leadership of the new government was completely socialist and that the Cabinet had set as its immediate task the realization of the socialist program. The actual measures enacted, however, as well as the guidelines enunciated for the future policies of the government contained little that could not have been just as easily carried out by a progressive democratic regime. A series of laws was promulgated which in effect simply established the civil liberties one expects to find in a democratic state, many of which had already existed in pre-war Germany. In addition, the manifesto declared that the eight-hour day would become compulsory by the first of the year. The Cabinet futher promised that measures would be enacted to curb unemployment, to extend health insurance, to relieve the housing shortage, to insure adequate food supplies and to maintain production. The propertied classes were assured that they would be protected against seizures by private individuals or groups. The manifesto also declared that all future elections would be conducted on the basis of universal suffrage and according to a system of proportional representation. A final, but very important sentence added that the new electoral system would be utilized in the election of delegates to the constituent assembly.[7]

The program of November 12 did indeed, as Scheidemann declared, represent a massive step forward for German democracy. Many of the objectives for which the S.P.D. had so long and so ineffectually struggled were thereby achieved overnight.[8] Nevertheless, it could hardly be considered an appropriate program for a revolutionary socialist government. Although the omission is understandable given the chaotic condition of the economy, it is noteworthy that it contained not a word about the prospective socialization of the means of production. No reference was made to the establishment of a democratically organized defense force. Perhaps most important, it at least implied that a constituent assembly would be convened in the near future, and, as many moderates and even conservatives realized, a constituent assembly could be expected to act as an effective dam to any radical extension of the revolution.[9]

It was at this point that the fundamental disparity between the attitudes of the two factions within the Cabinet toward the revolution began to merge. While the majority socialists were convinced that with the enactment of the measures contained in the program of November 12 the revolution had been essentially completed, the Independents considered them to be simply the first small steps in a continuing process which they hoped would lead to the realization of full-scale social democracy.[10] And as the struggle between these incompatible points of view evolved, the basic weakness of the position occupied by the Independent Cabinet members became increasingly manifest.

The extent of this weakness was clearly reflected in the areas of responsibility assigned to the various Cabinet members at one of their first meetings. Haase assumed direction of foreign affairs, while Ebert chose the ministries of war and the interior as his fields of special concern. Responsibility for government information agencies was assigned to Landsberg, while Scheidemann was placed in charge of finances. Dittmann was given the task of overseeing demobilization, justice, and health, while Barth, appropriately, accepted responsibility for social policies.[11] Under normal conditions the fields allotted to the Independents might well have been considered as important as those delegated to the majority socialists. This was, however, a revolutionary government, and it soon became evident that the positions of real and immediate power had been delivered into the hands of those least anxious to make use of it to complete the revolution.

One can perhaps understand Haase's decision to focus his attention upon foreign affairs at such a moment. He had, after all, devoted much of his energy to this field for many years, and it was apparent that the fate of Germany now lay to a large extent in the hands of the victorious Entente. It is probable that he also hoped that Germany's enemies would respond positively to the decision to place an outspoken opponent of the war in charge of the new government's foreign relations.[12] Yet his willingness to permit the key positions in domestic affairs to be placed in the hands of the majority socialists at a time when he fully recognized that the German revolution was far from complete also appears to have reflected a pessimistic assessment of his party's strength and thus of its ability, at least for the time being, to carry that revolution through to ultimate success.

The relative weakness of Haase's position in the Cabinet is reflected in the minutes of its meetings. From the beginning, Ebert seized the initiative, chairing most meetings,[13] determining the agenda[14] and reporting on the most important questions facing the government.[15] Haase was not even supreme in his own field of foreign relations. As early as November 18, he was compelled to ask Ebert to intervene with the Foreign Secretary, Wilhelm Solf, to obtain the dismissal of two of Solf's more reactionary aides.[16] To some extent, of course, Ebert's ability to play a dominant role in the new government may be ascribed to the strength of his personality. On the whole, Haase appears, at least at first, to have reverted to his old policy of conciliation and compromise. Ebert, on the other hand, generally assumed an aggressive posture, as did his majority socialist colleagues. Symptomatic of this difference in attitude is the fact that Ebert moved into the chancellery while Haase remained in his private home.[17]

More important than the personality factor, however, was the fact that both Ebert's increasing confidence and Haase's moderation were based upon a realistic assessment of the relative power of the two socialist parties. The Independents, whose agitational efforts had been much more severely limited by wartime restrictions, emerged from the war with barely 100,000 members.[18] As late as December the party was publishing only some twenty daily newspapers.[19] Moreover, its strength was very unevenly distributed. Despite its success in a number of the great industrial centers, in other crucially important areas the U.S.P.D. was hardly represented at all. Its progress was further hampered by a lack of trained leaders, since many of its most experienced spokesmen had been recruited into the various branches of the government. Despite frantic attempts to expand its organization in November and December, the membership had risen to only 300,000 when the Independent representatives resigned from the government.[20]

Perhaps equally significant was the fact that the S.P.D. enjoyed at least the temporary support of most of the elements in the population which had formerly barred the way to the triumph of Social Democracy. This was reflected in the frequent references in the non-socialist press to the Ebert rather than to the Ebert-Haase regime. Of far more immediate importance was the active support of both the officer corps and the majority of the government officials held over from pre-revolutionary times as "experts."[21] The incident involving Ebert's intervention with Solf was just one example of many which could be cited as evidence that the bureaucracy stood squarely on the side of the S.P.D. Haase was painfully aware of this fact from the beginning. Writing to his son on November 26, he declared that one of the major reasons he had rejected the suggestion that the Independents take power alone was that he had recognized that if Ebert were not in the Cabinet, a large number of the bourgeois specialists in the bureaucracy would pursue a policy of active sabotage.[22] The cooperative relationship between the military leaders and the S.P.D. was still more explicit. To be sure, at the time the military forces of the Reich were in the process of apparent dissolution, but as the weeks passed and a modicum of order was re-established, this alliance became increasingly significant. Ultimately it proved decisive.

The very system of parity, of course, also militated against the Independents. United in their efforts to maintain the status quo, the majority socialists possessed the clear advantage of being able to veto any measure of which they disapproved. Any hopes that Haase and his Independent colleagus may have had that they could play an innovative role in the government were thus effectively frustrated. The old orthodox Marxist warning against entering a coalition with non-socialist reformists appeared to have been amply confirmed by the situation in which they now found themselves.

Haase's reluctance to challenge Ebert for the leadership of the government becomes more understandable if these circumstances are kept in mind. If he had insisted upon his formal prerogatives as co-chairman of the cabinet, he would only had succeeded in becoming more clearly identified with the government's policies, many of which he did not in fact support. Moreover, he would thereby have further alienated that growing segment of his party that opposed the U.S.P.D.'s continued participation in the government. He therefore gravitated toward his accustomed role of opposition rather than asserting himself in ways which, in his view, could only have exacerbated an already difficult situation.

Among the many questions dividing the Cabinet, one of the most important concerned the proper role to be assigned to the workers' and soldiers' councils. The issue was both immediate and central, for not only had councils been formed throughout the Reich, but the Cabinet based its principal claim to legitimacy upon the endorsement of the Berlin councils. Moreover, in the Berlin Executive Council which had been created at the Zirkus Bush meeting of November 10, the government confronted an institution which insisted upon exercising at the very least a right of review over the actions of the Cabinet. The Independents, of course, were from the beginning much more sympathetic to the claims of the councils than the majority socialists.[23] Indeed, despite the success of the S.P.D. in imposing the principle of parity upon the selection of the Berlin Executive Council members, it did develop a somewhat more radical complexion than the Cabinet and might therefore have been expected to serve as an important source of support for the Independent representatives in the government.

Unfortunately, the Independent members of the Executive Council were little concerned to support their colleagues in the Cabinet. The most influential of these, Ledebour, Richard Müller and Ernst Däumig, all opposed the participation of the U.S.P.D. in the coalition government. Haase and his colleagues in the Cabinet, therefore, found themselves without any effective representation in the one body which might have assisted them in their efforts to drive their coalition partners toward the left. Indeed, the Independent members of the Executive Council at times seemed intent upon making the continuation of the coalition impossible. They made little attempt to differentiate between the Cabinet members in their numerous and vehement public attacks upon the activities of the government.[24] More important, their constant intervention in the affairs of the executive was often conducted in such an irresponsible and disruptive manner that the Independent Cabinet members found themselves hard pressed to defend the legitimate claims of the council in the Cabinet. The result was that the authority of the council rapidly declined, and its majority socialist members, under the able leadership of Hermann Müller were able to exert increasing influence.[25]

In the Cabinet, the Social Democrats consistently decried the behavior of the council, and the Independents were reduced to arguing somewhat apologetically for understanding and forbearance. During a joint meeting of the council and the Cabinet on December 7 even Haase complained about actions of the council which had tended to discredit the Cabinet. By December 11 the situation had degenerated to the point where the S.P.D. threatened to withdraw from the Cabinet if the council did not halt its disruptive interventions. Haase could only reply by pointing out that the Berlin council would soon be replaced by a central council representing the entire Reich.[26]

Ultimately more significant was the question of what role the councils should play in the future constitution of the new republic. Intimately related to this issue was the debate which developed concerning the calling of a constituent assembly. The majority socialists, uneasy about the extremist agitation of the left and eager to retain the support of the middle classes, urged that such an assembly be convened at the earliest possible moment. They distrusted the councils and wanted to return to the simpler and more familiar pattern of parliamentary democracy. The councils, which had served their purpose in helping to maintain order during the interregnum, could then be disbanded or at most given a limited function in industry. Thus, as early as November 15, Ebert proposed that the assembly be convened during the first weeks of January.[27]

Haase also recognized the necessity of convening a constituent assembly. He repeatedly declared in his public speeches that political democracy was a necessary concomitant of socialism.[28] He soon came to the conclusion, however, that the councils should be preserved as a necessary check and control on the parliamentary institutions. Moreover, he conceived of the revolutionary government in Marxist terms as a dictatorship of the proletariat which should be maintained until a firm socialist as well as democratic basis had been established for the new republic.[29] He and Dittmann therefore insisted during the course of a combined meeting of the Cabinet and the Berlin Executive Council on November 18 that a National Congress of Councils be convened as early as possible.[30] They also sought to postpone the election of the constituent assembly as long as possible.[31]

Once again, however, Haase found himself opposed by a significant portion of his own party. Several of the most influential Independent leaders, including most of those involved in the Berlin Executive Council, were drawn by the Russian example to advocate the establishment of a conciliar republic which would totally eliminate any return to parliamentary forms of democracy.[32] Haase was thus forced into the position of struggling in the Cabinet for a postponement of the constituent assembly while simultaneously conducting a public campaign for the acceptance of the principle of parliamentary democracy by his own party. The final result was a political debacle for the U.S.P.D. Under the pressure of public opinion and the majority socialists' threats to resign, Haase and his colleagues agreed late in November upon February 16 as a tentative compromise date. They appeared to have gained a significant concession when they compelled the majority socialists to agree to leave the final decision to the National Congress of Councils.[33] Even this victory was Pyrrhic, however, for the delegates to the congress proved to be just as eager as the majority socialists in the Cabinet to abdicate their power and responsibility.

The economic issues faced by the Cabinet were much less clearly defined than the political. Haase was convinced that the government should and could take immediate steps toward the socialization of those major industries that were ready for it. Progress in this direction, he believed, would constitute the most effective kind of propaganda for socialism. He therefore demanded that concrete measures be carried out without delay, despite the economic dislocation caused by the war.[34] The majority socialists were, of course, also at least verbally committed to socialization. They tended, however, to urge caution and careful preparation and clearly shared little of Haase's sense of urgency. Their principal concern was to prevent any further disruption of the economy, and they were reluctant to undertake any radical measures which might too deeply alienate their middle-class supporters.[35] It must, therefore, be considered at least a limited victory for Haase's point of view that upon his insistence the Cabinet voted on November 18 to establish a commission which was to prepare plans for the socialization of those industries which were "ripe."[36] Resolutions, however, are cheap, and actual progress proved to be very slow indeed. Haase continued to campaign publicly for immediate action, but to little avail. No concrete steps toward socialization had been taken before the Independents left the government.

In Haase's own field of special responsibility, foreign affairs, the differences between the coalition partners again revolved largely around questions of emphasis rather than basic policy. Moreover, Haase's ability to seize the initiative in this area was severely circumscribed both by Germany's extremely awkward international position and by his inability to effectively control the activities of the supposedly non-political experts in the foreign office.

The problem of dealing with the victorious Entente, of course, overshadowed all else. Haase's hopes that the allies would react positively to a regime which included outspoken critics of the German war effort proved to be unfounded. In fact, the almost paranoiac anti-communism of some of the allied leaders was put to effective use by Haase's domestic opponents. Once the armistice had been signed, Germany appeared to be entirely at their mercy, and it was upon this point that both the majority socialists and the professionals in the foreign office placed their greatest stress.[37] The Foreign Secretary, Wilhelm Solf, even went so far as to encourage allied threats which could be used in the struggle both against the Bolsheviks abroad and the Spartacists and Independents at home.[38]

It was, of course, in Eastern Europe, and particularly in Russia and Poland, that the new German government seemed to have its greatest freedom of movement. But it was there, too, that the anti-communism of the allies could be put to most effective use by the foreign office. During the war, Haase had been, as we have seen, not unsympathetic to the Bolshevik regime. Once in power, however, he appears to have been deeply influenced both by the strongly anti-Bolshevik sentiments of his friend Kautsky and by allied opposition to the Soviets.[39] When the question of reestablishing relations with the Russian government was raised,[40] he was among those who advised that the matter should be handled in a "dilatory" manner.[41] He responded to the repeated attempts on the part of the Russians to obtain permission for their embassy officials to return to Berlin at first with silence and then with obviously obstructionist bickering about matters of form and questions of secondary importance.[42] Moreover, he joined his majority socialist colleagues in rejecting a Russian offer to send several trainloads of grain to Germany[43] and in refusing to permit them to send delegates to the National Congress of Councils which met in Berlin in mid-December.[44] Virtually the only evidence to be found in the Cabinet minutes which suggests that Haase had not totally abandoned his earlier stance is that on a number of occasions he spoke out against lending German support to allied and Polish attacks upon the Bolshevik regime.[45]

Haase's policy with regard to Poland was somewhat more positive. The problem of establishing amicable relations with the Poles was particularly acute at this time both because of the large number of German troops who were still in the east and because of the very real danger of Polish intervention in Upper Silesia which would have threatened the supplies of gas and coal upon which Berlin depended. In the course of many Cabinet debates on the issue, Haase consistently favored a conciliatory policy and opposed the insistent majority socialist demands for active military intervention to protect German interests. Although increasingly critical of Polish policies, he urged his colleagues to try to understand the Polish point of view and avoid any unnecessarily provocative acts. As a participant in negotiations with local Silesian leaders on November 22 he helped to reduce tensions in the area at least temporarily.[46] Although Polish-German relations remained uneasy, it was not until the end of December, just as Haase was preparing to resign, that a major crisis developed as fighting broke out between Poles and Germans in the Prussian province of Posen.[47]

Whatever Haase's personal proclivities, however, there was little chance that he could develop a successful policy as long as the foreign office remained independent of his control. Wilhelm Solf, who had been appointed Foreign Secretary by Prince Max, was by no means representative of the most reactionary holdovers from the old regime. During the war he had consistently urged the government to adopt a moderate policy which he hoped might lead to an early peace of reconciliation. When the revolution came, he concluded that he could in conscience support the new republic and was easily persuaded to remain at his post. Moreover, he developed a deep respect for and friendship with Ebert.[48] Indeed, Solf's relative moderation and his close relationship with Ebert contributed significantly to Haase's difficulties. A more clearly reactionary figure might have been easily disposed of or at least compelled by a united Cabinet to obey the directives of his superiors. Solf, however, confident as he was of Ebert's support, was in a position to defy or disregard the instructions of his chief.[49]

The tension between Haase and Solf reached its first climax during a conference of representatives from the various state governments which was convened at Haase's suggestion on November 25. The primary purpose of the conference was to reassert the essential unity of the Reich which had been severely shaken by the revolution and by the antipathy which had arisen in many quarters towards the hegemony of Berlin and Prussia, an antipathy which was being actively fostered in some areas by the Entente. Although the conference revealed a generally favorable attitude toward the policies of the central government, it provided an opportunity for Haase's friend and party comrade, Kurt Eisner, to launch a vehement attack upon Solf. Eisner, who was engaged in an attempt to conduct a semi-independent foreign policy from his post as Prime Minister of Bavaria, labeled both Solf and the chairman of the armistice commission, Matthias Erzberger, as hopelessly compromised by their support of the German war effort. Ebert replied with an enthusiastic defense of Solf, but Haase, speaking for both himself and Kautsky, echoed many of Eisner's criticisms.[50] The latent antagonism between Haase and his Foreign Secretary had thus been brought out into the open, and Solf, returning from the conference "utterly broken," drafted what was in effect an ultimatum to the Cabinet upon the acceptance of which would depend his willingness to remain in his position.[51]

The issue was debated during the Cabinet meetings of December 2 and 4 without any clear conclusion being reached. At the end of the session of December 4 Ebert was delegated to speak with Solf about remaining in the foreign office while simultaneously efforts were to be made behind the scenes to find a successor.[52] Apparently Haase was satisfied with this arrangement, for during a joint meeting of the Berlin Executive Council and the Cabinet on December 7 he urged the council to withdraw a motion calling for the immediate removal of Solf. The problem, he declared, would be solved within the next few days.[53]

The conflict was, however, not to be resolved without another painful flareup between Haase and Solf. When the Cabinet met on December 9, Solf demonstratively refused to shake Haase's hand. The immediate cause of Solf's indignation was the claim by the former Russian ambassador, Adolf Joffe, that Haase and Barth had been among the recipients of Russian funds prior to the revolution. A stormy scene ensued. Solf obdurately refused to accept Haase's and Barth's denials.[54] After such a clash there could no longer be any question of Solf's remaining at his post. His resignation was finally accepted on December 13, shortly after the Cabinet had agreed to appoint Count Brockdorff-Rantzau, the ambassador to Denmark, as his replacement.[55] Whether the new secretary could have worked more effectively with Haase than had Solf is a moot question, for before Brockdorff could become firmly established in the foreign office the Independents had resigned from the government.

Far more divisive than questions of foreign policy were those raised by the problem of rapidly demobilizing an immense army while simultaneously preserving domestic order. Military defeat and political revolution had, of course, severely shaken the Prussian-dominated German officer corps. Paradoxically, the supreme command was aided in its efforts to preserve its role in the state by its two implacable enemies, the victorious Entente and the Spartacists. By insisting upon an extremely rapid withdrawal of German troops in the West, the allied leaders made it difficult for the revolutionary government to disband the officer corps which alone possessed the technical ability to accomplish this mammoth task in the time allotted. On the other hand, by fomenting disorder at home and thus creating at least the appearance of serious danger to the regime from the left, the Spartacists and their allies lent considerable weight to the argument that an alliance had at least temporarily to be maintained between the government and the old military establishment.

The basis for such an alliance had been established on November 10 when Groener called Ebert at the Chancellery to offer "his" government the support of the army.[56] From the beginning, however, the relationship which was thus established had many of the characteristics of a pact negotiated between equals. The army did not offer its support unconditionally. Groener made it clear to Ebert that the supreme command expected the government to provide assistance in maintaining discipline and to conduct an active campaign against the rise of Bolshevism in Germany. During the weeks that followed, he and Hindenburg made every effort to hold Ebert to these terms.[57]

In effect, of course, this alliance was not with the government as a whole, but rather with Ebert and the S.P.D. The extent to which Haase was aware of the special relationship which developed between Ebert and Groener is open to conjecture.[58] In any case, it is clear that Haase conceived of the concessions which the Cabinet made to the supreme command as unfortunate and temporary expedients made necessary by the conditions imposed by the

Entente.[59] In contrast to the majority socialists, he and his Independent colleagues emphasized that the most serious danger to the revolution came from the right rather than the left.[60] In the Cabinet, he voiced with increasing frequency his suspicions concerning the activities of the officer corps and tried to insist upon their absolute subservience to the government.[61] Unfortunately, his efforts remained largely verbal, and he failed to force a decisive confrontation on the issue until it was too late to do so with any hope of success.

Perhaps the Independents' greatest mistake in this regard was that they made no concerted effort to create a new military force loyal to the revolution. Soon after the collapse of the monarchy, a project to create a "red guard" which had been initiated by the Berlin Executive Council shattered upon the opposition of the Cabinet and the Berlin garrison.[62] When the government itself took steps to establish a popular defense force early in December, the initiative apparently came from Ebert. His proposal that a popular force (*Volkswehr*) of 11,000 volunteers be organized was supported by the Independents, but not uncritically. Haase questioned in particular the majority socialists' suggestion that detailed plans for the execution of Ebert's proposal be worked out by the war ministry which, he insisted, could not adapt itself to the new ways of thinking. A new man was needed to organize the popular force, he argued, someone who was "filled with the modern spirit." In the end, however, the Cabinet agreed to delegate Ebert to ask the war ministry to work out a detailed plan, and on December 6 it unanimously passed a law providing for the establishment of the new unit.[63] As was so often the case, Haase and his colleagues then failed to insist upon the proper execution of this plan which might have made it possible to avoid at least some of the tragic events of the next few months.[64] The *Volkswehr* never became a viable force,[65] and when the regime faced its greatest test a few weeks later, it was all but defenseless unless it chose to call upon the supreme command for assistance.

The revolutionary government was thus beset from its very inception by a wide variety of virtually insoluble problems, all of which contributed to the increasing strain which threatened to break the tenuous bonds holding the coalition together. During November there appeared to be at least some possibility that the socialist alliance could nevertheless be maintained. As December wore on, however, a series of crises arose which, on the one hand, drastically eroded the confidence of the Independent Cabinet members in their coalition partners and, on the other hand, forced them gradually to abandon their earlier moderation.

The disintegration of the alliance can in large measure be traced to the growing impatience and confidence of the extremists of both left and right, who by their increasingly aggressive actions were able to draw the leaders of the two Social Democratic parties steadily away from their original course.

During the first days of December the number and gravity of the provocations on both sides mounted rapidly. Haase and Dittmann repeatedly voiced their uneasiness about the increasingly flagrant independence of the military.[66] A crescendo of propaganda against the "Bolshevik menace" flooded from the bourgeois and majority socialist press while the Spartacists' *Rote Fahne* attacked with growing vehemence everyone who did not share their views. Rumors of impending coups from both right and left swept the capital.[67]

The first major crisis erupted on December 6, apparently as a result of a series of rather macabre coincidences. On the afternoon of that day the Independent leaders gathered in the offices of the Prussian interior ministry to discuss the general political situation. In the course of the meeting, Liebknecht, Luxemburg and Ledebour unleashed a vehement attack upon the party's representatives in the Cabinet and demanded that they withdraw from the government. Tempers flared to such a degree that Ledebour had to be physically restrained from assaulting Haase. Scarcely had order been restored after this outburst when word was received that an attempted putsch was in progress and that fighting had broken out between Spartacists and government troops. The meeting broke up immediately, and Haase and Dittmann hurried to the Chancellery.[68]

There they learned that groups of soldiers and sailors had simultaneously tried to arrest the Berlin Executive Council and to proclaim Ebert President of the republic. The group which had sought to seize the council was soon persuaded that the Cabinet had not, as they had been informed, issued any such order. The group which had demonstrated before the Chancellery withdrew after receiving a noncommittal answer from Ebert. Unfortunately events occurring almost at the same time elsewhere in Berlin robbed the affair of its comic opera character. Troops sent by the majority socialist city commandant, Wels, to cordon off the center of the capital fired upon a demonstrating group of Spartacists, killing sixteen.[69]

The impact of these events upon the already restless population of Berlin was, of course, immense. The extent of the tension was revealed during the course of a long meeting of the Executive Council and the Cabinet on December 7. Although not even radicals such as Daümig and Ledebour went so far as to accuse the Cabinet of direct complicity in the affair, there was considerable criticism of the government for having allowed an atmosphere to develop in which such events could occur. Ebert was chastised in particular for having merely told the demonstrators who urged him to make himself President that he had to consult his colleagues before making any such decision. His explanation that he was acting under the pressure of the moment could not have been very satisfying to the suspicious Independents. A motion to remove him from the Cabinet, however, was easily defeated.[70]

For his part, Haase decried the use of troops in the streets of the capital.

He also used the occasion to express his lack of confidence in many elements active within both the military establishment and the foreign office where the plot to arrest the Executive Council had apparently been hatched. It had become clear, he declared, that many of the old generals were by no means prepared to abandon their former views. He proposed no real solution to this dangerous situation, however. He merely promised that, if necessary, the Cabinet would be prepared to intervene with a strong hand.[71]

The events of December 6 had shaken but not disrupted the governing coalition. Haase voiced what was apparently the feeling shared by most of the participants in the December 7 meeting when he declared that the Cabinet would stand or fall with the Executive Council. He therefore strongly urged that a formal statement be issued reasserting the determination of the two governing bodies to work together.[72] It was fully apparent from his remarks that despite his uneasiness, he was willing to accept the avowals of good faith made by his majority socialist colleagues and intended to continue to try to make the coalition work.

A potential Cabinet crisis was thus averted. The December 7 meeting, however, did little to calm the steadily mounting tensions in the capital. An investigatory commission instituted by the Cabinet and Executive Council failed to clarify the circumstances surrounding the mysterious events of December 6. The joint statement issued by the Cabinet and the council declared in essence only that the situation in the government remained unchanged.[73] On December 8 massive demonstrations organized both by various elements within the U.S.P.D. and by the majority socialists made it abundantly clear not only that the radicals were gaining increasingly widespread support among the most active segment of the Berlin working class, but also that a dangerous polarization was taking place within that part of the population pledged to support the revolution. The popular support available to those such as Haase who were trying to follow a middle path was being rapidly eroded.

One of the reasons for the growing uneasiness of many Independents was the supreme command's plan to bring substantial numbers of troops returning from the western front into the capital before demobilizing them. It was well known that these soldiers remained to a considerable degree apolitical, and many supporters of the revolution feared, not without justification,[74] that they might be used to carry out a coup against the regime. Haase's response to the situation both indicated how earnest he still was in his efforts to maintain the fragile governing coalition and reflected his apparent failure, despite his rapidly growing suspicions, to recognize the full magnitude of the dangers confronting the revolution.[75] Although he and his Independent colleagues raised questions about the plan, they permitted it to be carried out. That the returning troops were not, in fact, used for counterrevolutionary purposes appears to have been much more the result of inadequate leadership and their own eagerness to be demobilized than of any precautionary measures taken by Haase and the other Independents in the Cabinet.[76]

The striking contrast between the attitudes of Haase and Ebert toward the military was clearly reflected by their speeches to the returning troops as they entered Berlin. On December 10 Ebert delivered one of the most famous speeches of his career. Couching his message in highly patriotic terms, he expressed Germany's gratitude to the soldiers for the sacrifices they had endured and assured them that they had not really been defeated by any enemy, but had been forced to give up the struggle only by the tremendous superiority they faced in men and material. To be sure, he also declared that they returned to a new and freer Germany, but the speech as a whole was clearly directed toward buoying up their patriotism and their pride in their military accomplishments.[77]

Addressing another body of troops on the following day, Haase stressed rather the changes which had taken place since they had left their homeland. He condemned the "iron system of military dictatorship" which had plunged Germany into war. Under "the accursed system" of the old rulers, he declared, the life of the German people had been laid waste. Now they would be called upon to participate in the building of a new and better life for their homeland. He went on to emphasize that the red insignia worn by their comrades in the barracks symbolized the brotherhood of man to which the new socialist republic was dedicated. By stressing this point, Haase was indirectly throwing down a challenge to the many members of the officers' corps who had consistently resisted the use of such insignia. He told the soldiers, furthermore, that they had been to a large extent misinformed about the socialist society and those who had fought to create it. In fact, only a socialist society could be expected to rid the world of war. The task of the socialist republic, he declared, would be to construct a world free from exploitation and oppression. The success of the republic in achieving this goal would in large measure depend upon its returning soldiers.[78]

Speeches alone, however, were not enough to assure Haase's party comrades that he was truly and effectively representing their interests in the government. Ledebour and other well known Independents continued to press their demand that the party leave the coalition. The Spartacists, furthermore, were obviously approaching the point where they would sever the final loose ties which still bound them to the U.S.P.D. Despite the clamor of the left Independents, however, Haase still had at least the qualified support of the majority of his party. This became apparent during the course of a conference of Independent representatives from the Berlin metropolitan area which met on December 15.

The conference was dominated by a long debate between Haase and Rosa

Luxemburg in which he vigorously defended his conduct since the revolution. He reminded the delegates that in entering the Cabinet he had been obeying the obvious will of the overwhelming majority of the German proletariat. He pointed out that several of his most vehement critics had joined the Berlin Executive Council which was constituted, like the Cabinet, on the basis of a coalition with the S.P.D. and which also was a formal part of the government. He emphasized that he and his Independent colleagues would gladly resign if they thought it was in the interest of the proletariat to do so. They were, indeed, by no means satisfied with what the Cabinet had accomplished. They were also, however, convinced that the situation would be far worse if they had resigned or had refused to participate in the first place. The inevitable result would have been the establishment of a right socialist coalition with the bourgeoisie or even a purely bourgeois regime, either of which would have led to a rapid degeneration of the conditions under which the proletariat had to carry on its struggle for the continuation of the revolution.

He decried the Spartacists' slavish imitation of the Bolsheviks. Their fine sounding call for the giving of "all power to the councils" was simply irrelevant to German conditions as they would discover soon enough. Their attack upon the constituent assembly was understandable, but again was based upon a refusal to face the facts. Any call for a boycott of the elections to the assembly would be ignored by ninety-nine per cent of the proletariat. An attempt to disrupt the assembly would lead not to a struggle against the bourgeoisie, but to a fratricidal civil war within the working class. It was not true, as the Spartacists claimed, that the resignation of the Independents from the Cabinet would clarify the situation for the masses. The result would simply be that the party would lose contact with the overwhelming majority of the proletariat. The task now was not to divide the proletariat, but to unite it and to gain a majority for the Independents' point of view. At the moment a large proportion of the workers still looked to the S.P.D. for leadership. This fact could not be ignored. The U.S.P.D. must remain committed to the principles of democracy. Even if they should be unable to gain a socialist majority in the constituent assembly, they must continue the struggle on a realistic basis, using every tool at their command, including the institutions of parliamentary democracy.[79]

Despite Rosa Luxemburg's impassioned rebuttal, in which she vehemently attacked him and his colleagues, Haase's far more realistic appraisal of the situation was supported by a large majority of the delegates. Luxemburg's resolution, which included a demand for the immediate resignation of the Independents from the government, uncompromising opposition to the constituent assembly, and a call for all power to be given to the councils, was defeated by a two-to-one margin. Instead, a counter-resolution introduced by

Haase's friend Hilferding was passed which in effect endorsed the program outlined by Haase.[80]

The National Congress of Workers' and Soldiers' Councils which convened on the following day largely confirmed Haase's analysis. A large majority of the delegates were either sympathetic to or members of the S.P.D.[81] Indicative of their mood was the fact that Luxemburg and Liebknecht were not only not elected, they were explicitly denied permission to participate in an advisory capacity.[82] Moreover, the assembly obdurately refused to be cowed by a series of large and raucous demonstrations organized by the Spartacists and their left Independent allies.

Despite his victory on the previous day, Haase soon found himself at odds with the majority of the Independent delegates who generally turned to leaders of the left wing of the party for guidance.[83] Indeed, both he and Dittmann played the role of loyal representatives of the government at the congress and as such did not wholly escape the acid criticism which their party comrades heaped upon the majority socialists.

At Haase's suggestion, Dittmann had been delegated to report for the Cabinet as a whole.[84] Dittmann made it clear in his speech that the Cabinet members had not always agreed, but he avoided any explicit criticism of his majority socialist colleagues. He urged the delegates to consider party differences secondary and to go into the approaching electoral campaign united against the common enemies of their class.[85] Although his call for a fraternal alliance was greeted warmly, the course of the debates soon proved that his hopes were not to be fulfilled. By the end of the congress, the voices of conciliation had been effectively drowned out by a new flood of personal and partisan invective.

One of the principal tasks facing the congress was, of course, to set the date for elections to the constituent assembly. As Haase had feared,[86] it soon became apparent that a large majority of the delegates supported the S.P.D.'s demand that they be held on January 19 rather than on February 16 as proposed by the Cabinet. Nevertheless, in one of his few major speeches at the congress, Haase made a vigorous plea for a later date. He began by firmly rejecting the efforts of both the extreme left and the majority socialist leaders to state the question in absolute terms. The congress was by no means faced with the problem of making a decision as to whether Germany would be ruled solely by a conciliar or by a parliamentary regime. The Cabinet, he declared, had indeed come to the conclusion that a constituent assembly was a political necessity. This did not mean, however, that the councils would thereby become superfluous. On the contrary, there was little doubt that the councils would continue to play a fundamental role in German government and society.

The only step that needed to be taken at the moment, therefore, was to set a definite date for elections, and there were, he insisted, good grounds for selecting a later rather than an earlier date. The borders of the new Germany had not yet been established. Germans in the occupied zones had no opportunity to engage in free political activity. Furthermore, many soldiers had not as yet returned from the east, and they certainly had earned the right to participate in this most crucial of elections. Most important, it was necessary to provide time enough for large-scale political education to take place. Not only had the entire nation been misled by a "net of lies" for more than four years, but there were large numbers of new voters, women and youth, who had heretofore had no opportunity to participate in political life. Parties such as the U.S.P.D. had been the special victims of the lies propagated by the old regime and had had little opportunity to counteract them. The national assembly, he concluded, must represent a true expression of the will of the entire nation. Then, the whole world would be forced to admit that Germany was truly a democratic republic.[87]

Haase's efforts, however, were in vain. The congress voted overwhelmingly for the January 19 date proposed by the S.P.D.[88] The eagerness of the delegates to abdicate their position of power in the new republic had made a mockery of the extreme left's insistent demand that all power be placed in the hands of the councils.

Of more immediate practical significance was the dispute which erupted concerning the future relationship of the councils to the provisional government. Although a resolution was easily passed on the third day of the congress directing that the Cabinet continue its work under the "parliamentary supervision" (*Überwachung*) of a Central Council to be elected by the congress,[89] the Independents, some of whom had been directly involved in the frequently acrimonious conflicts between the Berlin Executive Council and the Cabinet, remained unsatisfied. They reopened the debate on the issue and insisted that the meaning of the term "parliamentary supervision" be precisely defined. It was Haase who presented the Cabinet's interpretation of the word and thereby came into conflict with the majority of the Independent delegation. The Central Council, he declared, would be provided with drafts of all legislation and would be explicitly consulted concerning all "important" laws before they were promulgated. The Cabinet expected that no irreconcilable differences would arise between itself and the council. If a compromise on some important measure could not be reached, however, the Cabinet reserved the right to act over the objections of the council. In such a case the only sanction the council could impose would be to force the Cabinet's resignation.[90]

Although Haase's interpretation represented a significant concession,[91] it aroused the immediate opposition of many Independents who felt that the

Cabinet was being given too much discretionary power. The Independent delegation retired to consider the matter just as Haase began his speech on the constituent assembly issue. Before he was able to join his party comrades, they had already voted to refuse to participate in the election of the Central Council if the Cabinet's interpretation was upheld by the congress.[92] The arguments of the Independents fell on deaf ears when presented on the floor of the congress, and a resolution was easily passed which explicitly endorsed Haase's statement concerning the relationship between the Central Council and the Cabinet. The Independent delegation thereupon carried out its threat and refused to nominate a list of candidates for membership on the council. The congress then simply elected the majority socialist list *en toto*.[93]

Undoubtedly Dittman was correct in his contention that many of those who voted to abstain from the elections to the Central Council did so primarily with the intention of forcing the Independents out of the Cabinet.[94] Although the tactic was not immediately successful, its effect was to weaken gravely Haase's position. Not only had he and his colleagues thus been left without partisan support in the Central Council; they had also been disavowed by the important elements of the U.S.P.D. represented by the Independent delegation to the congress. Haase's victory in the Berlin party organization meeting of December 15 was thus placed in question and his ability to play an effective leadership role in both the party and the government seriously impaired.

The congress was not, however, a total failure from Haase's point of view. On two crucial issues, the socialization of industry and the dissolution of the old military establishment, his position was fully endorsed by the delegates. The fact that the Independents could win such significant victories in an assembly ostensibly dominated by the majority socialists undoubtedly weighed heavily in Haase's mind when he decided to remain in the Cabinet despite his failure to secure the election of Independents to the Central Council.

The majority socialist leaders had hoped that the matter of socialization would not be debated at the congress, for it was apparent that their reluctance to support such a fundamental plank in the traditional Social Democratic program would not be well received even by their most dedicated followers. Their efforts to adjourn the congress immediately after the election of the Central Council, however, were thwarted by the outraged protests of the Independents,[95] and after effective speeches by Barth and by Haase's old friend Rudolf Hilferding who was now editor of *Freiheit*, the delegates unanimously adopted a resolution calling upon the government to "begin immediately *(unverzüglich)* the socialization of all industries, in particular the mining industry, that are ready *(reif)* for it."[96]

The congress' decision on the military question provided at least as compelling grounds for Haase to remain in the Cabinet. As in the case of the socialization issue, the delegates turned to the Independents for leadership and passed a resolution directing that, among other things, insignia of rank be eliminated, that full responsibility for the maintenance of discipline be vested in the soldiers' councils, that most officers be elected by their troops, that the Cabinet be explicitly given direct command over the armed forces and that the demobilization of the old army and the creation of a popular force be accelerated.[97]

Haase played an important role in securing the passage of these "Hamburg points." As chairman of the commission which prepared the resolution in its final form, he was at least partly responsible for the elimination of a final point which would have declared that its provisions were to be considered merely "general guidelines." Without this qualification the resolution took the form of a series of specific instructions to the Cabinet which would be difficult to ignore or circumvent. Moreover, in presenting the resolution to the delegates, Haase explicitly declared that it was the intention of the commission that it should be applied immediately.[98] Its obvious impact, if fully implemented, would have been to completely destroy the power of the officer corps which Haase considered the greatest threat to the revolution.

As Haase undoubtedly realized, however, the supreme command was in no mood to abdicate its still very formidable powers without a struggle. Hindenburg immediately sent a secret telegram to his commanders in which he declared that he refused to recognize the Hamburg points. He added that the army remained loyal to the "Ebert government" and expected it to continue to adhere to its agreements concerning the preservation of the army.[99] Moreover, Groener told Ebert in the course of a telephone conversation on the very day the resolution was passed that the supreme command would stand or fall on this issue. Ebert asked him to come to Berlin to argue his case, and two days later he appeared at the first meeting of the Cabinet with the newly elected Central Council ostentatiously dressed in full military regalia.[100]

After formally welcoming the members of the council, Ebert turned the floor over to Groener who unleashed a long and vehement attack upon the resolution. Any attempt to enforce it would, he declared, bring a complete catastrophe. Although admitting that the officer corps was not entirely blameless, he repeatedly warned that not only the supreme command, but most of the officers as well would resign if the government insisted upon obeying the directives of the congress.

The Independent Cabinet members at first sharply rejected Groener's arguments. Haase emphatically criticized the officers for bringing the action of the congress upon themselves by their refusal to accept the revolution. Dittmann and Barth still more strongly insisted that the Hamburg points be immediately enforced. Ebert and Scheidemann, however, argued for a policy of procrastination, and it soon became apparent that they enjoyed the support of most if not all of the members of the Central Council. The disastrous effects of the Independents' decision to boycott the council were already becoming manifest. Toward the end of the meeting even Haase, clearly impressed by Groener's threats, agreed to put off the execution of the resolution until specific detailed directives could be formulated. He emphasized, however, that these directives must be worked out as quickly as possible (*schleunigst*).[101] Groener could leave the meeting satisfied that with the aid of the majority socialists he had succeeded in at least temporarily forestalling what had appeared to be a total disaster for the old army.[102] As events were to prove, this kind of procrastination was all that was necessary.

The crisis which finally disrupted the government coalition erupted just a few days later. The immediate cause was a dispute concerning the status of the People's Naval Division, a unit made up of about a thousand men which had been quartered in the Hohenzollerns' Berlin palace since the early days of the revolution. Repeated complaints that the sailors were vandalizing the palace as well as an uneasiness concerning the presence of a large body of armed and relatively ill-disciplined men near the seat of the government led to demands that the division be reduced in size and moved to the royal stables. An agreement was finally reached with the sailors that they would move out of the palace and dismiss several hundred of their number as soon as they were given 80,000 marks in back pay by the city commandant, Otto Wels. This amount was to be turned over to the division leaders upon receipt by Wels of the keys to the palace.[103]

On December 23 the sailors appeared ready to fulfill their part of this agreement. Late in the afternoon, however, the commander of the sailors phoned Haase and expressed his fear that if he were to take the keys directly to Wels, the sailors who accompanied him might create some sort of unfortunate incident. Haase proposed as an alternative that the keys be brought to the Chancellery. Haase himself then had to leave for a meeting, but he left word for Ebert that he should direct Wels to pay the sailors as soon as the keys were delivered.[104]

Unfortunately, when the contingent of sailors finally arrived at the Chancellery, they delivered the keys to Barth rather than to Ebert. Barth thereupon telephoned Wels who refused to pay the sailors until the keys were brought directly to him or until he received authorization to do so from Ebert. Unable to find Ebert and enraged by Wels' recalcitrance, the sailors cordoned off the Chancellery and closed its switchboard. Ebert, using his direct telephone line, was, however, able to reach the supreme command, and troops under the command of General Lequis were soon set in motion to free him. A clash was nevertheless prevented by a series of involved negotiations, and early in the evening both the government troops and the sailors withdrew with the understanding that a final agreement would be worked out on the following morning. The Independent Cabinet members returned to their homes that night after having been informed that the affair had been at least temporarily settled.[105]

What happened next will perhaps never be satisfactorily explained. Groener later declared that during the evening he finally persuaded Ebert to undertake decisive military action against the sailors.[106] Ebert's official explanation was that he acted simply to free Wels, whom the angry sailors had arrested and incarcerated in the palace.[107] In any event, it is clear that Ebert, supported by Scheidemann and Landsberg and without having made any attempt to contact their Independent colleagues, issued an order to the War Minister which could only have been interpreted as a directive to initiate military operations against the People's Naval Division. Sensing the danger, the sailors contacted Ledebour, who made several unsuccessful attempts during the night to initiate negotiations with the majority socialist Cabinet members. He too, however, apparently made no attempt to contact the Independent members of the Cabinet.[108] By the next morning General Lequis had his troops in position, and at 7:50 A.M. he issued a ten-minute ultimatum to the sailors to surrender. When they refused, artillery fire was directed against the palace, and a battle raged for several hours. Lequis' troops, however, were unenthusiastic about the struggle, and little progress was made.

In the meantime, Haase and Dittmann arrived at the Chancellery. They found Barth engaged in an excited exchange with their majority socialist colleagues who were already present. Ebert assured the Independents that he knew nothing of the attack which was in progress despite the fact that Barth had been informed by both the war ministry and by a participating officer that they had received their orders from the Cabinet.[109] Haase, his faith in his colleague's honesty apparently still unshaken, declared that it appeared to be a case of an arbitrary intervention by the military. He proposed that he call the war ministry to order an end to the attack. Ebert, however, insisted that he himself should make the call and did so. Negotiations were then initiated with the sailors and a new understanding reached before noon.[110]

The events of December 23–24 obviously constituted a stinging defeat for Ebert and his military allies. They had been unable to enforce their will against fewer than a thousand rebellious sailors and in the attempt to do so had once again fanned the flames of hatred and distrust within the most active segment of the Berlin working class. They now stood apparently defenseless against the outraged left wing leaders. Most important, once the circumstances surrounding these events began to come to light, the confidence of the moderate Independents in their majority socialist allies was so deeply shaken that a Cabinet crisis was unavoidable.

It was not until the afternoon of December 27, however, that Haase and his Independent colleagues received explicit confirmation of what they undoubtedly by this time suspected, i.e., that Ebert had given the order for the attack upon the People's Naval Division. They obtained this confirmation not from Ebert directly, but from a report published in *Vorwärts*, which sought to place the entire blame for the clash upon the sailors' refusal to release Wels.[111] With the publication of this report it became immediately apparent that the government would have to be reconstituted. The majority socialists had consciously and intentionally misled their Independent colleagues. A continuation of the coalition after such a betrayal of trust was out of the question. As an editorial in *Freiheit* pointed out on December 27, it was now up to the Central Council to decide which party should assume sole control of the government.[112]

The final confrontation between the leaders of the two parties took place during a joint meeting of the Cabinet and the Central Council on December 28. Ebert opened the debate with a lengthy description of the events of December 23 and 24.[113] Although the Independents directly contradicted some of Ebert's testimony, the discussion soon moved from points of fact to the question of whether the majority socialists had acted wisely and in good faith. Haase, supported by Dittmann, complained sharply that the information which Ebert now presented had been withheld from the Independents despite their repeated inquiries. The majority socialists, he declared, had made a grievous error in giving unrestricted orders to the War Minister. They certainly should have realized what the representatives of the old regime would do under the circumstances. Moreover, their failure to contact their colleagues in the Cabinet, who were readily available for consultation, or even to inform them about what had happened after the fact was totally inexcusable.[114]

For their part, the majority socialists were unable to present more than a token defense. They maintained that they had no idea that Lequis would mount the kind of assault he did. They lamely insisted that they had not contacted the Independents merely because of the time element involved.[115] They made essentially no defense against the charge that they had withheld information from their colleagues. They devoted most of their energy to criticizing vehemently the behavior of the sailors, a matter which, under the circumstances, was only a side issue.

After a lengthy debate which appeared to be getting nowhere, a break was called in mid-afternoon. The Independents returned with a well developed plan of action. Haase opened the second session with a long polemic against his majority socialist colleagues for having failed to effectively curb the old military establishment. His remarks extended the debate far beyond the events of December 23 and 24. Groener's reaction to the Hamburg points, he declared, had made it abundantly clear that the supreme command was trying to expand its power. The discovery that Hindenburg had sent a secret telegram to his commanders preemptorily rejecting the action of the National Congress of Councils had simply confirmed this impression. Such insubordination was intolerable.

Haase went on to criticize his colleagues strongly for their failure to agree to the complete demobilization of the old army before the end of the year as the Independents had demanded.[115] Their failure to carry out the order to create a popular defense force was also inexcusable. Such a force would have provided ample protection for the government. The government was weak, Haase conceded, but it was weak primarily because it had capitulated to Hindenburg and Groener. It must not continue to follow such a path. It must base itself in the future upon the support of the masses in Berlin, and in order to gain that support, it must make a clean break with the old system.[116]

Not long after Haase delivered this stinging attack upon his colleagues, Dittmann brought the situation to a head by presenting a list of eight questions to the Central Council. The Independents, he declared, would decide whether they could continue to participate in the government on the basis of the replies which they received to these questions. The first two asked whether the council approved of the actions taken by the majority socialist Cabinet members and General Lequis on December 23–24. The remaining questions, however, dealt with a wide range of issues which went far beyond those directly raised by the clash with the sailors. They asked the council whether it supported the immediate and strict execution of the National Congress of Councils' resolutions calling of the National Congress of Councils resolutions calling for the elimination of insignia of rank and the introduction of a prohibition against officers carrying sidearms while off duty,[117] whether it approved of the supreme command's secret orders directing that the congress resolutions be ignored, whether it supported the demand now being made by the majority socialists that the seat of the government be removed from Berlin,[118] whether it approved of the War Ministry's plan to keep a significant part of the old army under arms rather than demobilize it completely, and whether the council agreed with the Independents that a socialist government should rely exclusively upon a democratically organized popular force for military support. Finally, they asked whether the council was prepared to support immediate legislative action to socialize appropriate industries.[119]

Early in the evening the Council retired to consider these questions. Its replies were communicated to the Independents at 11:00 P.M. As was to be expected, the council members came down clearly on the side of their majority socialist comrades.[120] Meeting in Haase's office, the Independents required less than an hour to draft their statement of resignation.[121]

The final session was brief and dramatic. After making a short opening statement, Haase turned the floor over to Dittman who read the formal explanation of their decision to resign. He and his colleagues had decided to leave the Cabinet, he declared, because, although the council had condemned the military measures undertaken on December 24, it had sanctioned the irresponsible actions of the majority socialist Cabinet members which had led to them. Moreover, although the council had declared that the National Congress of Councils resolutions on military reorganization should be carried out, it had not explicitly insisted that they be immediately and strictly enforced. The council had refused to take a position on the questions posed by the Independents concerning the removal of the government from Berlin, the complete demobilization of the army and the necessity of establishing a democratic people's military force and were thus endangering the achievements of the revolution. Finally, the council's reply to the question concerning immediate socialization offered little hope that the National Congress of Councils' resolution on that issue would actually be carried out. When Dittmann was finished, Haase characteristically assured the council and his former colleagues that he sincerely hoped that they would be successful in their efforts to lead Germany safely through the trying days ahead.[122]

On January 1 Haase published an article in *Frieheit* entitled "The First Phase of the Revolution" which provides a summary analysis of his participation in the revolutionary government as he viewed it. Much as in his December 15 speech, he began by strongly defending his decision to enter the government. Once that decision had been made, he continued, it was the obvious responsibility of the party to support its representatives in the Cabinet and thus to assist them to drive the majority socialists forward. Unfortunately, influential members of the party had chosen to pursue a different tactic. From the beginning these Independents had mounted a persistent and vehement attack upon their comrades in the Cabinet. The inevitable result was that his own and his colleagues' efforts had been rendered far less effective than they would otherwise have been. Moreover, the seeds of confusion had been sown in the ranks of the party, thus hindering its development into an effective political force. He was not denying, he added, that criticism of the government as a whole was appropriate. Indeed, such criticism could have played a very constructive role. But the attacks which had been directed specifically against the Independents in the Cabinet had constituted a grave political blunder.

During the war, he continued, the U.S.P.D. had been able to see through the fog of phrasemongering and to deal realistically with the crisis facing Germany. Since the revolution, however, a significant portion of the party membership had become enamoured of wholly abstract and artificial theories and in espousing them had squandered energies which could have been put to far better use enlightening the masses. To future observers, he predicted, it would appear incomprehensible that highly regarded leaders of the party had even gone so far as to question whether the U.S.P.D. should participate in the elections of the constituent assembly.

The decision to boycott the Central Council had already been proven a tactical error of the greatest magnitude. If the Independent delegates to the National Congress of Workers' and Soldiers' Councils had not ignored his advice, the party would now be in sole control of the government, for many of the majority socialist members of the Central Council had been severely shaken by the events of December 23–24. If the Independents had been able to force the resignation of the majority socialists, they would have immediately done away with the old power of command in the army, socialized important industries and adopted a foreign policy in keeping with the spirit of international socialism. The result would have been that the U.S.P.D. would have won over to its side the masses of workers who continued to support the old party.

But despite these grave mistakes, Haase concluded, all was not yet lost. The party must unite to gain as many seats in the constituent assembly as possible. It must pursue a clear and decisive policy. The revolution was not yet completed, and the U.S.P.D. would face immensely important tasks in the months ahead.[123]

There is much to be said for Haase's analysis of his brief tenure in the revolutionary government. It can hardly be denied that he and his Independent colleagues would have been in a far stronger position within the Cabinet if they had enjoyed the support of a united party. It is also apparent that the decision to boycott the elections to the Central Council was a blunder of the first magnitude. What Haase fails to consider, however, is what he himself might have done to overcome the extreme heterogeneity of the U.S.P.D. which, after all, had been one of its fundamental characteristics since the day of its birth. The confusion and dissension that developed within the ranks of the party was to be sure largely a result of the sectarianism evinced by the Independents' left wing. Nevertheless, at least some of the responsibility for the party's failure to come to grips with this problem lay on Haase's own shoulders, for in his eagerness to prolong the coalition and to maintain a collegial atmosphere within the Cabinet he failed to speak out as clearly and as forcefully as he might have on many of the questions that most troubled his followers. He thus failed to provide the kind of clear cut program that might have served as a focal point about which at least those who were not from the beginning intent upon disrupting the U.S.P.D. could have rallied.

Moreover, he and the other national leaders of the U.S.P.D. seriously neglected the basic organizational tasks so important to a rapidly growing party once they joined the government. Although this failure is understandable considering the demands upon their time and energy,[124] there is no evidence to suggest that they made a concerted effort to see that this work was delegated to others who could have performed it satisfactorily. Finally, Haase's hypothesis that had the U.S.P.D. chosen to participate in the elections to the Central Council, they would have been able to take over the government rests on questionable assumptions. Despite the evident disagreement within the Central Council concerning some of the policies of the majority socialists in the Cabinet, it is probable that if the majority socialist members of the council had been confronted with a united Independent delegation, they would have voted along party lines on important questions. The ultimate result would thus have been not very different from what actually occurred.

CHAPTER XIII

RETURN TO OPPOSITION

The dissolution of the government coalition was not the only event which signaled the end of the first phase of the revolution. Almost at the same time as the proletarian united front split down its center, a second convulsion occurred which led to the secession of its leftmost extremity. Relations between the Spartacists and the main body of the U.S.P.D. had, of course, always been strained. After November 9, however, they rapidly degenerated to the point where even Haase flatly declared during the Berlin party conference of December 15 that a split had become necessary.[1]

After the defeat of the radicals at the National Congress of Councils, opposition to the maintenance of formal ties with the U.S.P.D. rapidly grew among the Spartacists themselves. On December 22 the Spartacist central committee voted to call a national conference for December 30, and when the delegates gathered in Berlin on December 29, they voted overwhelmingly in a closed preliminary caucus to break with the Independents.[2] The conference which met during the following two days thus became the founding congress of the Communist Party of Germany (K.P.D.). The defection of the Spartacists, in turn, appeared to open the way for New attempts to establish a rapprochement between the S.P.D. and the U.S.P.D. Several of the moderate Independent leaders had, indeed, been making cautious gestures in this direction for some time. Dittmann reports that as early as mid-November he had raised the possibility of reunification, though with little success. More recently his conciliatory speech at the National Congress of Councils had represented a conscious effort to encourage cooperation.[3] Bernstein had gone so far as to rejoin the S.P.D. while at the same time remaining a member of the U.S.P.D.[4] Kautsky was also eager at the time to promote unity. In an article written around December 20, he expressed a point of view that was undoubtedly shared by many of the moderate Independents. The U.S.P.D. was, he argued, fundamentally "a child of the World War." It had been brought together solely by a negative force, the struggle against the war policy of the majority socialists. It included a wide variety of radically differing groups. On one side were those who wanted to hold fast to the teachings of Marx and Engels as incorporated in the Erfurt Program. On the other side were various elements which were convinced that new tactics and new programs were necessary. In fact, this latter segment represented a revival of the old Blanquist and anarchist views with which the S.P.D. had had to contend at an early stage in its development. The first group wanted to maintain proletarian unity as far as possible. The second had been consistently and consciously striving to divide the forces of Social Democracy. With the end of the war, the last bond holding these groups together had disappeared. At the same time, the end of the war had struck down the principal differences separating the moderate wing of the U.S.P.D. from the majority socialists.

The masses instinctively understood, Kautsky maintained, that the proletariat would have to rule united if it were to rule at all. They were now interested not in the war which stood in the past, but in the future. Unfortunately, those who demanded unity were being denounced as betrayers of the revolution by the sectarians. The differences between the moderates and the sectarians on this issue had finally reached the point where fruiful cooperation had become impossible. An immediate organizational reunification was, to be sure, impossible. The differences between the moderate Independents and the majority socialists were actually no greater than those which had existed prior to the split, but the added factor of personal distrust precluded any immediate return to the old party. These differences, however, would not prevent the moderates of both parties from constructing a unified proletarian front for the coming election. A final decision on unity could then be made by a party convention after the elections.[5]

Interestingly enough, it was Haase who persuaded Kautsky not to publish this article.[6] This fact does not, however, eliminate the possibility that the two friends may have been close to agreement on the question of unity. It is true that Haase had often publicly denied any intention of seeking to promote a movement toward organizational unity.[7] Moreover, it is almost certain that he was still both more sympathetic to the Spartacists and more suspicious of the majority socialist leaders than was Kautsky. Yet, tactical considerations may have been decisive in leading Haase to suppress Kautsky's article, and there is little reason to doubt that he shared Kautsky's fundamental conviction that the restoration of proletarian unity in some form was not only desirable, but also necessary for the success of the revolution.

Any possibility of establishing an immediate rapprochement with the majority socialists, however, was all but eliminated by the struggle that broke out in the streets of the capital early in January. Just as in December, the January disturbances developed as a result of confusion and misjudgment rather than careful calculation. The results, however, were far more tragic. The immediate cause of the crisis was the decision of the majority socialist Prime Minister of Prussia, Paul Hirsch, to replace the left Independent head of the Berlin police presidium, Emil Eichhorn. This move was certainly both technically completely legal and politically fully understandable, for Eichhorn clearly did not represent a reliable source of support for the Cabinet. Moreover, the resignation of the Independent Cabinet members had been followed by that of most of the Independents in the Prussian state government. Eichhorn, however, insisted that he was a local administrative official and refused to leave unless ordered to do so by the Berlin Executive Council.[8]

Recognizing the importance of Eichhorn's post and sensing the growing restlessness of the Berlin workers, the Revolutionary Shop Stewards, the Berlin U.S.P.D. organization and the Communists issued a call for protest demonstrations on Sunday, January 5.[9] The response to this appeal was so immense that a potentially revolutionary situation was created, and after a long and heated debate that evening, the leaders of the sponsoring organizations decided to make an effort to topple the regime if an opportunity arose to do so. A revolutionary committee was created and a call was issued for a general strike to take place on the following day.[10] Apparently acting independently, groups of armed workers under Communist leadership occupied the major Berlin newspaper offices that same evening.[11]

The government found itself placed in an extremely dangerous position by these events, for it soon became apparent that most of the troops in Berlin would at best remain neutral. Meeting in a private home to avoid the possibility of arrest, the Cabinet members decided to defend themselves until reliable military forces could be raised by calling for counter-demonstrations.[12]

Most observers agree that the revolutionary committee was in a position to seize control of the capital on January 6.[13] As on the previous day, immense numbers of workers, many of whom were armed, heeded the call. The only obstacle to an immediate seizure of power appeared to be a mass of largely unarmed loyalists who gathered to form a human wall around the Chancellery. But the revolutionary committee frittered away its advantage.[14] After long hours of waiting for instructions while the committee debated, many of the workers who had at first heeded its call became apathetic and withdrew. In the meantime, Gustav Noske was made commander-in-chief of the government forces in the area, and in cooperation with the supreme command he rapidly began to recruit loyalist troops outside of Berlin.[15]

While the hostile groups of demonstrators were still facing each other in the capital, the national leaders of the U.S.P.D., who had refused to become involved in the revolutionary movement, met to consider what action they might take to prevent a bloodbath.[16] As on November 9, Haase was away from the capital. He would, however, undoubtedly have concurred with the decision of his colleagues to attempt to mediate the dispute. When he reached Berlin on January 7 he immediately assumed a leadership role in the efforts to achieve a peaceful settlement of the crisis. By the eighth, when he first participated in a meeting with the Central Council, he and his colleagues had succeeded in persuading the revolutionaries to moderate their position sub-stantially. Whereas on the sixth, they had insisted upon maintaining control of the newspaper offices until negotiations with the government had been satisfactorily completed, they now were prepared to free all except the *Vorwärts* building as soon as the Cabinet agreed to enter into substantive negotiations. They were, moreover, willing to assure the government that the *Vorwärts* building would also be released as part of any settlement of their grievances.[17] It was obvious that the movement was rapidly losing its momentum.

The government had insisted on the sixth that full freedom of the press be restored before any substantive negotiations would be initiated. Haase pointed out to the Central Council members on the eighth, however, that the long-standing dispute over the ownership of *Vorwärts* placed it in a special category. He repeatedly emphasized during this meeting the extreme serious-ness of the situation. Everyone involved in the negotiations, he declared, was obligated to do everything possible to prevent bloodshed. The parties to the dispute should agree to enter negotiations without setting prior conditions. After so much had already been achieved, it would be inexcusable for the government to refuse to negotiate until the *Vorwärts* building was also freed. The central task at hand was to prevent a bloody civil war within the Berlin proletariat.[18]

The spokesmen of the Central Council, however, remained unmoved by the pleas of Haase and his friends. They questioned, with some justification, the ability of the mediators to enforce an agreement to vacate any buildings held by the Communists. But the ability of the Independent leaders to fulfill their commitments proved to be only a secondary issue, for the Central Council remained adamant in its insistence upon the reestablishment of complete freedom of the press before entering into any substantive negoti-ations.[19] That night, the mediators issued a statement charging that their efforts had been frustrated by the intransigence of the government.[20]

In the meantime, the situation of the rebels continued to deteriorate. Despite the Cabinet's promise on the sixth to refrain from aggressive acts, loyalist troops recaptured a number of weakly defended rebel outposts. On the eighth, the government published an extremely threatening manifesto, urging the populace of the capital to have patience and promising that before long force would be met with force.[21]

Desperately trying to prevent a major clash, Haase and his colleagues now sought to encourage a mass movement for proletarian unity, which, they hoped, would succeed in overwhelming the resistance of the majority socialist leaders. As the week progressed, *Freiheit* published enthusiastic reports of a growing stream of resolutions passed by workers of every party in their factories. The resolutions, probably stemming in large part from a conscious campaign by the U.S.P.D.,[22] condemned the policies of the Cabinet which had brought the working class to the verge of a bloody civil war. They demanded that the unity of the proletariat be restored, even if their nominal leaders had to be sacrificed in the process.[23]

The most important immediate consequence of this campaign was the creation of an interparty mediation committee made up of workers from the giant Schwarzhoff works. With the aid of the U.S.P.D. national leaders, this committee was able to obtain the agreement of both the Berlin Independent leaders and the Revolutionary Shop Stewards to a declaration, which, to some observers at least, appeared to represent a complete capitulation to the government.[24] In it the two most powerful of the rebellious groups proposed that a truce be established and promised that the Vorwärts building would be freed in advance of negotiations if the mediation committee received assurances that these negotiations would be conducted in a conciliatory spirit, if the government would agree to submit disputed points to a commission chosen on the basis of parity, and if they were assured that the new head of the Berlin police would be someone who was acceptable to the U.S.P.D.[25]

By this time it seems probable that the government was merely using these discussions with the rebels to gain time until it had gathered sufficient strength to crush the revolt by force.[26] In fact, constant pressure was being put on Noske to bring his troops into the capital at the earliest possible moment.[27] Whatever their intentions, the government leaders apparently avoided this new proposal until the early afternoon of January 11, by which time the Vorwärts building had been successfully stormed and Noske had entered Berlin at the head of the first contingent of his loyalist troops.

The meeting which took place on the eleventh between the Central Council and a mixed group of mediators[28] was a strange affair. While the Central Council members were aware that the Vorwärts building had been taken,[29] the mediators apparently were not. Thus Haase, who acted as the principal spokesman of the delegation, reiterated the assurance of the Shop Stewards and the Berlin Independents that the building would be vacated, while the spokesmen of the Central Council continued to insist that it be freed before any negotiations, even regarding the establishment of a truce, be initiated.[30] Haase's evident frustration at the complete intransigence of the government would undoubtedly have been compounded if he had known that the rebel garrison of the building had already been led off to imprisonment.

After the Vorwärts building had been recaptured and Noske's troops had begun their entry into Berlin, the position of the rebels was militarily hopeless. During the next several days, one building after another was assaulted and many of the most active revolutionaries were either killed or imprisoned.

Tragically, both Luxemburg and Liebknecht were among those who were brutally murdered by the forces unleashed by the majority socialist leadership. The dispute which Haase and his colleagues had tried to resolve through negotiations had thus for all practical purposes been settled by brute force.

Politically, however, the position of the government was by no means as secure as its military successes seemed to indicate. Throughout the so-called "Spartacus Week," resistance had been rising within the S.P.D. to the policy pursued by its leaders. This was reflected both by the occasional dissident voices raised within the Central Council and by the mass meetings of factory workers in which members of all of the parties had voiced their dissatisfaction with the policies of the government. Encouraged by these signs of dissension among the majority socialists, Haase and his Independent colleagues decided to continue their campaign for a grass roots movement which would go "over the heads" of the old party's leaders.

On January 12 *Freiheit* editorialized that the actions of the majority socialist leaders had destroyed the last remnant of trust they might have enjoyed among the Berlin workers. They had gained merely a Pyrrhic victory. The struggle would now become one in which the entire proletariat would be aligned against the government.[31] On the same day, Haase addressed a large U.S.P.D. meeting in Berlin in much the same terms. Scarcely two months after the victorious revolution, he declared, Germany found herself in the grip of a counter-revolution. Those who plunged Germany into a disastrous war now dared once again to raise their heads. The growing forces of counter-revolution had been nurtured by Ebert, Scheidemann and Landsberg. The national leaders of the U.S.P.D. had sought to bring about a peaceful resolution of the crisis which had gripped the capital during the previous week. One concession after another had been granted, but the government had rejected all negotiations. The result had been the terrible bloodbath which was still going on about them. This disaster could have been prevented, but it was not because the government had frivolously decided that it wanted to make a show of force. The Cabinet was dominated by the old authoritarian spirit, the spirit of Hindenburg and Ludendorff. It was for this reason that the workers were demanding the resignation of Ebert, Scheidemann, Landsberg and Noske. Many of the majority socialists also condemned the policy of their leaders. The main obstacle to unity was, therefore, the leaders. The workers must act over their heads. This was the demand which had been made in almost every factory. He himself, he added, would be happy to step down if it were shown that he represented such an obstacle.

Haase went on to urge that a unified social democratic party be created. This should not be mere foggy amalgamation of the old organizations, but a truly new party that was capable of uniting the workers on the basis of a program of international revolutionary socialism. He cautioned his audience, however, that along with the opportunism of the majority socialist leadership, they must also reject the methods of the Communists. Germany could not follow the path of Russia. The dictatorship of the proletariat could not be established by the exercise of brutal force by a single small group. The German workers must gain control by making use of the immense political and economic power which would be available to them once the proletariat had been united. Only thus could the German movement become what it once had been, the leader of the international proletariat.[32]

A few days later, the Independents carried their unity campaign into the Central Council itself, apparently in the hope that their agitation had eroded the support enjoyed by the Cabinet in that body. On January 13 and 14 a deputation of Berlin Independents confronted the council with a series of conditions on the basis of which, they declared, their party was prepared to consider establishing a new coalition with the majority socialists.[33] One of their demands, the appointment of a Berlin police director acceptable to the U.S.P.D., had been made in the course of the discussions of the previous week. The others, however, went far beyond the immediate issues raised by the local conflict. Most importantly, they insisted upon nothing less than the replacement of the current Cabinet members with men who had not been "compromised" and the immediate execution of the directives of the National Congress of Councils.[34]

Haase joined the debate on these proposals on the fifteenth, when he acted as the principal spokesman of the Independents. In the course of a wide-ranging discussion, he replied to majority socialist accusations that the U.S.P.D. was in fundamental agreement with the Communists by asserting that every true socialist must agree with the theoretical goal of Bolshevism which was, in fact, nothing less than the establishment of socialism. He pointed out, however, that the Independents rejected the tactics of the Spartacists which were unsuited to German conditions. He agreed with the Central Council that a socialist government was obligated to maintain order, but he insisted that this must be accomplished with the aid of sincere supporters of the regime rather than by turning to Hindenburg and his cohorts. He described the "unheard of" excesses of the government troops and repeatedly asked what the Central Council intended to do to put a stop to them. He maintained that the agitation among the proletariat would continue until the workers were convinced that action was being taken to carry out the directives of the National Congress of Councils. If they could agree that independent proletarian policies must be pursued, he argued, then general guidelines could immediately be established on the basis of the Erfurt Program.[35]

Although some of the Central Council members were apparently not unsympathetic to Haase's arguments,[36] his efforts to appeal over the heads of the majority socialist leaders in the Cabinet were doomed to failure by the government's success in restoring order in the capital, by the relative strength of the S.P.D. as reflected in the National Assembly elections and by the still effective force of party discipline. The meeting on the fifteenth ended with Central Council's agreement to Haase's suggestion that the Independents should draw up a practical program for action to serve as the basis for possible cooperation.[37] When, on January 29, the council finally discussed the program proposed by the Independents, however, they concluded that any further negotiations should be conducted directly between the two socialist parties.[38]

As Haase had feared,[39] the strength of the majority socialist leaders was dramatically confirmed by the elections which took place on January 19. The S.P.D. received more than eleven million votes and 165 seats in the constituent assembly. The Independents, on the other hand, were able to garner only some two million votes and twenty-two seats. The two Social Democratic parties received together only forty-seven per cent of the vote, thus ruling out the establishment of a new socialist coalition capable of dominating the constituent assembly.

Even if they had received a majority, however, the S.P.D. and the U.S.P.D. would in all probability have been unable to cooperate, for the events of "Spartacus Week" had effectively destroyed the few remaining bridges between the two parties.[40] Certainly Haase was little inclined to work with Ebert, Scheidemann and Noske once they had called in *"Soldateska"* to put down the revolt in Berlin. Writing to Else Brill a few days after the election, he even expressed his extreme misgivings at the prospect of having to meet with the majority socialist leaders during a forthcoming international conference in Bern.[42] And if Haase was unprepared to seek a reconciliation with his former colleagues, this was still more the case for an increasingly large proportion of his fellow Independents, for a second result of the government's repressive measures was to encourage a flood of radical new recruits into the U.S.P.D. These new members tended to be relatively young and politically inexperienced, and a majority gravitated toward the extreme left wing of the party.

The events of "Spartacus Week" thus led both to a further exacerbation of the differences within the German proletariat and to the rapid growth of the U.S.P.D. The hopes of many moderates in both parties that the departure of the Spartacists would lead to a rapprochement had been dashed. From Haase's point of view the only course of action now possible was to attempt to build up the U.S.P.D. to a point where it could successfully reunite the workers under its own banner. Despite the secession of the Communists, however, the party remained seriously weakened by internal divisions. The massive influx of new members and the government's increasing persecution of the left led to a new resurgence of extreme radical sentiment which coalesced around the old demand for the establishment of a councilar republic.

Haase was himself not unmoved by a feeling of loyalty to the councils. He was too realistic, however, to abandon, as the radicals demanded, any attempt to use the institutions of parliamentary democracy to further the interests of the working class. He thus found himself again in the position of having to placate the radicals in his party while at the same time he sought to keep the U.S.P.D.'s policy relevant to the actual political situation in Germany.

The debate on this issue reached its first peak during the long-awaited national congress which met in Berlin early in March. The congress, which had long been demanded by the radicals, met under conditions which were little suited to calm and sensible discussion. The wave of strikes and civil disturbances which had rolled through the industrialized areas of the Reich since January flowed back into Berlin on the second day of the meeting.[43] Once again Noske called in his *Freikorps*, and after bloody fighting order was finally restored, but not until long after the congress was concluded. Under these circumstances, it is perhaps remarkable that the Independent delegates were able to achieve anything at all. On the other hand, the dramatic struggle in the capital undoubtedly contributed to the sense of urgency which dominated the convention proceedings.

Haase was an extremely active participant in this, his last national congress. He spoke repeatedly and with passion to the many issues facing the party and on numerous occasions hurled interjections from the floor when others were speaking. His aggressiveness can undoubtedly to some extent be traced to the extreme tension which pervaded the capital at the time. Perhaps equally important was the fact that he was time and again compelled to rise to defend the actions of himself and his colleagues in the party leadership against the often very personal attacks of the radicals.

On the whole, however, Haase's mood does not appear to have been negative or defensive. On the contrary, his speeches reflected an apparently genuine confidence in the future of both the party and the revolution. His greatest concern was, therefore, not to reiterate the by now rather worn arguments about what had happened in the past, but rather to forge a clear program upon the basis of which the party could play the crucial role he envisioned for it.

Haase's principal opponent at the congress was Ernst Däumig, who had resigned from the executive committee of the party shortly before it convened. Däumig had successfully mobilized radical support for a dogmatic and exclusive endorsement of the conciliar system of government. He insisted that the party categorically reject parliamentary democracy. Any compromise on this issue would, he feared, provide a loophole for those who were "merely" radicals and not true revolutionaries. At most, he wanted Independent deputies to use their mandates to obtain a public hearing for the party's point of view.[44]

Haase shared much of Däumig's disillusionment with the parliamentary system, but he refused to abandon what he considered to be a most useful instrument for achieving positive gains for the working class. Parliaments were a necessary feature of a bourgeois society, he argued, and the party would be ignoring reality if it refused to make the fullest possible use of such institutions. He did not, of course, deny the importance of the councils. Indeed, he declared that they were the most important creation of the revolution. He therefore included in the program he proposed to the congress a demand that the conciliar system be expanded, that the councils be given extensive political as well as economic power and that they be securely anchored in the constitution of the Reich. Haase's position on this issue was not simply an attempt to still dissension within the U.S.P.D. through compromise. A careful reading of his statements on this and other occasions indicates that he sincerely believed that such a mixed system of government was a practical possibility at least on a temporary basis until the proletariat could be effectively mobilized to complete the revolution.[45]

The programmatic manifesto which emerged from the convention debate essentially followed the lines laid down in Haase's draft. To be sure, it included a flat declaration that the party endorsed the conciliar system, but it also explicitly sanctioned the use of parliamentary institutions in the struggle for Social Democracy. The program was passed against a minority of just eight votes despite Däumig's refusal to support it.[46] In addition to the key statement on the issue of councils, it included the standard Independent demands for the dissolution of the old military establishment as well as the *Freikorps*, the immediate initiation of socialization and the establishment of friendly relations with all countries. At Haase's insistence and over Däumig's objections, the manifesto also included a commitment to the theoretical section of the Erfurt Program.[47]

Despite its radical tone, therefore, the party's new program must be considered a clear victory for Haase. The election of co-chairmen which took place soon after the program was passed seemed at first to clearly confirm Haase's predominance, for he received 154 votes to Däumig's 109. Haase's reaction to this apparent vote of confidence, however, threw the assembled delegates into a state of utter confusion. Arguing that Däumig's views diverged too radically from his own to allow them to work together successfully, he refused to accept his election.[48] This move was wholly unexpected, even by Haase's closest associates.[49] For a time it appeared that the convention would accept Haase's decision. It soon became apparent, however, that many of those who had voted for Däumig had done so only with the understanding that his radicalism would be balanced off by Haase's moderation. After a long debate followed by a brief intermission, Däumig freed the delegates from their dilemma by declaring that he had changed his mind and would now refuse to accept election. A new election was then held, and the Württemberg radical, Arthur Crispien, was elected to share the party chairmanship with Haase.[50]

It is impossible to determine whether Haase really expected to give up his position in the party leadership when he threw his bombshell into the convention. Whatever his intentions, however, the end result clearly was another important victory for Haase. Not only had Däumig been compelled to retreat from the formal leadership of the party, but Crispien, as Haase predicted when asked whether the Württemberger would be acceptable to him, soon abandoned his apparent extreme radicalism and became a loyal and cooperative partner.[51]

Several weeks before the party congress opened in Berlin, the National Assembly had convened in Weimar, purposely isolated from the radicalism of the capital. Haase entered the assembly at the head of a delegation not significantly larger than that which he had headed in the old Reichstag. But it was not merely the size of his delegation which reminded him of his pre-revolutionary experience. Writing to a friend on February 17, he remarked that the assembly was dominated by both the same faces and the same way of thinking that had characterized the old Reichstag. The S.P.D., which had formed a coalition government with the Center and Democratic parties, was pursuing a policy that tended to strengthen both the clerical and the bourgeois elements by welding them together. The majority socialists clearly were convinced that the revolution was over, while in Haase's own opinion, it was simply a question of when its second phase would begin.[52]

Under the circumstances, the Independent delegation had little opportunity to play a constructive legislative role. The criticism which Haase and his colleagues frequently and vehemently levelled against the government was often received with derisive laughter or rude interjections reminiscent of the old Reichstag's reaction to Liebknecht and Rühle. The painful division in the ranks of German Social Democracy was all too clearly reflected in the assembly debates. The majority socialist spokesmen consistently sought to lessen the effect of the Independents' criticism by associating them with the Communists while the Independents did not hesitate to accuse their former colleagues of having sold out to the bourgeoisie.

Despite the difficulty of his position, however, Haase was able to make a significant positive contribution to the solution of the most immediate problem facing the National Assembly, the conclusion of a formal peace treaty with the allies. The first reaction of the government to the terms which were presented to the German delegation on May 7 was one of defiance. Several weeks earlier Haase had labelled the proposal that Germany refuse to sign as foolishness, and now he embarked on a vigorous campaign for ratification.[53] Addressing the National Assembly on May 12, Philip Scheidemann declared amidst stormy applause that his government considered the proposed treaty unacceptable. Speaker after speaker endorsed this position. The Independents alone were courageous enough to point out the absurdity of Scheidemann's point of view. Speaking for his colleagues, but also as an East Prussian who despite his fervent internationalism was still moved by feelings of loyalty and nostalgia for his native province which the allies proposed to sever from the main body of Germany, Haase sharply condemned the terms of the treaty. He added, however, that frivolous gestures of defiance would only lead to the imposition of still more draconic conditions. He emphasized that the workers would not again, as in 1914, be misled by nationalist frenzy. In any case, he predicted, the terms of the treaty would not be permanent. The victorious progress of the world revolution would before long make just as short shrift of the Peace of Versailles as it had of the Peace of Brest Litovsk.[54]

The campaign which Haase and his colleagues engaged in during the next several weeks helped to prevent a disastrous new outbreak of hostilities and to prepare the way for the eventual signing of the treaty. Certainly this was Haase's view.[55] The extraordinary confusion which reigned in the other parties even led to proposals that the Independents be empowered to sign the treaty.[56] Finally, under the pressure of an allied ultimatum, a new Center-S.P.D. coalition cabinet was formed which appealed to the National Assembly on June 22 for permission to sign. The new government, however, still hoped to gain concessions from the allies concerning the war guilt and war criminal clauses of the treaty. Haase once again pleaded for a realistic recognition of the fact that the allies were not prepared to make such concessions.[57] On the following day, when Haase's prediction proved completely accurate, the assembly agreed to unconditional acceptance of the peace.

During the summer Haase continued to use his position in the assembly to wage a vigorous campaign against the policies of the government. As usual, he was at the time personally involved in defending a considerable number of radicals who were being prosecuted by the government,[58] and his attacks upon Noske's repressive policies were thus particularly vehement in tone. He dealt with many other topics as well, however. He rejected the timid initiatives of the government in the direction of socialization as tending in fact to strengthen the capitalist system. He urged the government to finally establish normal relations with the Russian regime and sought to expose the machinations of the *Freikorps* in the Baltic as a particularly shameful and dangerous manifestation of the counter-revolutionary spirit which was making such rapid strides in Germany.[59]

Haase's experience in the National Assembly during this period must have been particularly frustrating in view of the continued growth of his party. The majority socialists' endorsement of Noske's repression of the radicals, combined with their obvious timidity in dealing with the forces of reaction, kept the flood of new members into the U.S.P.D. from ebbing. Yet this new strength could not be reflected in the parliament until new elections were held, and despite Haase's protest that the National Assembly had outlived its mandate,[60] there was little prospect of a new appeal being made to the electorate before the following year.

Moreover, the growing confidence and numerical strength of the U.S.P.D. did little to ease the tensions which continued to mount within the party. Despite his victory in March, Haase was faced with a constant struggle against the radicals. His letters indicate that he strongly sympathized with those who wanted to initiate immediate and forceful action against the "wave of reaction," but that he feared the consequences if the workers should allow themselves to be provoked into acting prematurely.[61] He defended his views in a major speech at a national party conference held in Berlin on September 9–10. He decried the efforts of some radicals to commit the party to a revolutionary upheaval in the immediate future. They must not put all of their eggs into one basket, he declared, but rather remain flexible, employing whatever means were appropriate at a given moment.[62] Although the conference was not empowered to pass resolutions, the discussion which followed Haase's speech and that of his principal opponent on this occasion, Kurt Geyer, appeared to indicate that a large majority still endorsed the point of view of their chairman.[63]

A new and more crucial test of strength was set for November when a national congress of the U.S.P.D. was scheduled to convene. But Haase was not destined to participate. On October 8, as he approached the Reichstag building where he planned to deliver a new exposé of rightist activities in the Baltic, he was shot down by a mentally disturbed worker. At first his wounds did not appear to be particularly dangerous, and he continued his political activity for a time from his sick-bed. Before long, however, complications set in, and on November 7 he died. His murderer was declared legally insane and consigned to an asylum.

Haase's death came as a severe shock to many Social Democrats. Tens of thousands of workers joined the funeral procession which carried his ashes to the cemetery in Friedrichfeld where they were laid to rest next to the grave of Wilhelm Liebknecht.[64] Messages of condolence streamed into party headquarters from organizations and individuals throughout the Reich as well as from many foreign countries.[65] In addition to the sense of personal loss which was felt by many of his colleagues and friends, there was widespread recognition that Haase's death came at an extremely critical point in the development of the party he had helped to found. At the congress which met a few weeks after Haase's death, Dittmann reported that the party's membership had increased from three hundred thousand to seven hundred fifty thousand and the number of Independent newspapers had doubled since March.[66] This massive growth continued during 1920. The party reached the peak of its numerical strength that summer when it polled nearly five million votes in the election of a new Reichstag. In contrast, the majority socialists at that time found their electoral support reduced to slightly more than five and one half million votes, and not a few observers predicted that the German proletariat was about to be reunited under the banner of the U.S.P.D.[67]

Despite these impressive achievements, however, Haase's party was already stricken at the time of his death with what would prove to be a fatal affliction. The course of the congress which met in Leipzig at the end of November 1919 made it clear that the internal tensions which had been so evident in March continued to threaten the very existence of the party. To be sure, a new program was passed unanimously which appeared to reflect a willingness on the part of the moderates to make significant concessions to the left wing.[68] But when the delegates turned their attention to what was rapidly becoming the most divisive issue facing the U.S.P.D., its relationship to the badly splintered international socialist movement, a fragile compromise was the best that could be achieved. After a stormy and at times ugly debate, the delegates resolved to make a final and complete break with the Second International and to take steps toward the creation of a new revolutionary organization to replace it.[69] The strident demands of the left wing for an immediate affiliation with the Russian-dominated Third International were thus momentarily stilled. But the issue remained a festering sore in the side of the party during the following months.

Shortly after the U.S.P.D.'s startling success in the Reichstag elections of 1920, a delegation of party leaders journeyed to Moscow to investigate the possibility of cooperating with the Russians. They returned bearing a list of twenty-one conditions which in effect stipulated that the U.S.P.D. had to expel those leaders who had been most closely associated with Haase and accept Russian dictation before it would be permitted to join the Communist International. A vicious struggle erupted during the summer and early autumn concerning the party's reaction to the Russian demands. Energetically supported by the Russians and by the K.P.D., the left wing was able to gain a majority at the October convention. The party thereupon split. A large part of the membership went over to the K.P.D., thus making it a truly mass party for the first time. Most of the members of the smaller group which remained within the U.S.P.D. finally returned to the S.P.D. after several years of frustrating political isolation.[70]

CHAPTER XIV
THE GERMAN JAURÈS

Hugo Haase exemplified many of the most attractive features of the pre-war German socialist movement. In his firm commitment to democracy he reflected the orthodox Marxists' confidence that eventually the vast majority of the population would inevitably come to share the socialists' world view. In his passionate devotion to the rectification of injustice, reinforced as it was by his own training and experience, he served as a classic example of the traditional sympathy of Social Democrats for the downtrodden and oppressed. In his commitment to rational discourse and his belief that reasonable men could create a truly good society he reflected the optimistic view of human nature that the socialist movement had inherited from the Enlightenment. In his acceptance of the ultimate necessity of revolution he shared the widespread expectation among German Social Democrats that when the appropriate time had finally come, the transfer of power could be accomplished with a minimum of pain and bloodshed. Finally, in his consistent rejection of chauvinistic nationalism, he served as one of the most effective spokesmen for the Social Democratic vision of a world in which the individual would owe his first loyalty to humanity rather than to the state.

While Haase thus exemplified many of the virtues of the movement he led, it is also true that he was bedeviled by many of its most fundamental weaknesses. Indeed, surveying his career as a whole, it would appear that it was beset, particularly in its later stages, by an overriding element of tragedy. The party he had been chosen to lead turned against him when it faced the most important crisis in its history. Having helped to divide that party in an effort to defend what he believed to be its traditional principles, he joined in creating a new party, only to discover once again that many of those who had chosen him as their leader interpreted these principles very differently than he himself did.

The revolution which Haase helped to foment appeared to give him a new opportunity to put his principles into practice. But, lacking the full and effective support of his own party and confronting men who shared few of his scruples, his accomplishments as a governmental leader were largely negative in character and to a considerable degree were obliterated by the rising tide of reaction which swept him out of power.

Carried still further to the left by the rush of events, Haase was in no position to create the kind of aggressive revolutionary force which might conceivably have checked the process of erosion that was already threatening the existence of the young republic. Even as it approached its greatest popular success the U.S.P.D. was so rent by internal discord that it was in no position to take advantage of its opponents' many tactical blunders. And within less than a year after Haase's death, the party whose creation must be considered his most significant concrete achievement entered its death throes. At that time the majority of Independents broke off and joined a movement which rejected even more emphatically than the S.P.D. the principles Haase had spent his life trying to uphold.

One question that immediately arises is whether Haase could have prevented the division and eventual demise of the U.S.P.D. had he lived. He was certainly the most widely respected of the party's leaders at the time of his death. His presence would therefore have undoubtedly increased the strength of the moderate wing of the U.S.P.D. Yet his friends pursued a policy which was entirely consistent with that which Haase had advocated,[1] and it is difficult to imagine how his prestige alone could have significantly altered the ultimate outcome.

Indeed, it would appear that, however unfortunate in a personal sense, Haase's death did not come at an inappropriate moment when viewed in the context of his entire career. Throughout his political life he had based his policies upon the Erfurt Program of 1891. That program now seemed to have lost its relevance, or at least its attractive power. It was just a few weeks after Haase's death that the party he had founded in order to uphold the principles embodied in the Erfurt Program officially abandoned it.[2] A few months later the German Social Democratic movement irretrievably split into two parts, both of which had moved beyond the centrist orientation which had dominated it during the period of Haase's rise to political prominence. The Communists looked to the Soviet Union for leadership while the majority socialists had in fact, if not as yet completely in theory, endorsed the revisionist point of view which had been decisively rejected by the party leadership before the war. Haase had consistently struggled against both of these tendencies. For a time he had appeared successful, but in the end the rapidly accelerating flood of events had proved too powerful. War, revolution and counterrevolution had made his backward-looking Marxist centrism an anachronism.

It would be possible to argue that Haase's failure to build a party capable of leading Germany into democratic socialism can to some degree be explained in terms of certain of his personality traits. Despite its attractiveness from a personal point of view, his essential modesty certainly made it more difficult for him to confront the aggressive self-confidence of a Scheidemann or an Ebert. Throughout his career he had been drawn into leadership roles almost against his will and had not been reluctant to abandon them when he could do so with a clear conscience. Moreover, his ingrained cautiousness made him hesitant to commit himself to any action until its full implications could be clearly perceived. He was frequently reluctant to make the daring gamble, especially when the fate of others was involved. More often than not, of course, his judgments appeared to have been justified by subsequent events, but because they so often involved a certain pessimism concerning his own chances of success, they may have led him at times to respond with less vigor than circumstances warranted.

Another personally attractive aspect of Haase's character which contributed on a number of occasions to his political difficulties was his profound commitment to certain ethical principles. His Marxism, though genuine and consistently held, was shot through with a Kantian spirit that may have limited his ability to act decisively in some crisis situations. It was not without justification that Maximilian Harden labeled him a "Jewish Christian socialist."[3] Although he was not a theoretical pacifist, he abhorred violence and was extremely reluctant to authorize its use even against his most dangerous enemies. Moreover, although he often theoretically endorsed the creation of a dictatorship of the proletariat, his interpretation of this term was so tempered by his commitment to democracy and his essential humanitarianism that it remained largely meaningless in the context of post-war Germany. Even if he had been in a position to exercise dictatorial power after the revolution, it is unlikely that Haase would have been willing to crush the sworn enemies of socialism who remained so numerous and so powerful. Haase's personality was, therefore, far better suited to opposition than to the exercise of governmental power, at least under the circumstances that prevailed in 1918 and 1919, and it was as German Social Democracy's most articulate opponent of the war that he felt most at ease and achieved his greatest successes.

In the last analysis, however, it would appear that these personal traits had far less to do with the fate of Haase's political activities than the conditions under which he worked. In the specific context of the German Social Democratic movement, he possessed the most important prerequisites for successful centrist leadership. Unfortunately, he was drawn into the leadership of the S.P.D. just as the centrist position was losing its viability. Even before the war Haase's abilities as a conciliator had been severely tried by the rapidly mounting factional strife within the party. The war had merely accelerated a process that was already well developed while simultaneously placing Haase in the position of having to defend the party's traditional principles against the vast majority of his colleagues.

The end of the war did not, as Kautsky and many others maintained, eliminate the basic cause of the differences which had developed between the U.S.P.D and the old party. Haase continued to defend the program of 1891 against those who were convinced that the events of 1914 or 1917 had made that program basically irrelevant. It was this tripartite division of the Social Democratic movement that doomed Haase's work to failure after the war. To be sure, his adherence to the pre-war dream of a truly socialist and truly democratic Germany contributed to this fateful division, but it seems unlikely that a willingness on his part to abandon his principles would have led ultimately to a more desirable outcome.

In an article published at the time of Haase's death, Kautsky aptly compared his friend's character and career with that of Jaurès.[4] Despite their differences in temperament and situation, the French and the German leader shared the same vision of a world in which every individual would have the opportunity to develop himself freely to his fullest potential and in which war would be consigned permanently to the rubbish heap of history. Partly as a result of the persistence with which they pursued this vision, they both died tragically at the hand of the assassin. Haase's fate was, however, in some ways still more tragic than that of Jaurès, for he lived on into the era of war and revolution and by the time of his death cannot but have sensed that the ideals that had guided his life work belonged to an age which had passed irretrievably from the scene.

APPENDIX

Dr. Walter Friedlander, who served as a member of the Berlin city council during the Weimar Republic and was later Professor of Social Welfare at the University of California in Berkeley, was kind enough not only to write a brief account of his memories of his uncle, but also to ask two of his friends, Dr. Ernest Hamburger (New York) and Dr. Peter Fleischmann (Professor of Medicine at the University of Haifa), who also knew Hugo Haase well, to do the same. These accounts are included in this appendix in an effort to provide a clearer and fuller picture of the personal side of Haase's character.

DR. ERNEST HAMBURGER

My wife and I came to know Hugo Haase when we were students at the university through his son, Ernst Haase, whom we had met in the "Academic Courses for Workingmen." In these courses, students taught manual laborers spelling, grammar, and literature. It was an encounter of young people in academic life with workingmen, which was quite unusual in Germany at that time. Benedikt Kautsky, the son of Karl Kautsky, also took part in these courses. We soon became friends with him and with Ernst Haase; both were somewhat younger than I. Through this friendship, we also became guests in the homes of Haase and Kautsky. Teaching these courses brought together a number of students who, though not yet members of the Social Democratic Party, were imbued with the ideas of the liberal left. Many of them were Jews. This is easily explained by the fact that a great number of non-Jewish students at that time—before 1914—belonged to various pan-German, nationalist, and anti-Semitic organizations, or were at least leaning toward these organizations.

My first impressions in Haase's home were of the close family life and Haase's lively interest in young people. He had a way with them. We never felt that he was talking down to us from a position of superiority, and so he never embarrassed us. We felt at home with him and his family and talked to him without a trace of timidity. This personal rapport with young people was also obvious in his party work. In the course of these casual meetings it was suggested that we should meet regularly, either at Haase's house or at Kautsky's, to discuss problems of socialism. We met about every other week in Haase's or Kautsky's house, but gave up the meetings at Kautsky's when Rudolf Hilferding pointed out that Kautsky, as an Austrian, was under police surveillance and always in danger of being expelled. From then on, we always met at Haase's. Hilferding attended almost all of our meetings; Kautsky as often as his time permitted.

Haase had a very special way of chairing these meetings almost unnoticeably. Usually one of us gave a short report, in which a connection was established between a subject of his special field of knowledge and socialist theories of the past or present. These meetings were a great experience for all of us. The elegant way in which Haase always kept the discussion to essentials impressed us greatly. In the course of these meetings friendships were formed that lasted a lifetime. Many of us became active socialists who played their part during the Weimar Republic. Not all of us followed in Haase's footsteps, especially in regard to his attitude during the war and in the short time left to him after it. But all believed to act in his spirit and even after his death felt bound to him in reverence, gratitude, and affection. Among these people were: Georg Flatow who, during the revolution, was the secretary of Rudolf Wissell, later *Ministerialrat* in the Prussian Ministry of Commerce and author of the best known commentary on the *Betriebsrätegesetz* (shop stewards law); Fritz Wittelshoefer, *Ministerialrat* in the Prussian Ministry of Public Welfare, and a specialist in this field; Hans Hirschfeld, Press Secretary in the Prussian Ministry of the Interior under Carl Severing as well as under Albert Grzesinski and, after the Second World War, Press Secretary in the Senate of Berlin under three governing mayors: Ernst Reuter, Otto Suhr, and Willy Brandt. Hilde Oppenheimer was also a member of this group; she did excellent work at the Reich Ministry of Labor and was one of the first women to receive the title *Regierungsrat*.

In my activities as a member of the Prussian Diet, as well as later, after I had emigrated to the United States, in the Division of Human Rights at the United Nations Secretariat, I often thought of Hugo Haase and of his ideas that were so deeply rooted in humanism.

I well remember Haase's speeches in the Reichstag, which I attended often, thanks to the tickets provided by his son. Haase always spoke clearly and more freely than most delegates. Contrary to most of them, he spoke from notes, never from a carefully prepared text. It has been said that Haase's voice was somewhat rough and hoarse, especially toward the end of a long speech. This may have been true during mass meetings in smoke-filled halls, when the speaker—in those days before the use of loudspeakers—had to shout to be heard. I never noticed it in Parliament. Haase spoke impressively and with characteristic honesty. A certain nervousness was noticeable in the way he played with the chain of his watch. He always commanded everyone's attention. And he became especially animated when dealing with such topics as peace, foreign policy, the fight against the reactionary tendencies of the

German bourgeoisie in comparison with England or France, and the customs of the duelling fraternities.

At our meetings at Haase's house we came into contact with many socialists of the older generation—contacts that were very important for our future development. Kautsky did not have those educational gifts that were natural to Haase. We respected Kautsky as a great scholar, but we did not feel personally close to him. One of his co-editors at the *Neue Zeit*, Emanuel Wurm, who was a member of the Reichstag, occasionally attended our gatherings. He was open-minded and courteous, and we learned much from him. Gustav Eckstein, also associated with the *Neue Zeit*, joined us from time to time. He was a somewhat younger scholar and socialist, a man between two generations. Occasionally some Russian socialists were also present. I vividly remember Rjasanoff, who seemed to us the prototype of a revolutionary. He presented his ideas in halting German, encouraged by Haase, whose benevolent manner was equally successful in establishing confidence and personal relationships with older people and those of his own generation.

With a heavy heart I recall the fate that befell the people of this fine group: assassinated, murdered in camps, forced to emigrate; only very few died of natural causes. Most of the Russians were "liquidated" by Stalin. At that time, however, inspired by Haase's positive outlook on life and the future, we were all optimists, looking forward to a fruitful life and work in the service of humanity. None of us suspected anything of the horrors awaiting us.

PROFESSOR DR. PETER FLEISCHMANN

The personality of people in the public limelight often appears in an entirely different light in the eyes of their close family and circle of friends. A proponent of good like Leo Tolstoy was, in the eyes of his wife, a terrible egotist. In the description by one of his grandchildren, Kaiser Wilhelm II sounded like a benevolent grandfather instead of a man harshly judged by history.

I was too young to be able to judge Hugo Haase the politician, since I was only fourteen years old when World War I broke out and separated my family in Kiev from contact with Germany. Until then my family was in constant intimate contact with Haase's family. For my parents he was one of the closest friends of a shared youth. For me he was always the beloved "Uncle Hugo." Even so, I knew that he played an important role in world politics, for he once took me along to an executive committee meeting of the Social Democratic Party so that I could, as he smilingly told me, learn to know "men of influence." And on a walk through the Berlin Tiergarten we met an elegant gentleman, and Uncle Hugo asked me in an amused tone whether I was aware that we had just been greeted by the Prussian War Minster. So I was aware from an early age that there were two personalities contained in Hugo Haase: I knew that he was the feared fighter in the arena of politics and jurisprudence, while at home he was careful never to hurt the feelings of family or friends. In his home I learned reverence for classical and modern art and for philosophy. The philosophy of Marx, Kant and Hegel were an integral part of daily life in his household. Even at the table conversation was never wasted on irrelevant or idle subjects.

I was not able to diagnose the split in Hugo Haase's personality until my mature years. His intellectual acceptance of the necessity for a radical, ruthless battle for the furthering of social progress, and his emotional tendency to spare each individual pain, were not always reconcilable. This division caused him great sorrow on those occasions when friends turned into enemies, and he bore this sorrow only in the realization that he had to follow his designated path as he deemed right.

This insight did not come to me on the basis of the observation of a fourteen year old boy, but came as a result of later conversations with my parents and close friends. However, once I personally experienced Haase's despairing inner conflict while making a decision in one of the most severe crises of his life. A few days before the outbreak of the First World War I was a guest in his house. He spoke with me as with the grown-ups, and, young as I was, I recognized the severe dilemma which fate had placed before him.

It was on that occasion and from his mouth that I heard the term "chauvinism" for the first time. He knew that a victory for Imperial Germany would mean a step backward for western politics. But he shrank from the alternative of a capitulation of Germany and particularly of East Prussia before the hordes of czarist occupation and foresaw the dangers of a pauperization of the populace and the nameless personal tragedies in the lives of individuals. While we stood at the window and looked down at the street through which the hysterical chauvinist groups paraded, he explained both aspects to me and weighed them against each other. The question arises whether this ability to empathize and not only to make cool detached decisions cost him the "hero's role" in history.

DR. WALTER FRIEDLANDER

Hugo Haase was my godfather, his wife, Thea née Lichtenstein, the youngest sister of my mother. Since my early childhood both were my most beloved relatives. As a member of the Reichstag, Uncle Hugo frequently came to its sessions from Königsberg. His arrival in Berlin always was an event of special importance to my parents, myself and my younger brother.

Not just we as his close relatives were impressed by the warmth and the sun-like glow of his personality. After the Second World War, when I revisted Berlin, the mother of a friend, who had been a member of the Reichstag during the persecutions of the Social Democrats under Bismarck, told me that she had been accused of high treason and arrested at that time. When she was sitting in despair in her dark prison cell, Hugo Haase who had agreed to be her defense lawyer entered the dark room, and it suddenly appeared with his conforting words as if the sun had entered.

When I was nine years of age, in the summer of 1901, Uncle Hugo and Aunt Thea invited me and my brother Erich to join them in Königsberg for the school vacation. During tha visit I learned even more to appreciate what a wonderful person Uncle Hugo was in his own environment. I saw not only his warm understanding of others, his outstanding kindness, but also his superior intelligence, his strong sense of responsibility and his warm optimism. His magnificent popularity among the working people was evidenced whenever we walked together on the streets of the city by the warmth with which people greeted him everywhere. After the First World War, one of my friends living in Bonn wrote to me: "Years ago I worked in the same office with a lady whose mother was working woman in Königsberg. She told me that as a child her mother walked several hours to attend every meeting in which Hugo Haase spoke to the people because she did not want to miss his words and that her mother, after walking home for over an hour, often wakened the children from their sleep in order to share with them what Haase had told the meeting." This report confirms how much he was loved by the working class in Königsberg.

Haase and his wife did not belong to a synagogue. But his moral convictions based upon his own philosophical thought and his sincere tolerance led him to a positive attitude toward Judaism. His oldest daughter was an ardent Zionist. His attitude was also proven by the choice of his closest friends. Dr. Oscar Cohn, the president of the German section of the Poale Zion, Dr. Julius Magnus, president of the German National Bar Association and editor of the leading legal journal, the *Juristische Wochenschrift*, Dr. Kurt Rosenfeld, noted attorney at law and Prussian Minister of Justice after the revolution of November 1918, Dr. Siegfried Weinberg, attorney and representative of the trade unions, Emanuel Wurm, member of the Reichstag; all of these individuals were within the closest circle of Haase's friends, and all were active Jews.

Professor Calkins has emphasized Haase's respect for the religious feelings of his parents and his parents-in-law. Recently my friend, Dr. Ernest Hamburger, recalled to may attention the fact that Haase sharply stigmatized the anti-Semitic propaganda campaign during a session of the German National Assembly in Weimar on July 26, 1919 and vehemently protested against the undisturbed distribution of anti-Semitic pamphlets in railway stations and military barracks.

How much Haase was acknowledged as an outstanding lawyer is reflected by the fact that not only his close party associates but also leading radicals such as Rosa Luxemburg, Clara Zetkin and Karl Liebknecht, chose him as their defense attorney as did the famous poet Ernst Toller when he was accused of high treason in Munich in 1919.

Personally I experienced the extent of Hugo Haase's reputation as a leading socialist personality when after the November revolution the noted Göttingen philosopher Leonard Nelson and the poet Ernst Toller came to Berlin and asked me to introduce them to Haase. I fulfilled their request, and both men, neither of whom had joined a political party before that time, joined the U.S.P.D. after their visit with Hugo Haase.

ENDNOTES

Sources are given with the name of author and/or shortened title.

ABBREVIATIONS:

A.A.	– Politisches Archiv des Auswärtigen Amtes, Bonn-Bad Godesberg
Ad.	– Adler
A.S.D.	– Archiv des sozialen Demokratie, Bonn-Bad Godesberg
Ba.	– Bundesarchiv, Koblenz
Dtt.	– Dittmann
Dv.	– David
E.H.	– Ernst Haase
Frakt.	– Reichstagsfraktion der Deutschen Sozialdemokratie
H.H.	– Hugo Haase
Inf.	– Informant
I.I.S.H.	– International Institute for Social History, Amsterdam
N.Z.	– *Die Neue Zeit*
P.A.	– Protokolle der Sitzungen des Parteiausschusses
Prot.	– Parteitagsprotokoll
R. Vb.	– Rat der Volksbeauftragten
Rt.	– *Verhandlungen des Reichstages*
S.A.	– *Sozialistische Auslandspolitik* (entitled *Der Sozialist* after Nov. 22, 1918)
Sch.	– Scheidemann
T.H.	– Thea Lichtenstein Haase
Zr.	– Zentralrat der deutschen sozialistischen Republik

PREFACE

1. Fortunately, there has recently been a surge of interest in the U.S.P.D., and this significant gap in the history of the German left is now beginning to be filled. For helpful surveys of the literature, see Morgan, pp. 468ff., and Krause, pp. 5ff.

I. FROM DISTANT KÖNIGSBERG

1. Matull, *Ostpreussens Arbeiterbewegung*, pp. 4ff.; Matull, "Anfänge . . .," pp. 224ff.; Gause, pp. 168ff.

2. E.H., p. 1. Haase's relatives recall that Hugo's father was "rather well to do" but not wealthy. Infs.: Friedlander (nephew of H.H.), Freyer (niece of H.H.), Hans Haase (nephew of H.H.).

3. E.H., p. 1. None of Haase's brothers or sisters were as socially conscious as he was. Inf., Friedman (grandaughter of H.H.).

4. H.H. to T.H., June 6, 1891, E.H., pp. 186ff.

5. E.H., pp. 4f.

6. Haase defended the Königsberg Social Democratic newspaper sixty-four times in seventeen years. *Leipziger Volkszeitung*, No. 251, Nov. 7, 1919. In addition to taking on such political cases, however, he was able to establish a very profitable civil practice which allowed him both to maintain a confortable home and to contribute substantially to the local party. Infs.: Hans Haase and Boenheim (later partner of H.H.).

7. E.H., p. 8.

8. *Ibid.*, pp. 3f.; Infs.: Friedlander and Freyer.

9. For a description of Haase's work as a lawyer, see *Leipziger Volkszeitung*, No. 251, Nov. 7, 1919.

10. For his most extensive theoretical discussion of the subject, see *Prot. S.P.D.*, 1906, pp. 360ff.

11. Infs.: Hans Haase, Friedlander, Freyer, Dresel (eldest daughter of H.H.). These traits are also reflected in his correspondence and the minutes of many of the meetings in which he participated. See also a letter to Matull from Charlotte Melzer, whose father worked closely with Haase in Königsberg, which is quoted at length in Matull, *Ostpreussens Arbeiterbewegung*, p. 47.

12. Infs.: Friedlander and Freyer.

13. E.H., p. 8 and particularly two letters from Haase to his cousin, Oct. 2, 1891 and Oct. 11, 1891, E.H., pp. 191ff.

14. *Ibid.*, p. 8

15. Hamburger, pp. 376f.

16. Inf., Freyer

17. Inf., Friedlander; Matull, *Ostpreussens Arbeiterbewegung*, p. 47.

18. Inf., Friedlander, who participated in some of these sessions.

19. The marriage produced three children. Deeply committed to the general principles to which his father dedicated his life, his son, Ernst, became a psychiatrist. He remained in Germany until 1939. He finally settled in the U.S. The two daughters, Gertrud and Hilda, also shared something of their father's idealism if not his belief in the ability of international socialism to cure the world's ills. They became involved in the Zionist movement and settled in Israel. Haase, himself, was opposed to Zionism throughout most of his life. He had many friends who were Zionists, however, and a few months before his death he is reported to have praised Theodor Herzl as an "idealist and prophet." Infs.: Friedlander, Freyer, Friedman.

20. Toury, p. 212.

21. *Ibid.*, pp. 213ff.; Hamburger, pp. 404ff. For two extensive, if not completely satisfying, analyses of the apparent high degree of interest in socialism among Jews, see Knütter, pp. 39ff., and Wistrich, ch. I. For a discussion of the attractiveness for many Jews of the U.S.P.D., organized under Haase's leadership in 1917, see Angress, pp. 212ff.

22. Hamburger, pp. 442f.

23. Inf., Friedman.

24. For instance, in the early 1890s he provided the necessary financial support for the publication of a party newspaper in Königsberg. Matull, "Hugo Haase und Otto Braun," p. 175.

25. Osterreth, p. 44; Inf., Friedlander.

26. E.H., p. 10.

27. Ibid., p. 11. See also the Königsberg police report of Feb. 26, 1894, complaining about the encouragement that the local Social Democrats could be expected to draw from Haase's election quoted in Matull, *Ostpreussens Arbeiterbewegung*, pp. 44f.

28. Noske, *Aufstieg* . . ., p. 17.

29. *Ibid.*, pp. 21f.; Sch., *Memoiren* . . ., I, 158ff.; Severing, I, 156ff.

30. Sch., *Memoiren* . . ., I, 161.

31. For the emergence of the "Marxist center," see Matthias, "Kautsky und der Kautskyanismus," pp. 178ff.; Roth, pp. 185ff.; Schorske, pp. 185ff.; Groh, p. 60.

32. Rt., CLXXXVII, 371ff., CLXXXVIII, 1347ff., 1395ff.

33. Ibid., CLXXXVII, 385ff.

34. See newspaper excerpts in Eisner, pp. 500ff.

35. For selections from the protocol of the trial, see *ibid.*, pp. 215ff.

36. See, for instance, his statement at the 1900 congress vigorously supporting Social Democratic participation in Prussian state elections. *Prot. S.P.D.*, 1900, pp. 220f.

37. *Prot. S.P.D.*, 1906, pp. 360ff. The main points of this speech, drawn up in the form of a resolution, were endorsed by a large majority. At Paul Singer's suggestion, the congress also voted to publish the speech as a pamphlet. *Ibid.*, pp. 140ff, 377f.

38. For what is perhaps the most incisive analysis of Kautsky's views, see Matthias, "Kautsky und der Kautskyanismus," pp. 151–197. See also: Groh, pp. 156ff., 185ff., 207ff.; Holzheuer; Brill; B. Kautsky.

39. Schorske describes Haase as "a tried and true representative of the Erfurt ideology." Schorske, p. 210. For Kautsky's analysis of the Erfurt Program, see his *Das Erfurter Programm*.

40. H.H. to T.H., Sept. 27, 1906, E.H., pp. 93f. It should be noted, however, that on the following day Haase joined the large majority in voting for an amendment to the general resolution on union-party relations which made just such a statement. *Prot. S.P.D.*, 1906, p. 304.

41. The party's Reichstag delegation was reduced from 79 to 43. For an analysis of this election, see Crothers.

42. Braunthal, I, 340ff.; Joll, pp. 13ff.

43. H.H. to T.H., Aug. 23, 1907, in E.H., pp. 96f. See also Bebel's reference to Haase's assistance in *Prot. S.P.D.*, 1911, p. 345.

44. *Protokoll über die Verhandlungen des internationalen Sozialisten-Kongresses zu Stuttgart, August 18–24, 1907*, pp. 64–66.

45. He attributed this defeat to the excellent theoretical arguments developed by Kautsky. H.H. to T.H., Aug. 22, 1907, E.H., p. 96. For an extensive discussion of this incident, see H.-C. Schröder, pp. 191ff.

46. H.H. to T.H., Aug. 24, 1907, in E.H., p. 97.

47. *Prot. S.P.D. Preussens*, 1907, pp. 9ff.

48. Schorske, pp. 97ff.

49. In May of 1908 representatives of the party and the unions persuaded delegates to an emergency meeting of the sourthern "League of Young Workers of Germany" to dissolve their organization. In June, a resolution was passed at the triennial trade union congress which declared that no special organization was required for the cultivation of youth and provided for the establishment of local joint party-union committees to organize activities for young workers. *Ibid.*, pp. 104f.

50. The executive committee's resolution was simply a somewhat watered down version of the resolution passed by the unions at Hamburg. *Ibid.*, p. 107.

51. *Prot. S.P.D.*, 1908, p. 226.

52. *Ibid.*, pp. 450f., 551.

53. *Prot. S.P.D.*, 1901, p. 99f.

54. H.H. to T.H., Sept. 17, 1908, E.H. p. 98.

55. *Prot. S.P.D.*, 1908, p. 189.

56. *Ibid.*, p. 426. See also Keil, I, 216ff.

57. Dtt., pp. 273ff. Concerning the origin in 1906 of Haase's long and productive relationship with Dittmann, see *ibid.*, pp. 195ff.

58. *Ibid.*, pp. 274f.; text in *Prot. S.P.D.*, 1910, p. 179.

59. *Prot. S.P.D.*, 1910, pp. 238ff., 259ff., 288ff.

60. Dtt., pp. 287f.

61. *Prot. S.P.D.*, 1910, p. 360.

62. *Ibid.*, pp. 366f.

63. *Ibid.*, p. 367

64. Dtt., p. 291

65. *Prot. S.P.D.*, 1910, p. 378.

66. Dtt., p. 288. Frank remarked during the debate that he was surprised that Haase had lost his usually calm attitude. *Prot. S.P.D.*, 1910, p. 371

II. THE CALL TO BERLIN

1. *N.Z.*, XXIX, Part I (1910–11), 649ff.; Hamburger, pp. 419ff.

2. Inf., Friedlander.

3. W. Schröder, pp. 47ff., Schorske, pp. 116ff., Nipperdey, pp. 326ff. For Ebert's role in particular, see Kotowski, I, 150ff.

4. Kautsky was certainly of this opinion. Writing to Haase early in 1909, he complained that Bebel had been "for years the only fighter and politician on the executive committee." Unfortunately, he was now "dead tired," yet refused to admit it. Kautsky to H.H., Feb. 19, 1909, Ratz, "Briefe . . .," pp. 438ff.

5. Dittmann, for instance, reports that he was urged at that time by many of the radical leaders to seek a place on the executive committee. Dtt., p. 297.

6. Toury, p. 232.

7. Nettl, I, 445ff.

8. *Prot. S.P.D.*, 1911, pp. 371f.

9. Kautsky to H.H., Feb. 14, 1909, Ratz, "Briefe . . .," pp. 437f.

10. Kautsky to H.H., Feb. 25, 1909, *ibid.*, pp. 445ff.

11. H.H. to Kautsky, March 9, 1909, *ibid.*, pp. 468f.

12. H.H. to Kautsky, March 18, 1909, *ibid.*, p. 477.

13. H.H. to Kautsky, June 5, 1909, I.I.S.H., Kautsky Nachlass (KD XII, No. 10).

14. These letters are not available, but that they both had approached him is clear from Haase's letter to Kautsky of Feb. 12, 1911, I.I.S.H., Kautsky Nachlass (KD XII, No. 14).

15. *Ibid.*

16. *Ibid.* Concerning Haase's relationship to Braun, see Matull, "Hugo Haase and Otto Braun," pp. 173ff.

17. Zetkin to Dittmann, Feb. 12, 1911, in Dtt., pp. 322f.

18. *Ibid.*

19. *Ibid.*, p. 323.

20. *Ibid.*

21. Bebel to Kautsky, Aug. 5, 1911, K. Kautsky, Jr., pp. 265ff.

22. Luxemburg to Dittmann, June 17, 1911, A.S.D., Nachlass Dittmann (Photokopien vor 1918, No. 106). A letter of July 28 is more specific on this question. In it, Luxemberg lists Haase's candidacy as one of those concerning which all of their "friends" were agreed. Luxemburg to Dittmann, July 28, 1911, A.S.D., Nachlass Dittmann (Photokopien vor 1918, No. 107).

23. H.H. to Dittmann, July 26, 1911, Dtt., pp. 324f.

24. H.H. to Kautsky, Aug. 5, 1911, I.I.S.H., Kautsky Nachlass (KD XIII, No. 15). 15).

25. Kautsky to H.H., Aug. 11, 1911, I.I.S.H., Kautsky Nachlass (KC, No. 436).

26. Writing to Dittmann in June of 1911, Haase remarked that majority support for expansion of the executive committee had already been achieved at Magdeburg. H.H. to Dittmann, June 26, 1911, Dtt., pp. 324f.

27. According to Dittmann, Ebert, fearing that Dittmann himself might be elected to the committee, claimed that he was by no means overloaded with work and that therefore no expansion was necessary. *Ibid.*, p. 298.

28. *Prot. S.P.D.*, 1911, pp. 160, 269f.

29. Dtt., p. 336. Haase explicitly voiced his satisfaction with Braun's candidacy. He also expressed support for Robert Dissmann and Gustav Hoch, both of whom were later to be closely associated with him in the Social Democratic opposition to the war. H.H. to Dittmann, July 26, 1911, *ibid.*, pp. 324f.

30. *Prot. S.P.D.*, 1911, pp. 371ff., 410.

31. Earlier in the convention Bebel had clashed with leading representatives of the extreme left over Luxemburg's attacks on the executive committee for its handling of the Moroccan crisis of the previous summer. *Ibid.*, pp. 204ff. It was apparent that a serious break had occurred in the left-center alliance which in the past had usually prevailed when crises arose during party congresses. See also Kotowski, I, 214.

32. Dtt., pp. 337f.

33. Kotowski, I, 217. See also Groh, pp. 203f.

III. THE CRISIS FORESHADOWED

1. *N.Z.*, XXX (1911–12), Part I, 581.

2. Bebel to Adler, Jan. 12, 1912, Ad., pp. 544f.

3. *Ibid.*

4. *Prot. S.P.D.*, 1912, pp. 98ff.; see also Groh, p. 311.

5. Haupt, p. 52.

6. Rt., CCLXXXIV, 1310ff.

7. His practice in Berlin was devoted largely to criminal cases and was never as successful financially as it had been in Königsberg. Infs.; Hans Haase and Boenheim.

8. Kautsky to Adler, May 21, 1913, Ad., pp. 564ff.

9. Kautsky to Adler, June 26, 1913, *ibid.*, pp. 573f.

10. Sch., *Memoiren . . .*, I, 81f.

11. Kautsky to Adler, Oct. 8, 1913, Ad., pp. 582ff.

12. See, e.g., Bebel's statement to this effect at the 1912 party congress. *Prot., S.P.D.*, 1912, p. 392.

13. Dtt., p. 371.

14. He received 438 votes as compared to the 452 received by Bebel. *Prot. S.P.D.*, 1912, p. 516. It should be noted, however, that it was almost axiomatic that a party leader, once elected to such a post, became all but irremovable. Michels, *Zur Soziologie . . .*, pp. 74ff.

15. For a summary of this debate, see Ratz, "Karl Kautsky und die Abrüstungskontroverse. . .," pp. 199ff.

16. *Prot. S.P.D.*, 1912, pp. 403ff.

17. In so doing, he was again following the lead of Kautsky. Ratz, "Karl Kautsky und die Abrüstungskontroverse . . .," p. 225; Schorske, p. 246.

18. Schorske, p. 264.

19. See, for instance, the speeches of the revisionist Bernstein and the left wing leader Liebknecht. *Prot. S.P.D.*, 1912, pp. 419ff., 425ff.

20. Ratz, "Karl Kautsky und die Abrüstungskontroverse . . .," pp. 208ff.

21. *Prot. S.P.D.*, 1912, pp. 415ff.

22. *Ibid.*, p. 434. For text of Haase's resolution, see *ibid.*, pp. 529f.

23. Haupt, pp. 63ff.

24. H.H. to "Friends," Nov. 13, 1912, E.H. pp. 98f.

25. Haupt, p. 71

26. *Protokoll über die Verhandlungen des ausserordentlichen internationalen Sozialistenkongress zu Basel, November 24–25, 1912*, p. 12. It was in such terms that Haase spoke of revolution throughout his career.

27. *Ibid.*, pp. 12f.

28. *Ibid.*, pp. 29f.

29. *Ibid.*, pp. 23ff.

30. Haupt, p. 85.

31. *Rt.*, CCLXXXVI, 2520ff., 2534f.

32. Haupt, pp. 90f.

33. H.H. to E.H., March 2, 1913, E.H., pp. 99ff.

34. *Ibid.* Concerning the origins of this manifesto, see Bebel to Adler, Feb. 28, 1913, Ad., pp. 562f.

35. Haupt, p. 92.

36. *Stenographisches Protokoll der deutsch–französischen Verständigungskonferenz 11 Mai 1913 zu Bern*, pp. 29ff.; E.H., p. 23; Haupt, p. 93; Schulz, "Die deutsche Sozialdemokratie . . . ," pp. 114f.

37. Haupt, p. 93, Hamburger, p. 452.

38. *Rt.*, CCLXXXIX, 4517ff.

39. For a summary of this debate and the actions taken by the delegation, see the delegation's report to the party congress. *Prot. S.P.D.*, 1913, pp. 169ff. For a thorough analysis, see Groh, pp. 434ff.

40. Rt., CCLXXXX, 5926f.

41. *Prot. S.P.D.*, 1913, pp. 515f.

42. Among those who signed a resolution condemning the action of the delegation were his old Königsberg friend Alfred Gottschalk and such future leaders of the U.S.P.D. as Arthur Crispien, Arthur Stadthagen and Ewald Vogtherr. *Ibid.*, p. 197. Among those who supported the delegation were Kautsky and Emanuel Wurm. *Ibid.*, pp. 481ff. Haase suffered at the time from a severe intestinal disorder which required two operations and several months' stay in a hospital. He was not fully recovered until late in the fall. E.H., p. 24. For an analysis of the opposition group, see Groh, pp. 441f.

43. H.H. to E.H., March 2, 1913, E.H., pp. 99ff.

44. Schorske, pp. 257ff.; Groh, pp. 468ff.

45. *Frakt.*, I, 306; Dtt., pp. 402f.

46. *Frakt.*, I, 307.

47. The aging Hermann Molkenbuhr was the third co-chairman. See also Ratz, *Georg Ledebour*, p. 84.

IV. THE UNEXPECTED CATASTROPHE

1. Groh, pp. 537ff.; Berlau, pp. 69f., Varain, pp. 69f., Schorske, pp. 258ff.

2. *Schulthess' . . .*, LV, 312. The Social Democratic deputies had hitherto left the chamber on such occasions. See also Groh, pp. 543ff.

3. H.H. to Vaillant, "May, 1914," E.H., pp. 101f.

4. H.H., *Grundzüge . . .*, pp. 1ff.

5. H.H. to Vaillant, "May, 1914," E.H., pp. 101f.

6. Haupt, p. 116.

7. "Polizeiprotokoll über die Sitzung des Vorstandes der Sozialdemokratischen Partei Deutschlands am 29. Juni 1914," Kuczynski, pp. 187f.

8. Sch., *Memoiren . . .*, I, 232ff.

9. Kautsky to Adler, July 25, 1914, Ad., pp. 595ff.

10. E.H., pp. 24f. Ebert expressed his satisfaction with this proclamation in a letter written at this time. Ebert to "Colleagues," July 27, 1914, Ebert, *Schriften . . .*, I, 309.

11. *Vorwärts*, Nr. 200a, July 25, 1914.

12. Vice Chancellor Clemens von Delbrück arranged this meeting after consulting with the right wing Social Democratic leader Albert Südekum. Delbrück reports that Südekum strongly recommended that Haase be included although he realized that Haase was "little suited to establish the necessary relationship (*Fühlung*) with the government." Delbrück, pp. 105f. See also: Groh, pp. 577ff.; Zechlin, pp. 25ff.; Mommsen, pp. 120f,; Jarausch, pp. 168f., Erdmann, pp. 168f.

13. Reported by Haase at the S.P.D. conference of September 1916. *Protokoll der Reichskonferenz . . .*, p. 60.

14. *Vorwärts*, No. 204, July 29, 1914. But see also Groh, p. 637, who provides evidence that the attendance at these meetings was uneven.

15. Ebert had also been invited to attend. Haupt, p. 157. Although he arrived back in Berlin on the afternoon of the 28th, he decided after consulting with other party leaders not to go to Brussels. Buse, "Ebert and the Coming of World War I . . .," pp. 440f.

16. The Spanish delegate Fabra-Ribas reported that Haase was "particularly angered" by Adler's pessimism. Haupt, p. 158. For the "Protokoll der Sitzung des I.S.B. vom 29. bis 30. Juli 1914 in Brüssel," see *ibid.*, pp. 177ff. For Adler's statement, see *ibid.*, pp. 178f.

17. *Ibid.*, pp. 179f.

18. Most of the other delegates apparently shared Haase's optimism. Haupt, pp. 159f.

19. *Ibid.*, pp. 188f.

20. *Ibid.*, p. 181. This, despite the fact that, according to Ebert, he and his colleagues in the S.P.D. leadership had sent him a telegram directing him to support the indefinite postponement of the congress. Buse, "Ebert and the Coming of World War I . . .," p. 440.

21. Haupt, p. 186.

22. For Haase's proposed resolution and the final, slightly altered version, see *ibid.*, pp. 191f.

23. *Le Peuple* (Brussels), July 30, 1914, quoted in LaChesnais, pp. 25f.

24. Grotjahn, p. 150.

25. Südekum to Bethmann-Hollweg, July 29, 1914, Kuczynski, pp. 78f.

26. Haupt argues with considerable cogency that the exclusion of Haase may well have been intentional. Haupt, p. 169.

27. "Protokoll der Sitzung des K. preussischen Staatsministeriums am 30. Juli 1914," Kuczynski, p. 80f.

28. *Ibid.*, p. 81.

29. Sch., *Memoiren . . .*, I, 245. In his diary Ebert does not mention a formal meeting of the executive committee, but simply reports that Scheidemann and Hermann Müller were of the opinion that he and Braun should leave and that they did so that afternoon. Buse, "Ebert and the Coming of World War I . . .," p. 442. It seems unlikely, however, that such an important decision would have been made informally. Ebert returned to Berlin on August 4. *Ibid.*, p. 444. Paul Löbe, who was at the time an

editor of the *Breslauer Volkswacht*, reports that he and his colleagues also fully expected the police to take action against them. Löbe, pp. 66f.

30. *Rt.*, CCCLXXXVI, 2507ff.

31. Dv., pp. 3f.; Sch., *Memoiren* . . ., I, 247.

32. Stampfer, *Erfahrungen* . . ., p. 170; Sch., *Memoiren* . . ., I, 238f. Scheidemann dates this incident erroneously on July 30.

33. Kautsky to Adler, July 25, 1914, Ad., pp. 595ff.

34. Miller, "Zum 3. August 1914," pp. 519ff.

35. Sch., *Memoiren* . . ., 247; Dv., p. 4. When Müller reached Paris, he was apparently still convinced that the S.P.D. would either vote against war credits or abstain. De Man, p. 114. Grünberg, pp. 39ff.

36. Dv., pp. 4ff.

37. *Ibid.* For the text of the Kaiser's speech, see Lutz, I, 4.

38. Dtt., p. 422.

39. Sch., *Memoiren* . . ., I, 248f.; Dv., pp. 6f.

40. Zechlin, pp. 27ff.

41. Varain, p. 72.

42. Liebknecht, *Klassenkampf* . . ., p. 14.

43. Dv., pp. 7ff.

44. Sch., *Memoiren* . . ., I, 249ff.; Delbrück, pp. 108f.

45. Although not a member of the delegation, Kautsky had been invited as an "expert." For a sympathetic discussion of Kautsky's proposal see Miller, *Burgfrieden* . . ., pp. 64f.

46. An official list of those who voted in the negative was never published. The eyewitness sources agree on the following eleven names: Bock, Geyer, Haase, Henke, Herzfeld, Kunert, Ledebour, Lensch, Liebknecht, Rühle, Vogtherr. For a discussion of the historiographical problem involved and the names included on various lists, see Miller, *Burgfrieden* . . ., pp. 59ff. For an analysis of the dissident group, see Groh, pp. 692f.

47. This was Scheidemann's suggestion. Dv., p. 9.

48. *Ibid.*, pp. 7ff. See also *Frakt.*, II, 3f.; Sch., *Memoiren* . . ., I, 250ff.; Liebknecht, *Klassenkampf* . . ., pp. 14f., 87f.; Dtt., pp. 426ff. In contrast to the sources cited above, Keil claims that the minority did not fight with their usual passion. Keil, I, 301.

49. Dv., pp. 10ff.

50. Sch., *Memoiren* . . ., I, 257; Dtt., pp. 429f. Heine claims, however, that Haase agreed to read the statement in order to "sabotage" the position of the party. He argues that Haase thereby hoped to weaken the impact of the statement. Heine, pp. 105f.

51. Liebknecht, *Klassenkampf* . . ., pp. 87f.

52. E.H., p. 28.

53. Dv., p. 11.

54. *Rt.*, CCCVI, 5ff.

55. Dtt., pp. 431f.

56. Dv., p. 12

57. Dtt., p. 431; *Frakt.*, II, 4. For the text of the statement as read by Haase, see *Rt.*, CCCVI, 8f.

58. See, e.g., Bartel, p. 177.

59. Dittmann considered it simply a skillful maneuver on the part of the government. Dtt., pp. 436f.

60. *P.A.*, June 30, 1914 . . ., p. 12. The minutes of party council meetings were published in various sections. They will be cited by the date of the first meeting recorded in the section to which the citation refers.

61. Dv., pp. 12f.

V. WALKING A TIGHTROPE

1. Rosenberg, pp. 73ff.

2. *Ibid.*

3. *N.Z.*, XXXII (1913–14), Part II, 843. See also the articles that he published on the impact of the war in September. *Ibid.*, 937ff., 969ff.

4. Roth, pp. 288ff., Schorske, pp. 290f.

5. Haenisch, pp. 152f.

6. At the S.P.D.'s 1917 party congress, David, for instance, described the vote of August 4 as an act of "world historical significance." *Prot. S.P.D.*, 1917, p. 316. For two perceptive analyses of the motivations of the Social Democrats at this point, see Groh, pp. 718ff. and Miller, *Burgfrieden* . . ., pp. 68ff.

7. Dv., pp. 16f., 2ff., 45, 53f.; Heine to Vollmar, Oct. 8 and Nov. 14, 1914, I.I.S.H., Vollmar Nachlass (No. 873). These are two of a series of reports which Heine sent to Vollmar between October 1914 and February 1916. All are listed under the same number in the I.I.S.H. and will hereafter be cited simply by date followed by the initials of the archive. See also Kuczynski, pp. 207ff.

8. Dv., p. 17.

9. Liebknecht, *Klassenkampf* . . ., pp. 16ff.; Kuczynski, pp. 97f., 164, 211ff.; Nettl, II, 609ff.

10. See, e.g., Severing, I, 203f.; Stampfer, *Erfahrungen* . . ., p. 171; Scheidemann, *Memoiren* . . ., I, 303f.

11. For Haase's emphasis upon the importance of refusing to abandon time-tested policies and programs, see in particular H.H. to E.H., Oct. 30, 1914, E.H., p. 103.

12. Dv., p. 14.

13. *Ibid.*, p. 15.

14. Sch., *Memoiren* . . ., I, 267f., 298.

15. Prager, pp. 30f.; Koszyk, *Zwischen* . . ., pp. 44f.

16. Among them were Heinrich Ströbel, Ernst Däumig, Arthur Stadthagen and Rudolf Hilferding, all of whom later became leaders in the U.S.P.D.

17. Sch., *Memoiren* . . ., I, 267.

18. *Ibid.*, I, 270.

19. E.H., p. 29; Koszyk, *Zwischen* . . ., p. 29.

20. *P.A.*, June 30, 1914 . . ., pp. 3ff. For an analysis of the role of the party council, see Nowka, pp. 31f.

21. *P.A.*, June 30, 1914 . . ., pp. 11f.

22. Dv., p. 62.

23. *Ibid.*, pp. 69f.

24. *Ibid.*, p. 72.

25. *Ibid.*, p. 73.

26. Liebknecht, *Klassenkampf . . .*, p. 89.

27. Adler to Kautsky, Nov. 26, 1914, Ad., pp. 602ff.

28. Dv., p. 70.

29. Kautsky to Adler, Nov. 28, 1914, Ad., p. 606.

30. Dittmann to H.H. (for the executive committee), Nov. 15, 1914, Dtt., pp. 449f.

31. Gay, pp. 280ff.; Dv., pp. 50f., 65. Kurt Eisner also spoke out against the war at this point. Mitchell, pp. 60f.

32. Kautsky to Adler, Nov. 28, 1914, Ad., pp. 605ff.

33. Dtt., p. 452.

34. *Ibid.*, pp. 452f.

35. Sch., *Memoiren . . .*, I, 318ff.

36. *Ibid.*, I, 320.

37. E.H., pp. 29f.

38. Haase was joined by Kautsky, Hoch and Ledebour in opposing the majority's draft. Dv., p. 74; Heine to Vollmar, Dec. 10, 1914, I.I.S.H.

39. *Ibid.*, Dv. pp. 76f.

40. *Frakt.*, II, 7.

41. Dtt., pp. 458f.

42. *Ibid.*, p. 459; Dv. p. 74; *Frakt.*, I, 7.

43. Sch., *Memoiren . . .*, I, 21. Haase told his colleagues that he had expressed a willingness to make minor editorial changes. Dtt., p. 462.

44. Sch., *Memoiren . . .*, I, 321f.; Dv., p. 75.

45. Dv., pp. 77f.

46. Dtt., p. 465.

47. Sch., *Memoiren . . .*, I, 322f.

48. *Ibid.*, p. 323; Dv., pp. 78f.

49. Dtt., pp. 460ff.

50. Dv., p. 79.

51. Dtt., p. 464.

52. *Ibid.*, Dv., pp. 79f. Ebert was among those who urged Haase to speak for the S.P.D.

53. Sch., *Memoiren . . .*, I, 326f.

54. *Rt.*, CCCVI, 20f.

55. Dtt., p. 469; Dv., p. 80.

VI. COLLAPSE OF THE CENTER

1. Haase repeatedly expressed this conviction throughout the war, but see in particular H.H. to E.H., April 17, 1915, E.H., pp. 106f.

2. See, e.g., Dv., p. 16; Heine, pp. 105f.

3. H.H. to E.H., July 21, 1915, E.H., pp. 108f.

4. Kautsky to Adler, Feb. 11, 1915, Ad., pp. 610f.

5. Dv., p. 91.

6. P.A., June 30, 1914 . . ., p. 42.

7. Dv., p. 60.

8. Sch., *Memoiren . . .*, I, 358ff.

9. H.H. to E.H., Oct. 1, 1915, E.H., p. 110.

10. See, e.g., Sch., *Memoiren . . .*, I, 360f.

11. Dv., p. 85.

12. *Ibid.*

13. Dtt., p. 479.

14. Dv., p. 92.

15. Dtt., p. 476.

16. Sch., *Memoiren . . .*, I, 328f.

17. *Ibid.*, pp. 374ff.

18. *P.A.*, June 30, 1914 . . ., pp. 26f., 34.

19. *Ibid.*, pp. 27, 35.

20. *Ibid.*, pp. 31ff.

21. *Ibid.*, p. 42.

22. Dtt., pp. 482f.

23. Dv., pp. 101f.

24. Dtt., pp. 489f.

25. *Frakt.*, II, 27f.

26. *Ibid.*, pp. 32ff., Dtt., pp. 502f. Heine had feared that the opposition would gain a majority on the issue. Heine to Vollmar, Feb. 5, 1915, I.I.S.H.

27. *Frakt.*, II, 34.

28. Kautsky to Adler, Feb. 11, 1915, Ad., pp. 610f.

29. Dv., p. 101.

30. Heine to Vollmar, Feb. 5, 1915, I.I.S.H.

31. Dv., p. 108.

32. H.H. to Ebert, March 5, 1915, E.H., p. 105.

33. *P.A.*, June 30, 1914 . . ., pp. 45ff.

34. Dv., pp. 109f.; Sch., *Memoiren . . .*, I, 332; Heine to Vollmar, March 22, 1925, I.I.S.H.

35. Dtt., pp. 510ff.

36. *Ibid.*, pp. 515ff., *Frakt.*, II, 43.

37. Dv., p. 110. David reports that the margin was 52 to 48. Other sources do not mention this vote.

38. *Frakt.*, II, 43.

39. *Rt.*, CCCVI, 45ff.

40. *Ibid.*, p. 48.

41. Dtt., p. 524.

42. Heine to Vollmar, March 22, 1915, I.I.S.H.

43. Prager, p. 62.

44. Dv., p. 111.

45. *Schulthess'* . . ., LVI, 131.

46. Dtt., pp. 521ff.

47. Haase had made this proposal earlier during a meeting of the executive committee of the delegation. Dv., p. 108.

48. Dtt., pp. 526ff.

49. *Ibid.*, p. 530.

50. *Ibid.*, pp. 531f.

51. *Ibid.*, p. 533; *Frakt.*, II, 46. Five others, who were absent, later declared that they also rejected the majority point of view. Prager, p. 58.

52. Dv., p. 113.

53. *Vorwärts*, No. 80, March 21, 1915.

54. Dv., p. 113.

55. *Ibid.*, p. 118.

56. H.H. to E.H., April 17, 1915, E.H., p. 106.

57. Dv., pp. 122f. For what is apparently another account of this meeting, see Wachenheim, pp. 60f.

58. Dv., p. 124.

59. Sch., *Memoiren* . . ., I, 336ff.; Dtt., pp. 542f.

60. Dv., pp. 125f.

61. Kautsky, *Sozialisten* . . ., pp. 538f.; Braunthal, II, 51ff. For texts of official statements from this period, see *The Bolsheviks* . . ., pp. 264ff., 273ff.

62. Schöpflin informed David that Ebert had told him that he intended to prevent agreement on any international resolution for the time being. Ebert also claimed on the same occasion that he had succeeded in isolating and repeatedly embarrassing Haase during a recent meeting at the Hague. Dv., p. 118. See also Sch., *Memoiren* . . ., I, 340ff.

63. H.H. to E.H., April 17, 1915, E.H., pp. 106f.

64. Dtt., pp. 544ff.

65. *Ibid.*, pp. 554ff.

66. *Ibid.*, p. 562.

67. *Rt.*, CCCVI, 171f.

68. *Ibid.*, pp. 172ff.

69. "An den Vorstand . . .," I.I.S.H., Nachlass Otto Braun (No. 22); *Dokumente und Materialien* . . ., Reihe II, Vol. I, 169ff. For its origins, see Liebknecht, *Klassenkampf* . . ., pp. 94f.

70. Among the signatories were many who later became leaders of the U.S.P.D., including Henke, Crispien, Däumig, Ledebour, Stadthagen, Adolf Hoffmann, Prager and Zietz. According to Dittmann, he and Haase discussed at length the wisdom of adding their own signatures, but came to the conclusion that, although they supported its general tone and purpose, their positions in the party leadership made it impossible for them to endorse a document which contained certain statements which they knew to be inaccurate. Dtt., p. 572. Haase's later statements and his vote to condemn the petition, however, suggest that his objections went considerably beyond these inaccuracies.

71. Dtt., p. 576. See also Gay, pp. 285f.

72. It was also distributed as a leaflet. Dt., p. 575.

73. *Leipziger Volkszeitung*, No. 139, June 19, 1915.

74. Dv., p. 134.

75. *Vorwärts*, No. 170, June 22, 1915.

76. Sch., *Memoiren . . .*, I, 340; Keil, I, 327.

77. Sch., *Memoiren . . .*, I, 340.

78. It was published in *Vorwärts* (No. 181) on July 3, 1915 and as a leaflet entitled *Gegen Parteizerrüttung*.

79. Dv., p. 136.

80. *Ibid.*, pp. 134f.; *Vorwärts*, No. 174, June 26, 1915.

81. Dv., pp. 134f.

82. *P.A.*, June 30, 1914 . . ., pp. 83ff.

83. *Ibid.*, pp. 88f.

84. *Ibid.*, pp. 99ff.

85. *Ibid.*, p. 104.

86. H.H. to "Friends," July 17, 1915 and H.H. to E.H., July 21, 1915, E.H., pp. 107ff. For an enthusiastic endorsement from the leaders of the S.P.D.'s lower Rhine district, which included the electoral districts of both Ebert and Scheidemann, see Buse, *Parteiagitation . . .*, pp. 89ff.

87. In his letter of July 21, Haase remarked that at the moment it was impossible to tell which side had a majority of party members behind it. E.H., pp. 108f.

VII. THE GAUNTLET THROWN DOWN

1. Dtt., pp. 633f.

2. David and Bernstein had been invited by the executive committee to prepare foreign policy theses to serve as the basis for discussion. David's theses quickly became the focus of the debate. *P.A.*, June 30, 1914 . . ., pp. 107ff.,; Dtt., pp. 579ff.

3. *Rt.*, CCCVI, 229ff.

4. H.H. to E.H., Aug. 25, 1915, E.H., p. 109. See also Kautsky's comment in a letter to Adler of Aug. 30, 1915, Ad., pp. 626ff.

5. Koszyk, *Zwischen . . .*, p. 62.

6. Dtt., p. 640; Koszyk, *Deutsche Pressepolitik . . .*, p. 149.

7. *N.Z.*, XXXIV (1915–1916), Pt. I, 129ff., 161ff.

8. *Leipziger Volkszeitung*, No. 270. Nov. 27, 1915.

9. *N.Z.*, XXXIV (1915–16), Pt. I, 264ff.

10. Prager, pp. 86f.

11. Dv., pp. 144f. See also Scheidemann's statement to this effect as reported by Dittmann, p. 661.

12. Dv., pp. 145f.

13. H.H. to Brill, Nov. 27, 1915, E.H., pp. 112f.

14. Haase defended Liebknecht's right to interpellate the Chancellor. Dtt., p. 653.

15. For texts, see *ibid.*, p. 660.

16. *Ibid.*, pp. 660ff.

17. Several of those who had signed the opposition draft later declared that they had done so solely in order to insure that it would get a hearing. *Frakt.*, II, 87.

18. Dtt., pp. 668f.

19. *Rt.*, CCCVI, 430ff. Scheidemann claims that Haase complimented him on the speech. Sch., *Memoiren . . .*, I, 381.

20. *Rt.*, CCCVI, 434ff.

21. *Ibid.*, pp. 438; H.H. to Brill, Dec. 16, 1915, E.H., pp. 113f.

22. *Rt.*, CCCVI, 442ff.

23. Dv., p. 147.

24. Dtt., p. 673.

25. H.H. to Brill, Dec. 16, 1915, E.H., pp. 113f.

26. Dittmann reports that after several days the total opposing a vote for credits reached 44. Dtt., p. 684.

27. *Ibid.*, pp. 677ff., 684f.

28. Dv., pp. 147f.

29. Dtt., pp. 685ff.

30. *Ibid.*, p. 686.

31. *Frakt.*, II, 104.

32. Dtt., pp. 686ff.

33. Dtt., pp. 695ff.; *Frakt.*, I, 134.

34. Dv. 148.

35. H.H. to "Friends," Dec. 21, 1915, E.H., p. 114. At about the same time he expressed similar views to his son and added that events continued to confirmed his analysis. H.H. to E.H., "end of December," 1915, *ibid.*, p. 115.

36. Dtt., p. 691.

37. *Rt.*, CCCVI, 506f.

38. Liebknecht, *Klassenkampf . . .*, pp. 91f. See also his "An die Neunzehn!" Liebknecht, *Gesammelte Reden . . .*, VIII, 436f.

39. *Spartakusbriefe*, pp. 86ff.

40. *Ibid.*, pp. 11 ff. They were originally the work of Luxemburg. Nettl, II, 639.

41. Ledebour to "Werte Genosse," Dec. 21, 1915, A.S.D., Nachlass Dittmann.

42. Bartel, pp. 375ff.

43. Kautsky, *Mein Verhältnis . . .*, p. 6.

44. H.H., *Reichstagsreden . . .*, p. 9.

VIII. THE DELEGATION DIVIDED

1. *P.A.*, June 30, 1914 . . ., pp. 147ff, 173.

2. *Frakt.*, II, 153ff.

3. Dtt., p. 173.

4. Most of the opposition abstained on this vote or cast blank ballots. *Ibid.*, p. 70f.; *Frakt.*, II, 152.

5. H.H. to Brill, Feb. 3, 191 6, E.H., pp. 116f.

6. He received only 25 votes to Ebert's 43 and Scheidemann's 45. *Frakt.*, II, 165.

7. The government was preparing new tax legislation, but since it was not

expected to be ready for action by the Reichstag until early in the summer, a temporary budget had been introduced to cover the intervening period.

8. Dtt., pp. 741ff.; *Frakt.*, II, 166ff.

9. Dtt., p. 74 . Liebknecht consistently was denied permission to speak on substantive issues in the Reichstag.

10. H.H. to Brill, March 25, 1916, E.H., p. 119.

11. *Rt.*, CCCVII, 841ff.

12. The best description is to be found in *Vorwärts*, No. 84, March 25, 1916. See also Dv., p. 168; *Frakt*, II, 170ff.

13. *Rt.*, CCCVII, 844f

14. *Ibid.*, p. 845.

15. *Frakt.*, II, 173ff.; Dtt., pp. 745ff.

16. Dtt., p. 749; *Vorwärts*, No. 84, March 25, 1916; Berger, p. 27.

17. Dv., p. 168.

18. *Ibid.*; H.H. to Brill, March 25, 1916, E.H., p. 119.

19. *Ibid.*

20. *Vorwärts*, No. 88, March 29, 1916.

21. *Die Bildung.* . . .

22. Kautsky admitted, however, that it was unavoidable. Kautsky, *Mein Verhältnis* . . ., pp. 7f.

23. Eight deputies joined the S.A.G. or the Independent delegation after March 1916. See the table in *Frakt.*, I, CLIIIff.

24. Dtt., p. 756; Prager, pp. 100f. See also *Prot. S.P.D.*, 1917, pp. 235f.

25. Haase was certainly of the opinion that the initiative of the opposition forced the majority to take a much more critical attitude toward the government. See, e.g., H.H. to E.H., May 4, 1916, E.H., pp. 120f.

26. Kautsky to Adler, Aug. 7, 1916, Ad., pp. 630f.

27. H.H. to Brill, March 25, 1916, E.H., p. 119.

28. *Rt.*, CCCVII, 850ff.

29. *Ibid.*, pp. 857ff.

30. *Ibid.*, pp. 896f. David attributed the success of the U-boat resolution largely to the "splitting off of the Haase group." Dv., p. 170.

31. *Rt.*, CCCVII, 881ff.

32. *Ibid.*, pp. 889ff.

33. S.A., April 12, 1916.

34. H.H. to Brill, "May 1916," E.H., p. 122.

35. S.A., April 12, 1916.

36. H.H. to Brill, "May 1916," E.H., p. 122. Dittmann reports that the speech made an immense impact on the masses. Dtt., p. 754.

37. *Rt.*, CCCVII, 952f,; Dtt., pp. 757ff.

38. *Rt.*, CCCVII, 979ff.; H.H. to Brill, "May 1916," E.H., p. 122.

39. *Rt.*, CCCVII, 1026ff.

40. *Ibid.*, pp. 1028ff.

41. H.H. to Brill, May 2, 1916, H.H. to Gottschalk, July 2, 1916, H.H. to Brill,

July 9, 1916, E.H., pp. 120, 123ff., 125ff. The wife of the Communist leader Eugen Levine confirms Haase's continuing personal sympathy for even some of his severest critics on the left. Levine-Meyer, p. 71.

42. H.H. to Gottschalk, July 2, 1916, and July 15, 1916, H.H. to E.H., July 19, 1916, E.H., pp. 123ff., 127ff.

43. The Spartacists negotiated with the centrists concerning the possibility of joint action on May 1, but the two groups could not reach agreement. Nettl, II, 648.

44. *Illustrierte Geschichte* . . ., pp. 139f.

45. H.H. to Dittmann, June 26, 1916, Dtt., pp. 770ff.

47. See, e.g., Adolf Braun to H.H., Aug. 22, 1916, a carbon copy of which is in the Kautsky Nachalass, I.I.S.H. (KDXII). Braun appears to have assumed that Haase would be negatively inclined.

48. H.H. to Gottschalk, July 2, 1916, E.H., pp. 123ff.

49. Buse, *Parteiagitation* . . ., pp. 105f.

50. H.H. to Gottschalk, July 2, 1916, E.H., pp. 123ff; H.H. to Dittmann, June 26, 1916, Dtt., pp. 770ff.

51. A collection of these, *Aus Flugschriften* . . ., was published by the majority leaders for the delegates to the national conference.

52. Kotowski is uncertain whether Ebert was at the time pressing for a split. Kotowski, p. 263. From time to time David expressed doubts in this regard. See, e.g., Dv., p. 188. Haase appears, however, to have been convinced that the majority leaders were determined to drive out the opposition. See, e.g., H.H. to "Friends," June 21, 1916, H.H. to Gottschalk, July 15, 1916, E.H., pp. 123, 127.

53. *P. A.*, July 20–21, 1916, p. 54.

54. *P. A.*, Aug. 18, 1916, pp. 38ff.

55. See, e.g., Kautsky to Adler, Aug. 7, 1916, Ad., pp. 629f.

56. *P. A.*, Aug. 18, 1916, p. 37.

57. *Reichskonferenz*, pp. 5ff., 13ff.

58. Dtt., p. 777.

59. *Reichskonferenz*, pp. 35ff.

60. *Ibid.*, pp. 53ff.

61. *Ibid.*, pp. 85ff.

62. *Ibid.*, pp. 168f. This gives at least some indication of the relative strength of the two factions. It should be noted, however, that some of those who shared the views of the opposition apparently voted against the motion in the vain hope that some measure of reconciliation could still thereby be achieved. S.A., Sept. 27, 1916.

63. *Ibid.*

64. Dv., p. 200.

IX. THE FINAL BREACH

1. Koszyk, *Zwischen* . . ., pp. 79ff.

2. *Ibid.*, pp. 84f.; Stampfer, *Erfahrungen* . . ., pp. 205f. The minority claimed that the executive committee actually went far beyond the original intent of the military authorities. Prager, pp. 116ff.

3. Koszyk, *Zwischen* . . ., p. 85.

4. The campaign to gain control of the opposition press was pressed throughout the Reich with considerable success. The *Leipziger Volkszeitung*, which because of its corporate independence could not be coerced by the majority leadership, proved to be the exception rather than the rule. Koszyk, *Deutsche Pressepolitik* . . ., p. 149.

5. H.H. to Eisner, Nov. 4, 1916, E.H., p. 130.

6. H.H. to "a friend within the delegation majority" (i.e., Gustav Hoch), Nov. 16, 1916, *ibid.*, pp. 131ff. It should be noted that some of the members of the opposition who had remained within the old delegation also protested. Dv., p. 208. The dispute was also carried to the floor of the Reichstag. *Rt.*, CCCVIII, 1956f.

7. Hoch to H.H., Jan. 29, 1917, letter in possession of Dr. Fritz Hoch, Kassel-Wilhelmshoehe, copy in archives of Leo Baeck Institute, New York.

8. H.H. to E.H., Nov. 21, 1916, E.H., pp. 134f. See also H.H. to Brill, Nov. 25, 1916, *ibid.*, pp. 135f.

9. Feldman describes the concessions obtained by the majority socialists and their allies as a "triumph of labor." Feldman, pp. 197ff.

10. *Rt.*, CCCVIII, 2290ff.

11. *Ibid.*, 2294ff.

12. It is notable that 21 majority socialists opposed its acceptance and that a number of these abstained when the vote was finally taken in the Reichstag. *Frakt.*, II, 239f,; Feldman, p. 247.

13. H.H. to E.H., Dec. 13, 1916, E.H., p. 138. During the opposition conference on Jan. 7, 1917, he declared that he had never been "so deeply moved" as he was by the majority's reaction to the Fatherland's Service Law. *Prot. U.S.P.D.*, 1917, p. 88. A report of this conference is included as an appendix to this protocol.

14. There has been considerable debate concerning the sincerity of the German initiative. See, e.g., Fischer, pp. 381ff,; Vietsch, *Bethmann Hollweg*, pp. 245ff,; Mommsen, p. 155.

15. *Rt.*, CCCVIII, 2331ff.

16. The S.A.G. immediately issued a manifesto declaring that the note was meaningless as long as the German conditions were not revealed; see Haase's report to the Jan. 7 conference, *Prot. U.S.P.D.*, 1917, p. 87. The peace offensive was also decried as a swindle by Hans Block in *S.A.*, Jan. 11, 1917. Neither of these statements, however, could have been expected to reach more than a relatively small number of Social Democrats.

17. This was just what Bethmann hoped to avoid. As early as Dec. 14 he wrote to Conrad Haussmann that he expected his initiative to be politically and morally very useful as long as the other parties did not follow the example of "those around Haase, who are already demanding a public clarification of our conditions." Mommsen, p. 155.

18. H.H. to E.H., Dec. 14, 1916, E.H., pp. 136ff. Ten days later he wrote to friends expressing his pessimism concerning the possibility of negotiations being initiated; H.H. to "Friends," Dec. 24, 1916, *ibid.*, pp. 138f.

19. See, e.g., an article by Stampfer in which he declared that there was no longer any reason to doubt that Germany was conducting a defensive war. *Vorwärts*, No. 4,

Jan. 5, 1917. See also Ebert's speech to the party council on Jan. 18. *P.A.*, Jan 18, 1917, p. 1.

20. *Prot. U.S.P.D.*, 1917, pp. 84ff.

21. *Ibid.*, pp. 92ff. For text of these proposals, see *ibid.*, pp. 97f.

22. *Ibid.*, pp. 108ff.

23. *Ibid.*, pp. 117f. Nevertheless, a poll was taken on three organizational resolutions, the results of which give some indication of the relative strength of the opposition factions at the time. The proposal endorsed by the S.A.G. received 111 votes, the Spartacists' proposal was supported by 34 delegates, and 7 representatives endorsed a resolution submitted by Julian Borchardt, the Bremen radical who was even too extreme for the Spartacists. *Ibid.*, p. 118.

24. For text, see Prager, pp. 127ff.

25. *S.A.*, Jan. 11, 1917.

26. Dv., p. 217.

27. *P.A.*, Jan. 18, 1917, p. 41.

28. As quoted in Prager, p. 130.

29. *S.A.*, Jan. 25, 1917.

30. Prager, pp. 133ff.

31. *Ibid.*, pp. 135f. For a police report of the schism in the lower Rhine district at this time, see Buse, *Parteiagitation . . .*, p. 124.

32. H.H. to E.H., March 12, 1917, E.H., p. 140.

33. H.H. to E.H. March 21, 1917, *ibid.*, pp. 140f.

34. H.H. to E.H., Feb. 12, 1917, *ibid.*, p. 139.

35. See, e.g., his letter to Ernst Haase on March 21, 1917, *ibid.*, pp. 140f.

36. Vietsch, *Bethmann-Hollweg*, p. 264.

27. *Rt.*, CCCIX, 2889.

38. *Prot. U.S.P.D.*, 1917, p. 38.

39. *Unterirdische Literatur . . .*, pp. 86f,; Bartel, pp. 418f.

40. *Prot. U.S.P.D.*, 1917, p. 8.

41. This phrase was widely used during the pre-conference debates among the Spartacists concerning their future relationship to the S.A.G. *Illustrierte Geschichte . . .*, p. 148.

42. *Prot. U.S.P.D.*, 1917, pp. 9ff.

43. *Ibid.*, pp. 39ff.

44. *Ibid.*, pp. 46f

45. *Ibid.*, pp. 49f. Kautsky later insisted that the choice of this name was decisive in splitting the new organization off from the S.P.D. Kautsky, Mein Verhältnis . . ., p. 8. Emil Eichhorn, in his introduction to the Gotha convention protocol (p. 4), and Prager (p. 146) assert that Haase originally proposed the name.

46. *Prot. U.S.P.D.*, 1917, p. 71. Haase received 114 votes. Others elected to the committee were Zietz, Hofer, Wengels, Dittmann, Ledebour and Laukant. Thus, although the committee included a number of left-learning Independents, no actual Spartacists were elected, and Haase could count on the consistent support of is long-time friends Zietz, Dittmann and Wengels. Haase was chosen with Ledebour as co-chairman of the new party.

47. *Ibid.*, pp. 51ff.
48. *Ibid.*, pp. 61ff.
49. *Ibid.*, pp. 73f.
50. H.H. to Brill, April 8, 1917, E.H., pp. 141f.
51. For text, see *Prot. U.S.P.D.*, 1917, pp. 79ff.
52. Kautsky, *Mein Verhältnis . . .*, p. 8; Kautsky, *Sozialisten . . .*, p. 475.
53. *Ibid.*, pp. 474f., 479. Nettl, however, points out that "the fierce denunciations at the top did not penetrate far down into the amorphous Socialist membership." Nettl, II, 659.
54. Kautsky to Adler, Feb. 28, 1917, Ad., pp. 634f.
55. Kautksy to Adler, Aug. 7, 1916, *ibid.*, p. 630.

X. LEADER OF A NEW PARTY

1. See Haase's reference to such an incident in a Reichstag speech. *Rt.*, CCCX, 594.
2. Prager, p. 154.
3. For Kautsky's reaction, see his letter to Adler of Oct. 4, 1917, Ad., pp. 239ff. Haase predicted that the firing of Kautsky would strengthen the determination of many in the opposition, especially inasmuch as the selection of Heinrich Cunow as his successor made it clear that the journal had been surrendered to the "imperialistic wing" of the party. H.H. to "Friends," Oct. 1, 1917, E.H., p. 151.
4. The details of this persecution were often enumerated by Independent deputies in the Reichstag. See, e.g., Haase's speeches of July 19, 1917 and June 6, 1918. *Rt.*, CCCX, 3593ff., CCCXII, 5252ff. In some areas the U.S.P.D. leaders found it necessary to pursue their activities under the cover of front organizations. See, e.g., Sender, pp. 68f. For police and other official reports of efforts to suppress the activities of the U.S.P.D., see *Auswirkungen . . .*, II, 506, 511ff., 635f., 852, III, 951ff., 1047ff., 1078ff., 1116ff., 1317, 1416, 1529f. For additional similar documentation, see *Militär und Innenpolitik . . .*, I, 252, II, 726, 1143, 1286, 1294.
5. Prager, pp. 152ff.; *Auswirkungen . . .*, II, 294ff,; *Prot. S.P.D.*, 1917, pp. 235f. For an excellent analysis of the growth and distribution of U.S.P.D. membership, see Morgan, pp. 67ff.
6. Haase's letters of 1917 and 1918 reflect a cautious optimism concerning the growth of the party, but they also contain not a few expressions of frustration concerning the restrictions imposed upon his party's activities. See, e.g., H.H. to Gottschalk, May 24, 1917, H.H. to "Friends," Oct. 1, 1917, H.H. to Kautsky, Aug. 6, 1918, E.H., pp. 144, 151, 161.
7. For text of peace resolution, see *Rt.*, CCCX, 3573. Epstein argues that Erzberger "devised the Peace Resolution . . . partly with the purpose of strengthening Ebert's position against Haase." Epstein, p. 183.
8. H.H. to E.H., July 10, 1917, E.H., p. 148.
9. *Rt.*, CCCX, 3570ff.
10. *Ibid.*, 3575ff. Writing to his son, Haase condemned the behavior of the S.P.D. delegation as "contemptible." Their efforts to portray the Chancellor as being in essential agreement with their own policy was no longer simply a matter of self-

deception. Such tactics now involved "a crude deception of the workers." H.H. to E.H., July 27, 1917, E.H. p. 149.

11. Issued on March 27 by the Petrograd Soviet. Braunthal, II, 79ff.

12. *Rt.*, CCCX, 3585ff.

13. For the minutes of these conferences, see *Die Zimmerwalder Bewegung*, I, 95ff., 265ff. Haase attended neither conference. In the case of Zimmerwald, he was apparently not even invited because the primary organizer of the conference, Robert Grimm, considered him too moderate. Braunthal, II, 60. Although invited to Kienthal, he declined to attend because of his position in the International Socialist Bureau. Wheeler, p. 20.

14. Braunthal, II, 82ff,; *The Bolsheviks . . .*, pp. 582ff.

15. H.H. to E.H., May 6, 1917, E.H., pp. 145f. See also H.H. to Gottschalk, April 25, 1917, H.H. to Brill, June 17, 1917, *ibid.*, pp. 142ff., 146f.

16. H.H. to Gottschalk, April 25, 1917, H.H. to Gottschalk, May 24, 1917, H.H. to Brill, June 13, 1917, *ibid.*, pp. 142ff., 146f.

17. H.H. to E.H., June 24, 1917, H.H. to T.H., June 24, 1917, E.H., pp. 147f.

18. For text, see Rt., CCCX, 3590ff. For text of S.P.D. Stockholm memorandum, see Ebert, *Schriften . . .*, I, 365ff.

19. Braunthal, II, 105f.

20. Balabanoff, *Erinnerungen . . .*, pp. 167ff. She was a leading organizer of the conference. This mood is also reflected in Haase's letter to his wife of Sept. 9, 1917, E.H., pp. 149f. See also *Die Zimmerwalder Bewegung*, I, 456ff.

21. *Ibid.*, I, 482f.

22. In this context, see Haase's letter to "Friends" of Oct. 1, 1917, in which he complains of the lack of energy of the German workers, asks rhetorically when they will arouse themselves and argues that the Russian Revolution can be saved from its predicament only if socialist parties gain power everywhere. E.H., pp. 150f.

23. Balabanoff, *Erinnerungen . . .*, p. 169.

24. Balabanoff, "Die Zimmerwalder Bewegung . . .," pp. 402f.

25. Late in September Luise Zietz requested postponement of its publication because of the threat hovering over the U.S.P.D. at the time. It was finally published by Karl Radek in a Bolshevik-oriented Finnish paper without the permission of Balabanoff. *The Bolsheviks . . .*, pp. 666f; Balabanoff, *Erinnerungen . . .*, pp. 172f.

26. *Rt.*, CCCX, 3773ff.

27. *Ibid.*, pp. 3785f.

28. *Ibid.*, pp. 3794ff.

29. *Ibid.*, pp. 3803f.

30. Writing to his son on Oct. 15, Haase declared that he had been "almost in high spirits" during the session of Oct. 9. Ebert had "for the first time found energetic tones" because he had finally begun to realize that he and his friends were next in line for persecution if they should begin to stir themselves. E.H., pp. 151f. For detailed discussions of the incident, see Horn, pp. 94ff.; Vidil, pp. 104ff. See also Dittmann's testimony during proceedings initiated against Zietz in November as published in *Die Ursachen des deutschen Zusammenbruchs . . .*, IX, Part I, 200ff.

31. For official references to Haase's efforts to politicize the strike, see *Auswirkungen* . . ., II, 452, 459, 465. For similar references in a report of the General Commission of the Trade Unions, *ibid.*, pp. 467f.

32. See the discussions of the strike in the Reichstag by Oscar Cohn and Dittmann. *Rt.*, CCCIX, 3098f., CCX, 3145ff. See also Dtt., p. 807; R. Müller, I, 83; *Auswirkungen* . . ., II, 463.

33. Groener, pp. 363f.

34. According to Richard Müller, a leader of the "Revolutionary Shop Stewards," the principal reason that the strike was not carried out was that the Shop Stewards opposed it on the grounds that they had already lost too many leaders as a result of the April strike. R. Müller, I, 89.

35. Cohn declared that the April strike came as a complete surprise to the Independent leaders. *Rt.*, CCCIX, 3098.

36. For details concerning the planning of the strike, see *Der Ledebour-Prozess*, pp. 24f,; R. Müller, I, 100ff; Dtt., pp. 830ff,; *Auswirkungen* . . ., III, 1131ff.

37. For text, *ibid.*, III, 954f. According to Müller, Haase felt that a mass action for peace was necessary, that the U.S.P.D. should support it vigorously, but that a public call for a strike by the Independent delegation would destroy the entire party. Müller, I, 101.

38. Feldman estimates that some 400,000 Berlin workers went on strike. Feldman, p. 449.

39. For text, see *Vorwärts*, No. 29, Jan. 29, 1918.

40. Sch., *Der Zusammenbruch*, pp. 69ff. See also Scheidemann's report to the interparty committee on Feb. 5. *Interfraktionelle Ausschuss*, II, 194.

41. *Frakt.*, II, 364ff.; *Rt.*, CCCXI, 4161ff.

42. See, e.g., the testimony of Dittmann before the Reichstag investigatory commission in Nov. 1927 in which he maintained that both the S.P.D. and the U.S.P.D. sought to keep the strike under control. *Die Ursachen des deutschen Zusammenbruchs* . . ., V, 252.

43. *Auswirkungen* . . ., III, 1133.

44. *Frakt.*, II, 368ff,; Feldman, pp. 450ff.

45. *Ursachen und Folgen* . . ., I, 250

46. See, e.g., the apologetics of Scheidemann in the Reichstag. *Rt.*, CCCXI, 4164ff.

47. *Auswirkungen* . . ., III, 1134.

48. *Rt.*, CCCXI, 4057ff,; Dtt., pp. 832ff.

49. *Auswirkungen* . . ., III, 1108f.

50. H.H. to Brill, Feb. 10, 1918, E.H., pp. 157ff.

51. *Rt.*, CCCXI, 421 ff. See also the leaflet issued by the executive committee of the U.S.P.D. after the strike which is reprinted in R. Müller, I, 209f.

52. He was referring to the German ultimatum of Feb. 21, the terms of which were communicated to the Reichstag on Feb. 26. For details, see Fischer, pp. 668ff.

53. *Rt.*, CCCXI, 4208ff.

54. This phrase was used by David in the Reichstag. *Ibid*, 4431.

55. *Ibid.*, 4540ff.

56. Kautsky, *Mein Verhältnis* . . ., p. 9.

57. For a general discussion of the attitude of the Independents toward the Bolsheviks, see Lösche, pp. 144ff. See also Morgan, pp. 98ff.

58. See, e.g., H.H. to Eisner, Nov. 17, 1917, H.H. to Brill, Nov. 25, 1917, H.H. to E.H., Nov. 30, 1917, E.H. pp. 152f., 154, 155.

59. H.H. to E.H., May 15, 1918, *ibid.*, pp. 159f.

60. Kautsky actually published later in August. *S.A.*, Aug. 22, 1918. It should, however, be viewed in the context of a continuing debate in this journal. See also Kautsky's pamphlet, *Demokratie oder Diktatur*.

61. H.H. to Kautsky, Aug. 6, 1918, E.H., p. 161.

XI. THE COMING OF THE REVOLUTION

1. G. Ritter, IV, 381ff.

2. For evidence, especially of unrest among workers, see Bartel, pp. 555ff. For further documentary evidence, above all of the decline in military morale, see *Ursachen und Folgen* . . ., II, 283ff. See also Volkmann, pp. 18 ff., 313f. Haase is reported to have spoken on Aug. 17 in a private meeting of U.S.P.D. leaders in Königsberg of the "disintegration of the western front as a result of disobedience and desertion" and of the collapse of the Austro-Hungrian army. *Auswirkungen* . . ., III, 1529.

3. H.H. to E.H., Sept. 9, 1918, E.H., pp. 162f.

4. H.H. to Brill, Sept. 25, 1918, *ibid.*, pp. 163f. At the time Haase's name was among those of a list of proscribed "Hetzredner." *Militär und Innenpolitik*, II, 1281.

5. H.H. to Brill, Sept. 28, 1918, E.H., p. 164.

6. For good general summaries of the political developments in Sept. and Oct., see Eyck, I, 31ff.; Halperin, pp. 50ff.

7. *Frakt.*, II, 417ff.

8. Max von Baden, pp. 341ff.

9. H.H. to E.H., Oct. 8, 1918, E.H., p. 166. According to the rather questionable report of Colonel von Haeften, a representative of the high command who was present at the meeting, Ebert turned "deathly pale and couldn't say a word." Haase, on the other hand, rushed up to Ledebour after the meeting, according to Haeften, and declared, "Now we have them!" *Die Ursachen des Deutschen Zusammenbruchs* . . ., II, 376.

10. *Frakt.*, II, 463. See also David's description of the meeting in Ebert, *Kämpfe und Ziele*, pp. 363f.

11. Max von Baden, pp. 348ff.

12. As a result of the January strike movement, the leaders of the Berlin Metalworkers Association initiated a long series of negotiations aimed at achieving a reconciliation. They did not finally abandon their efforts until late in October, but it was fully apparent at least by the end of September that they had no chance of success, for the Independents absolutely refused to give up their demand that the S.P.D. cease its bloc politics. Bernstein, pp. 26ff. See also H. Müller, p. 46.

13. It contains a considerable number of phrases which Haase had used previously in his letters.

14. *Ursachen und Folgen* . . ., II, 55ff. In the course of a conversation with the historian Gustav Mayer on Oct. 5, Haase expressed himself as not being fundamentally opposed to a restoration of the unity of the German workers movement. He pointed out, however, that serious and basic differences divided the Independents from the majority socialists. Mayer reports that Haase was particularly embittered by the failure of the majority socialists to intervene immediately upon their entry into the government to obtain an amnesty for Liebknecht and others "who had worked for peace." Mayer, pp. 299f.

15. *S.A.*, Oct. 10, 1918.

16. H.H. to E.H., Oct. 10, Oct. 20, 1918 and H.H. to Brill, Oct. 21, 1918, E.H., pp. 164ff.

17. Max describes him as speaking with "Schadenfreude." Max von Baden, p. 487.

18. *Rt.*, CCCXIV, 6181ff. Speaking in Frankfurt on Oct. 27, he again exuded a sense of triumph. Lucas, p. 16.

19. Dtt., pp. 853ff.

20. Morgan, p. 111.

21. *Unterirdische Literatur* . . ., pp. 114ff.

22. Richard Müller traces the origins of the group back to the first months of the war. R. Müller, I, 125. Ledebour declared at his trial in 1919 that it had been formed sometime in 1917. *Der Ledebour-Prozess*, p. 28.

23. Since the January strikes, Ledebour had met regularly with the group. Däumig had also worked closely with the Shop Stewards since early in the summer. R. Müller, I, 126f. See also Barth, pp. 26ff. Barth's book is manifestly inaccurate on occasion and tends to overemphasize his own role.

24. R. Müller, I, 127; Barth, p. 43.

25. R. Müller, I, 129ff. Barth complains of the Spartacists' "dilettantism." Barth, p. 34.

26. *Der Ledebour-Prozess*, pp. 28f. Barth describes a meeting on Nov. 1 at which this decision was reached. He then reports that another meeting took place on the morning of Nov. 2 which Haase attended and at which specific plans for the uprising were discussed. Barth, pp. 46f. Concerning the plans of the Independents, see also Morgan, pp. 112f.

27. *Der Ledebour-Prozess*, p. 29. Dittmann claims that after hearing the reports of the factory representatives, even Liebknecht and Müller supported the position taken by Haase and himself, i.e., that the action should be postponed. Only Däumig among the party leaders supported Ledebour. Dtt., p. 855. Barth stresses Haase's opposition to immediate action and describes him as being pessimistic about the chances of success. Barth, pp. 47ff.

28. R. Müller, I, 139; Barth, p. 51.

29. R. Müller, I, 139. Barth claims that when pressed to make plans in October for the post-revolutionary period, Haase had maintained that nothing could be settled in advance. Barth, p. 35.

30. R. Müller, I, 139.

31. In a letter written on the following day, Haase described the gathering as an "important political meeting" which had lasted from eight p.m. until four a.m. without achieving any "positive result." H.H. to T.H., Nov. 3, 1918, E.H., pp. 170f. The very real danger that the letter might be intercepted may well explain this somewhat enigmatic statement.

32. Inf., Friedlander, who was with Haase when the call came in from Kiel.

33. H.H. to T.H., Nov. 5, 1918, E.H., pp. 171f. This letter is obviously misdated. It should read Nov. 6. Ledebour declared at his trial that he had been asked to go, but refused because he was the only activist among the Independent deputies and therefore felt that he was needed in Berlin. *Der Ledebour-Prozess*, p. 29.

34. Inf., Friedlander.

35. This is the explanation given by his son (E.H., p. 56) and by Hermann Müller, who accompanied him during much of the journey. H. Müller, p. 39.

36. H.H. to T.H., Nov. 5 (6), 1918, E.H., pp. 171f. For a description of the outbreak of the revolution in Hamburg, see Comfort, pp. 35ff.

37. H. Müller, p. 39. Noske claims that Haase, who appeared to be "terribly exhausted," said essentially the same thing to him. Noske, *Von Kiel . . .*, p. 27. He immediately sent a telegram to Berlin in which he reported that Haase had assured him that the unity of the socialists in Kiel would not be disturbed and expected the same (*Gegenleistung*) from the majority socialists in Berlin. The telegram is reprinted in Sch., *Der Zusammenbruch*, p. 197.

38. H. Müller, p. 39.

39. *Ibid.*, pp. 39ff.

40. *Ursachen und Folgen . . .*, II, 568.

41. *Krakt.*, Ii, 514.

42. See, e.g., the manifestoes published in *Vorwärts*, No. 304, Nov. 4, 1918 and No. 306, Nov. 6, 1918 and the S.P.D. leaflet of Nov. 8 reprinted in *Ursachen und Folgen . . .*, II, 568.

43. Sch., *Memoiren . . .*, II, 293.

44. Dtt., p. 863; Barth, pp. 52f.

45. For text, see *Ursachen und Folgen . . .*, II, 569.

46. Sch., *Der Zusammenbruch*, pp. 206f.

47. Sch., *Memoiren . . .*, II, 297ff.; *Frakt.*, II, 518ff.

48. Dtt., pp. 864f.

49. The fact that Ebert was thus provided with a formal tie to the old regime undoubtedly helped to secure the loyalty of the many officers and officials who continued to serve the revolutionary government. *R.Vb.*, I, XXVII.

50. Dtt., p. 867.

51. *Ibid.*, pp. 868ff.; Bernstein, p. 34; R. Müller, II, 27f.

52. Bernstein, p. 33; Ströbel, p. 66.

53. Dtt., pp 868ff.; Barth, p. 57; *Frakt.*, II, 518ff.

54. Dtt., p. 870. Ernst Haase also writes that his father had serious reservations about entering a coalition government. E.H., p. 58. Barth claims that Haase was at first opposed to participation because the weakness of the Independents' organization

would put them at a disadvantage. Barth, p. 58. Haase himself later declared that he had been reluctant to enter such a government. H.H. to E.H., Nov. 26, 1918, E.H., p. 173.

55. A clear majority had been obtained before Haase arrived, but the party leaders felt that no final decision could be made before he arrived. Bernstein, pp. 35f.; Dtt., p. 870.

56. For text, see *R.Vb.*, I, 20f.

57. Dittmann reports that the new U.S.P.D. list of conditions was drafted by Haase. Only a small minority led by Ledebour opposed it. Dtt., p. 871.

58. For text, see *R.Vb.*, I, 30f.

59. Dtt., p. 871; Barth, p. 60.

60. Dtt., p. 872. Barth seems to indicate that this meeting did not take place until after the Zirkus Busch meeting. Barth, p. 64.

61. R.Müller, II, 32f.

62. *R.Vb.*, I, 22.

63. H. Müller, pp. 61ff. Barth complains that the Independents made no effort to influence the soldiers. Barth, p. 60.

64. R. Müller, II, 36.

65. *Ibid.*, 37; Bernstein, p. 46.

66. R. Müller, II, 37f.; Barth, pp. 62f.; Bernstein, pp. 47f.

67. Bernstein claims that this name was selected by the cabinet members themselves after the meeting. Bernstein, pp. 47f.

68. Haase later claimed that he was the author. *Prot. U.S.P.D.*, March 1919, p. 82. Richard Müller and Hermann Müller, however report that it was drafted by Ernst Däumig. R. Muller, II, 36, 40; H. Müller, p. 72. It may well be that they worked on it together.

69. For text, see *R.Vb.*, I, 31ff.

70. Dtt., p. 872; Barth, p. 64.

71. Rosenberg, p. 271.

XII. THE CRITIC IN POWER

1. Hamburger, pp. 509ff.; Angress, pp. 164ff.

2. *R. Vb.*, II, pp. XXXIXf.; Morgan, pp. 457.

3. Dittmann reports that the Cabinet members did not allow their differences to descend to the personal level. Dtt., p. 931. See also Haase's statement to the same effect in a joint meeting of the Cabinet and the Central Council on Dec. 28. *R.Vb.*, II, 88. This is not to suggest, however, that personal antagonism between the various members of the Canbinet was wholly avoided. For a description of conflicts that did develop, see *ibid.*, pp. LXXIIf.

4. *Ursachen und Folgen* . . ., III, 11.

5. *Ibid.*, p. 498. Dittmann claims that th telegram was drafted by Ebert. Dtt., pp. 881f.

6. Dtt., p. 88 .

7. *R.Vb.*, I, 37f.

8. Sch., *Memoiren* . . ., II, 325.

9. The convening of a constituent assembly quickly became a principal demand of the non-socialist as well as of the majority socialist press. For Independent reactions to this development, see *Mitteilungs-Blatt* . . ., No. 24, Nov. 24, 1918. See also Haase's remark on Nov. 18 that "counterrevolutionary forces" were working to bring about a precipitous calling of a constituent assembly. *R.Vb.*, I, 95.

10. In a letter to his son less than two weeks later, Haase wrote that "the revolutionary process is just in its beginning stages. The forms in which it will further develop itself depend upon the work that the government will accomplish." H.H. to E.H., Nov. 26, 1918, E.H., p. 173.

11. It should be noted that the Cabinet members did not thereby intend to assume the responsibilities hitherto fulfilled by the various secretaries of state. Rather, what was involved was simply a division of labor within the cabinet. *R.Vb.*, I, p. XLVII. Scheidemann and Landsberg exchanged positions on Nov. 19. *Ibid.*, pp. XLVIf.

12. This was in keeping with the policy advocated most vigorously by Kurt Eisner, who was now the Independent Prime Minister of Bavaria. See, e.g., Eisner's statements at the national conference of state representatives on Nov. 25. *Ibid.*, II, 179f. See also similar statements at the same meeting by Kautsky (p. 167), Bernstein (p. 170) and Crispien (p. 177). Kessler reports that Haase assured him on Nov. 13 that the French knew that he had opposed the war from the beginning. Kessler, p. 29. This view was also consistently expressed by the editors of *Freiheit*.

13. Haase took the chair only on two occasions. In both cases, Ebert was absent. *R.Vb.*, I, 344ff., II, 44ff.

14. Brecht, p. 200. Brecht was an important official in the chancellery at the time.

15. For discussions of the relationship between Haase and Ebert in the Cabinet, see: *ibid.*; Barth, pp. 78f.; Oehme, pp. 36f., 42f,; Elben, p. 28; Kolb, p. 123.

16. *R.Vb.*, I, 102f., 136.

17. E.H., p. 63.

18. *Prot. U.S.P.D.*, March 1919, p. 50.

19. Prager, p. 183.

20. *Prot. U.S.P.D.*, March 1919, p. 50. See also Morgan, pp. 179ff., 199f.

21. According to Oehme, who was an official in the chancellery at the time, all of the personnel considered Ebert to be the Chancellor. Oehme, p. 34.

22. H.H. to E.H., Nov. 26, 1918, E.H., p. 173. Haase also complained in this letter that the majority socialists had permitted bourgeois bureaucrats to retain even the most important positions.

23. Note Haase's statement during a joint meeting of the Cabinet and the Berlin Executive Council on Nov. 18 that "the source of all power is in the workers' and soldiers' councils; the government derives its power from this source; it cannot continue to exist without the confidence of the workers' and soldiers' councils." Even then, however, he emphasized that the councils must not intervene in the administrative affairs of the Cabinet. Otherwise, he remarked, "the entire organism will come to a halt." *R. Vb.*, I, 95.

24. This complaint was often made by Dittmann and Haase, but it was also emphasized by Hermann Müller. Dtt., pp. 877ff., 893; H. Müller, p. 100. For a

similar statement by Haase, see, e.g., his article in *Freiheit*, No. 1, Jan. 1, 1919.

25. H. Müller, pp. 108ff,; R. Müller, II, 53ff.

26. *R.Vb.*, I, 293, 314.

27. *Freiheit*, No. 3, Nov. 16, 1918.

28. See, e.g., *Freiheit*, No. 10, Nov. 20, No. 11, Nov. 21, No. 21, Nov. 26, No. 57, Dec. 16, and No. 59, Dec. 17, 1918.

29. It was at the national party congress of the following spring that Haase most clearly expressed the view that the councils should assume a permanent place in Germany's political structure. At that time he also declared that the revolutionary government had constituted a "dictatorship of the proletariat." *Prot. U.S.P.D.*, March 1919, pp. 87, 213f, 244. It is undoubtedly true that both he and his party had moved considerably to the left by that time. Nevertheless, according to his son, Haase had expressed essentially the same point of view as early as Nov. 25. E.H., pp. 64f. Dittmann maintains that the Independents viewed the councils as merely transitional organizations. He adds, however, that they considered them the guarantors of the revolution which should have been preserved until the revolution had been consolidated. Dtt., p. 892. Kautsky espoused a view much closer to that of the majority socialists. See, e.g., his comments in *Freiheit*, No. 37, Dec. 5, and No. 39, Dec. 6, 1918.

30. *R.Vb.*, I, 72, 88, 95.

31. The Independent Cabinet members argued during the decisive meeting of Nov. 29 against setting any date for elections. *Ibid.*, p. 227. In a speech to a Berlin party meeting on Dec. 15 Haase declared that they had urged that the elections be set for April at the earliest. *Freiheit*, No. 57, Dec. 16, 1918.

32. See, e.g., Richard Muller's statement that the road to the constituent assembly would have to pass over his dead body. *Freiheit*, No. 10, Dec. 20, 1918.

33. *R.Vb.*, I, 227f. Zietz later reported that the Independents had decided to resign if this concession were not granted. *Prot. U.S.P.D.*, March 1919, p. 173. See also Sch., *Memoiren . . .*, II, 37.

34. He made this demand in virtually all of his public speeches. See also his strong statement in this regard during the Cabinet meeting of Nov. 18. *R.Vb.*, I, 103f.

35. In the Cabinet, the S.P.D. representatives consistently stressed that socialization required careful planning. At times, they went so far as to decry the propaganda for immediate socialization. See, e.g., Scheidemann's statement on Nov. 21 that it was "impossible" to carry out any immediate socialization and that the constant discussion of such measures had a bad effect upon the industrialists. *R.Vb.*, I, 117. Several of the Independent leaders shared the majority socialists' cautious attitude to some degree. See, e.g., Bernstein's and Kautsky's articles in *Freiheit*, No. 13, Nov. 22 and No. 19, Nov. 25, 1918, respectively. The U.S.P.D. executive committee, however, consistently demanded that immediate steps be taken. See, e.g., *ibid.*, No. 22, Nov. 27; No. 43, Dec. 8; No. 72, Dec. 24, 1918.

36. *R.Vb.*, I, 103f.

37. Kolb, pp. 184ff.; A. Mayer, pp. 97ff., 101ff. For Solf's attitude toward domestic politics and their relationship to Germany's international situation during

this period, see the following materials to be found in Ba., Nachlass Solf: No. 59, pp. 81ff. and 228ff (copies of memoranda addressed to Ebert and dated Nov. 17 and Dec. 10, 1918); No. 156, pp. 79f. (answers to questions directed to Solf by Max von Baden and dated Jan. 15, 1931).

38. Solf apparently had the active support of Ebert in these efforts. A. Mayer, p. 101; Kolb, pp. 184ff. See also Barth, p. 68; R. Müller, II, 50; Oehme, pp. 255f. A collection of reports, dated Nov. 25, 1918, from foreign embassies and other foreign sources emphasizing the possible repercussions of any movement to the left in Germany is to be found in Ba., Nachlass Solf, No. 59, pp. 1 4ff. See also Haase's references to such reports in *R.Vb.*, I, 94f., 98f.

39. Kautsky had been named political representative (Beigeordneter) for the U.S.P.D. in the foreign office. *R.Vb.*, I, pp. LXIIf. Concerning Kautsky's influence upon Haase, see Barth, p. 77. For a perceptive analysis of the U.S.P.D.'s relationship to the Bolshevik regime at this point, see Wheeler, pp. 45ff.

40. Relations between the two governments had been severed after a box addressed to the Russian embassy had been intentionally broken open on Nov. 4 to reveal a quantity of revolutionary pamphlets which, in fact, had been placed there by German police. Scheidemann played a central role in initiating this incident. For details, see Baumgart, pp. 354ff.,; Carr, III, 94f.; Nadolny, pp. 62f.

41. *R.Vb.*, I, 98f. Though apparently suspicious, he was clearly impressed by the argument that the Entente would not look with favor upon the establishment of close relations with the Bolsheviks.

42. See Haase's teletype exchanges with various Soviet officials on Nov. 16 and 18 in A.A., Deutschland, No. 131, Vol. 55, pp. 50ff., 131ff. Of course, the Russians provided numerous excuses for procrastination. Among other things, they broadcasted an appeal for the formation of a government under Liebknecht on Nov. 11 (*Dokumenten und Materialien . . .*, II, 360) permitted the temporary arrest of German consular officials and refused to recognize them as the diplomatic representatives of the new German government. A. Mayer, pp. 238ff.,; Carr, III, 98ff.

43. See draft of telegram dated Nov. 16, 1918 from Haase to the Russian Commissar of Foreign Affairs Chicherin in A.A., Deutschland, No. 131, Vol. 55, pp. 73f.

44. *R.Vb.*, I, 303.

45. See, e.g., *ibid.*, I, 62, 100; II, 40f., 44, 51. See also Haase's explanation of his attitude in *Prot. U.S.P.D.*, March 1919, pp. 82f.

46. *R.Vb.*, I, 119, 122, 131f., 1 8.

47. Kessler, p. 71; Roos, p. 51.

48. Vietsch, *Wilhelm Solf*, pp. 212ff., 219f. See also Rosenfeld, p. 147.

49. See Haase's complaints at the conference of state representatives on Nov. 25. *R.Vb.*, I, 198. See also Oehme, pp. 43, 238; Barth, pp. 74f.; Nadolny, pp. 65f.; Kolb, p. 186.

50. *R.Vb.*, I, 110, 164f., 179f., 181, 198.

51. Vietsch, *Wilhelm Solf*, pp. 218f. Haase complained on the following day in a letter to his son that he had not yet been successful in getting rid of Solf. H.H. to E.H., Nov. 26, 1918, E.H., p. 173.

52. *R.Vb.*, I, 243, 254. According to Vietsch, however, Ebert urged Solf on Dec. 6 to withdraw his resignation. In his opinion Solf would have done so if he and Haase had not clashed on Dec. 9. Vietsch, *Wilhelm Solf*, p. 219.

53. *R.Vb.*, I, 296.

54. *Ibid.*, p. 300. For Haase's public denial of these charges, see *Freiheit*, No. 45, Dec. 9, 1918. For Barth's denial, see *ibid.*, No. 48, Dec. 11, 1918. Late in December Haase's friend Oskar Cohn explained that it was he who had received the money. He declared, however, that he had used it for propaganda purposes and not for the purchase of weapons. The most important relevant documents are reprinted in *Ursachen und Folgen . . .*, II, 534ff. For Haase's reaction to a second such broadcast by Joffe, see *R.Vb.*, I, 394f. See also Haase's discussion of the incident in *Prot. U.S.P.D.*, March 1919, pp. 242f.

55. *R. Vb.*, I, 302, 371f. Hermann Müller reports that both Haase and Scheidemann thought highly of Brockdorff. H. Müller p. 157. Concerning further negotiations between Brockdorff and the Cabinet, see *R. Vb.*, I, 397ff. See also Stern-Rubarth, pp. 52ff.

56. Groener, p. 467; Herzfeld, p. 384. In this, the second part (pp. 196ff.) of his book, Herzfeld reprints extensive excerpts from the testimony given at the so-called "Munich *Dolchstoss* trial" of October and November 1925. Actually, Ebert had exchanged expressions of mutual support with the supreme command before his conversation with Groener on Nov. 10. See, e.g., *Ursachen und Folgen . . .*, III, 495ff. See also Kluge, pp. 134ff.

57. Herzfeld, p. 384. Groener undoubtedly portrayed the "pact" as being far more explicit that it, in fact, was. For further discussion of this alliance, see: Kluge, pp. 136ff.; Morgan, pp. 151ff.; Carsten, pp. 18ff.; Schüddekopf, pp. 14ff. See also *Ursachen und Folgen . . .*, III, 500ff.

58. Ernst Haase claims that his father soon suspected that Ebert was intriguing with the military behind the backs of his colleagues. E.H., p. 63. Haase's actions, however, seem to reflect a fundamental trust in Ebert's honesty, if not his judgment, which was only very gradually shaken. In support of this analysis, see Oehme, p. 21.

59. See, e.g., Haase's statements to this effect at a Berlin party meeting on Dec. 15. *Freiheit*, No. 57, Dec. 16, 1918.

60. See, e.g., Haase's statements at the same meeting. *Ibid.* This point of view was constantly stressed by editorials in *Freiheit*. Under the editorship of Haase's friend Rudolf Hilferding, *Freiheit* can be considered a reasonably accurate reflection of Haase's point of view at this time. *Vorwärts*, on the other hand, emphasized the danger on the left.

61. See, e.g., *R.Vb.*, I, 240, 242, 248, 293; II, 9f., 107ff.

62. H. Müller, pp. 118f. The official explanation for the abandonment of this plan was that the troops of the Berlin garrison felt that it implied a lack of trust in their loyalty to the revolution. *Vorwärts*, No. 314, Nov. 14, 1918.

63. *R.Vb.*, I, 247ff., 276.

64. Haase apparently simply assumed that it would be carried out. See, e.g., his statements to the Berlin party meeting of Dec. 15 as reported in *Freiheit*, No. 59, Dec. 17, 1918.

65. Dittmann argues that the war minister, Scheüch, persuaded the majority socialists not to carry out the plan. Dtt., p. 898. On Dec. 28 Ebert explained his failure to execute the plan as resulting from Scheüch's decision in mid-December to resign as soon as a successor could be found. *R.Vb.*, II, 109. For further information concerning the fate of the popular force, see: H. Müller, p. 187; Kolb, p. 177; Schulze, p. 18; Kluge, pp. 247ff.

66. For Dittmann, see, e.g., *R.Vb.*, I, 240; II, 95. For Haase, see *supra*, n. 61.

67. Haase remarked on Dec. 7 that the Cabinet received warnings about a coup nearly every day. *Ibid.*, I, 292.

68. Dtt., pp. 895f.

69. Practically all of the memoir literature of the period deals at least cursorily with these events. Although there is some disagreement concerning details, most of these sources agree with the sketch presented here. My principal source, however, is the minutes of the meeting of the Cabinet with the Berlin Executive Council held on Dec. 7. *R.Vb.*, I, 285ff.

70. *Ibid.*

71. *Ibid.*, pp. 293f.

72. *Ibid.*, p. 296.

73. *Freiheit*, No. 46, Dec. 10, 1918; H. Müller, p. 148.

74. The supreme command did, indeed, hope to use these troops against "radical" elements in Berlin. Moreover, Ebert was apparently informed of this plan, and, although he remained ambivalent about it, he did nothing to prevent its execution. Morgan, pp. 186f. See also: Herzfeld, pp. 385f.; Konnemann, pp. 316ff.; the excerpt from the memoirs of Colonel von Haeften in R.Vb., I, 316ff.; *Die Wirren . . .*, pp. 27ff.

75. A few days after the troops began arriving he publicly declared that General Lequis, the commander of the returning soldiers who was intimately involved in these machinations was "completely harmless," although he added that some of his officers could not be trusted. *Freiheit*, No. 57, Dec. 16, 1918.

76. *Die Wirren . . .*, pp. 33f.; Konnemann, p. 1599; Morgan, pp. 187f.

77. *Vorwärts*, No. 340, Dec. 11, 1918.

78. *Freiheit*, No. 49, Dec. 11, 1918.

79. The above remarks are taken from both his major and his concluding speeches. *Ibid.*, No. 57, Dec. 16, and No. 59, Dec. 17, 1918.

80. *Ibid.*, No. 57, Dec. 16, 1918.

81. Of 489 delegates, 292 joined the majority socialist delegation. The Independent delegation had only 94 members, but they were supported by 10 members of the "United Revolutionary" delegation. *Zr.*, pp. XXVIIf.

82. *Allgemeiner Kongress . . .*, p. 6.

83. The Independent delegation's two chief spokesmen were Kurt Geyer, who had regularly criticized the Independent Cabinet members in the *Leipziger Volkszeitung*, and Otto Brass of Düsseldorf, who stood firmly on the left and had been engaged in a struggle with Dittmann for control of the party in his area.

84. Dtt., p. 904. Although Barth claims (pp. 78, 91) that Haase had written this speech, Dittmann maintains that he had not discussed its contents with Haase before he delivered it. Dtt., p. 878.

85. *Allgemeiner Kongress* . . ., pp. 19ff.

86. He had predicted such an outcome during one of his speeches to the Berlin party conference. *Freiheit*, No. 57, Dec. 16, 1918.

87. *Allgemeiner Kongress* . . ., pp. 127f.

88. *Ibid.*, p. 141.

89. *Ibid.*, pp. 78f.

90. *Ibid.*, pp. 88f, 126.

91. *Zr.*, p. XXXI.

92. He tried desperately, but unsuccessfully to persuade the delegation to reverse this decision. E.H., p. 69; Bernstein, p. 95; R. Müller, II, 210.

93. *Allgemeiner Kongress* . . ., pp. 150ff. For an analysis of the membership of the Central Council, see *Zr.*, pp. XXXVff.

94. Dtt., p. 919.

95. *Allgemeiner Kongress* . . ., pp. 152ff. See also *Zr.*, p. XXVIII.

96. *Allgemeiner Kongress* . . ., p. 182.

97. *Ibid.*, p. 95. For final text, see *ibid.*, p. 181 and *Zr.*, pp. 2ff. See also Herwig, pp. 150ff.

98. *Allgemeiner Kongress* . . ., pp. 90f. Haase also emphasized this point during a Cabinet meeting on Dec. 18. *R.Vb.*, I, 396.

99. Groener, p. 475. For text, see *Militarismus* . . ., p. 184.

100. Groener, p. 475; *Die Wirren* . . ., pp. 22f.; *R.Vb.*, I, 396. For other protests of the supreme command, see *Militarismus* . . ., pp. 181ff.

101. *R. Vb.*, II, 4ff., 7, 9ff., 14f.

102. In his memoirs, Groener praises Ebert extravagantly for his success in dealing with this situation. Groener, p. 475.

103. Again, there are a large number of sources which discuss these events. My description is taken largely from the minutes of the joint meetings of the Cabinet and the Central Council on Dec. 28. *R.Vb.*, II, 73ff. The most useful accounts by participants are: Bernstein (for background), pp, 103f.; Dtt., pp. 932ff.; Barth, pp. 98ff. For an analysis of the role played by Otto Wels, see Adolph, pp. 94ff.

104. See Haase's testimony at the Dec. 28 meeting. *R. Vb.*, II, 85f.

105. *Ibid.*, pp. 86f. See also Dtt., p. 936; Barth, pp. 99ff.; *Die Wirren* . . ., pp. 34f.

106. Herzfeld, pp. 387f. The authors of *Die Wirren* . . . claim (p. 36) that the decision was reached during a conference between the War Minister and the "moderate" members of the Cabinet which began at about 10:30 p.m. It seems likely that Ebert acted at least partly in response to the strong pressure being exerted upon him by the military.

107. *R.Vb.*, II, 82f.

108. *Ledebour-Prozess*, p. 40.

109. Barth, pp. 104ff. See also the transcript of a telephone conversation between Barth and Major von Harbou, dated Dec. 24, 9:15 a.m. A.S.D., Nachlass Barth, Kassette I, No. 44. See also Barth's testimony at the Dec. 28 meeting. *R.Vb.*, II, 93.

110. Dtt., pp. 932f.; Barth, pp. 106f.

111. *Vorwärts*, No. 326, Dec. 27, 1918; Dtt., pp. 939f.; Haase's testimony on Dec. 28, *H.Vb.*, II, 87.

112. *Freiheit*, No. 76, Dec. 27, 1918.

113. *R.Vb.*, II, 74ff.

114. *Ibid.*, pp. 83, 88, 89ff.

115. *Ibid.*, pp. 87, 95, 98ff., 102.

116. For details concerning the majority socialists' plan to keep a considerable number of men under arms and the Independents' opposition to it, see Barth, pp. 94f.; *Zr.*, p. 79, n. 40. See also Ebert's and Haase's remarks during the Dec. 28 meeting. *R.Vb.*, II, 111f, 128.

117. It is not clear why they chose to demand the immediate execution of just these, rather than all of the Hamburg Points. It seems probable that they considered these to be the easiest to carry out and thus the most likely to receive the support of the Central Council.

118. The majority socialists first made this proposal on Dec. 23. It was opposed by Haase and the other Independents, and it was decided that it should be discussed with the Central Council. Barth, pp. 97f.; *R.Vb.*, II, 35.

119. *R.Vb.*, II, 125f.

120. *Ibid.*, pp. 133f.

121. Dtt., p. 945.

122. *R.Vb.*, II, 141.

123. *Freiheit*, No. 1, Jan. 1, 1919.

124. Dtt., p. 902; Morgan, pp. 199f.

XIII. RETURN TO OPPOSITION

1. *Freiheit*, No. 57, Dec. 16, 1918.

2. *Der Gründungsparteitag der K.P.D.*, pp. 32ff.

3. Dtt., pp. 877, 910.

4. Bernstein, p. 130.

5. Kautsky, untitled handwritten ms., dated "approximately Dec. 20, 1918," I.I.S.H., Kautsky Nachlass, K.A., No. 83.

6. Kautsky noted this on the ms.

7. See, e.g., his speech at the Berlin party conference of Dec. 15, 1918. *Freiheit*, No, 57, Dec. 16, 1918.

8. Eichhorn, pp. 57, 67ff.

9. *Freiheit*, No. 8, Jan. 5, 1919.

10. *Der Ledebour-Prozess*, pp. 50ff. The chairmen of this committee were Ledebour, Liebknecht and the Revolutionary Shop Steward Paul Scholze. It should be noted that Ledebour resigned from the co-chairmanship of the U.S.P.D. Ratz, *Georg Ledebour*, p. 191.

11. *De Ledebour-Prozess*, pp. 62f.; Eichhorn, p. 71.

12. Noske, *Von Kiel . . .*, pp. 67f.

13. See, e.g., *ibid.*, p. 69; H. Müller, p. 257; Bernstein, pp. 140f.

14. The expected support of the garrison failed to materialize. *Der Ledebour-Prozess*, p. 52; Morgan, pp. 213ff.; Kluge, pp. 268f.

15. Noske, *Von Kiel . . .*, pp. 68ff.

16. Dtt., p. 986; Bernstein, p. 140.

17. *Zr.*, pp. 250f., 252ff.

18. *Ibid.*, pp. 255ff.

19. *Ibid.*, pp. 256ff.

20. *Freiheit*, No. 15, Jan. 9, 1919.

21. *Ibid.* For a description of military actions against the rebels, see *Die Wirren* . . ., pp. 59ff.

22. This was the opinion of the majority socialists. See, e.g., Robert Leinert's testimony before the investigatory commission of the Prussian Constituent Assembly. *Sammlung der Drucksachen* . . ., XV, 8029.

23. Many were published in *Freiheit*, No. 14, Jan 8, 1919, *et seq.*

24. Eichhorn, p. 79.

25. *Freiheit*, No. 18, Jan. 10, 1919.

26. This was the opinion expressed by the editors of *Freiheit* (*ibid.*, No. 14, Jan. 8, 1919) and by Dittmann (p. 993). It is challenged by Hermann Müller, among others. H. Müller, p. 266.

27. Noske, *Von Kiel* . . ., p. 73.

28. This delegation included two representatives each from the U.S.P.D., the S.P.D. (workers), the "Revolutionary Workers," and the K.P.D. *Zr.*, p. 325.

29. This was reported long before the delegation arrived. *Ibid.*, p. 317.

30. *Ibid.*, pp. 325ff.

31. *Freiheit*, No. 21, Jan. 12, 1919.

32. *Ibid.*, No. 22, Jan. 1 , 1919.

33. Apparently they were not willing to join a new coalition cabinet, but only to cooperate with a reconstituted majority socialist cabinet. *Zr.*, pp. 372, 401.

34. These demands appeared in various forms. See, e.g., *Frieheit*, No. 19, Jan. 11, 1919.

35. *Zr.*, 402ff.

36. *Ibid.*, pp. 410f., Kolb, pp. 244ff.

37. *Zr.*, pp. 410f.

38. *Ibid.*, 517f. Apparently nothing came of this proposal.

39. He predicted in the Central Council meeting of Jan. 15 that the campaign against the radicals would lead to a totally inaccurate reflection of public sentiment. *Ibid.*, p. 402.

40. This view is expressed by Dittmann (p. 1000) and by Kautsky, *Mein Verhältnis* . . ., p. 12.

41. H.H. to Brill, Jan. 16, 1919, E.H., pp. 173f.

42. H.H. to Brill, Jan. 23, 1919, E.H., pp. 174ff.

43. As usual, the U.S.P.D. took a middle-of-the-road position on these disturbances. The party spokesmen endorsed the general strike enthusiastically. They did not, however, favor taking up arms, although they did express sympathy for those who suffered as a result of their revolutionary action. See *Freiheit*, No. 112, March 3, 1919, *et seq.* There are references in the minutes of a Central Council meeting of March 5 that indicate that Haase sent out new feelers at this time concerning the possibility of entering the government in coalition with a reconstituted majority socialist leadership and that these feelers aroused some interest among council

members. Zr., pp. 769ff. Haase also discussed the developing domestic crisis with Foreign Minister Brockdorff-Rantzau on March 4, but apparently without achieving any constructive result. *Das Kabinett Scheidemann . . .*, pp. 40f.

44. *Prot. U.S.P.D.*, March 1919, pp. 95ff.

45. *Ibid.*, pp. 28f., 78ff., 212ff.

46. Däumig was not actually present for the vote, but later declared his opposition. *Ibid.*, p. 264.

47. *Ibid.*, pp. 3ff.

48. *Ibid.*, p. 254.

49. Dtt., p. 1029.

50. The dissatisfaction of many delegates with Haase's behavior was reflected by the vote. Crispien received 133 votes to Haase's 107. *Prot. U.S.P.D.*, March 1919, p. 265.

51. Dtt., pp. 1031f. Haase knew Crispien from his Königsberg days.

52. H.H. to Brill, Feb. 17, 1919, E.H., pp. 175f.

53. H.H. to Brill, April 22, 1919, *ibid*, pp. 176f. The Independents had even decided to call a general strike if the government refused to sign the treaty. Morgan, pp. 262ff. See also Wheeler, pp. 87ff.

54. *Rt.*, CCCXXVII, 1082ff, 1102ff.

55. H.H. to Brill, July 8, 1919, E.H., pp. 183f.

56. H.H. to T.H., June 18, 1919, E.H., pp. 178f.

57. *Rt.*, CCCXXVII, 1125ff.

58. See, e.g., Grossman (*passim*) which includes excerpts from the transcript of the trial in which Haase defended Ernst Toller. See also H.H. to E.H., July 17, 1919, E.H., pp. 184f.

59. The most important of his speeches, that of July 26, was published as a pamphlet and widely distributed. *Rt.*, CCCXXVIII, 1959ff., published as *Haases Anklagerede. . . .*Among the charges he made in this speech was that the majority socialists had failed to respond effectively to the rising tide of anti-Semitism. For a discussion of Haase's position on this issue and the majority socialists' response, see Niewyk, pp. 83ff. For other important statements by Haase, see *Rt.*, CCCXXVII, 1220; CCCXXVIII, 1710, 2033.

60. *Ibid.*, CCCXXVIII, 1832.

61. H.H. to T.H., July 2; H.H. to Brill, July 8, 1919, E.H., pp. 183f.

62. *Freiheit*, No. 436, Sept. 10, Nos. 438–9, Sept. 11, 1919; Prager, pp. 204f.; Krause, pp. 145ff.

63. Prager, p. 205; Dtt., p. 1063.

64. E.H., pp. 87f.; Dtt., pp. 1061ff.; *Freiheit*, No. 552, Nov. 14, 1919.

65. Many of these were reprinted in *Freiheit* during the week following his death.

66. *Prot. U.S.P.D.*, Nov. -Dec. 1919, pp. 80ff.

67. Kautsky, *Mein Verhältnis . . .*, p. 13.

68. For text, see *Prot. U.S.P.D.*, Nov-Dec. 1919, p. 533.

69. Prager, pp. 207ff.; Wheeler, pp. 164ff.

70. For details and analysis of the ultimate disintegration of the U.S.P.D., see: Morgan, pp. 341ff.; Krause, pp. 165ff.; Wheeler, pp. 213ff.

XIV. THE GERMAN JAURÈS

1. This was strongly emphasized by Crispien in an article published a year after Haase's death. *Freiheit*, No. 475, Nov. 11, 1920.

2. Dittmann stresses that the new program was passed "in Haase's spirit" (Dtt., p. 1071), and Haase might well have agreed to it for tactical reasons. It certainly did not go as far as the radicals wanted and retained a reference justifying parliamentary activity. Yet it did represent a formal break with the Erfurt Program and with the principles which Haase had consistently upheld.

3. Harden, pp. 229ff. In his autobiography, Leon Trotsky, who knew Haase "fairly well," writes that "in the realm of philosophy (Haase) called himself, somewhat shyly, a Kantian." Trotsky, p. 216.

4. *Freiheit*, No. 541, Nov. 7, 1919.

BIBLIOGRAPHY

The literature dealing with the political history of Germany during this period is, of course, immense. This bibliography is thus limited, in terms of published sources, to works which have been cited in the notes.

1. *Collected Papers*

Barth, Emil. A.S.D.
Bernstein, Eduard. I.I.S.H.
Braun, Otto. I.I.S.H.
Dittmann, Wilhelm. A.S.D.
Henke, Alfred. A.S.D.
Kautsky, Karl. I.I.S.H.
Landsberg, Otto. Ba.
Molkenberg, Otto. A.S.D.
Solf, Wilhelm. Ba.
Südekum, Albert. Ba.
Troelstra, P.J. I.I.S.H.
Vollmar, Georg von. I.I.S.H.

2. *Documents in the A.A.*

Deutschland, No. 131. "Verhältnis zu Russland." Vols. 53–58.
Europa Generalia, No. 82, No. 1. "Die Sozialdemokratie in Deutschland." Vols. 28–29.

3. *Interviews*

Boenheim, Kurt.
Freyer, Eva Lichtenstein.
Friedlander, Walter.
Haase, Hans.

4. *Correspondence with Relatives of Hugo Haase*

Dresel, Gertrud Haase.
Freyer, Eva Lichtenstein.
Friedlander, Walter.
Friedman, Annette.
Haase-Dubosc, Arnold.
Meisels, Hilde Haase.

5. *Periodicals*

Freiheit (Berlin). November 15, 1918–1920
Leipziger Volkszeitung. 1913–1920
Mitteilungs-Blatt des Verbandes der Sozialdemokratischen Wahlvereine Berlins und Umgegend. April 1917-December 1918.
Die Neue Zeit. 1900–1917.
Sozialistische Auslandspolitik. After November 22, 1918 entitled *Der Sozialist.* 1916–1920.
Vorwärts (Berlin). 1914–1919.

6. *Other Sources*

Adolph, Hans J.L. *Otto Wels und die Politik der deutschen Sozialdemokratie 1894-1939.* Berlin, 1971.

Allgemeiner Kongress der Arbeiter- und Soldatenräte Deutschlands. Berlin, 1919.

An den Vorstand der Sozialdemokratischen Partei Deutschlands! An den Vorstand der sozialdemokratischen Reichstagsfraktion, Berlin. Berlin, 1915.

Angress, Werner T. "Juden im politischen Leben der Revolutionszeit," in Werner E. Mosse, ed. *Deutsches Judentum im Krieg und Revolution 1916–1923* (Tübingen, 1971), 137–316.

August Bebels Briefwechsel mit Karl Kautsky. Karl Kautsky, Jr., ed. Assen, 1971.

Aus Flugschriften und Flugblättern der Parteiopposition. Berlin, 1916.

Die Auswirkungen der grossen sozialistischen Oktoberrevolution auf Deutschland. Leo Stern, ed. 4 vols. Berlin, 1959.

Balabanoff, Angelica. "Die Zimmerwalder Bewegung, 1914–1919," *Archiv für die Geschichte des Sozialismus und der Arbeiterbewegung,* XII (1926), 350–413; XIII (1928), 232–284.

———. *Erinnerungen und Erlebnisse.* Berlin, 1927.

Barth, Emil. *Aus der Werkstatt der deutschen Revolution.* Berlin, n.d.

Bartel, Walter. *Die Linken in der deutschen Sozialdemokratie im Kampf gegen Militarismus und Krieg.* Berlin (East), 1958.

Baumgart, Winfried. *Deutsche Ostpolitik 1918.* Munich, 1966.

Berger, R. *Fraktionsspaltung und Parteikrisis in der deutschen Sozialdemokratie.* München-Gladbach, 1916.

Berlau, A. Joseph. *The German Social Democratic Party 1914-21.* New York, 1949.

Bernstein, Eduard. *Die deutsche Revolution.* Berlin, 1921.

Die Bildung der Sozialdemokratischen Arbeitsgemeinschaft. Berlin, 1916.

The Bolsheviks and the World War. Olga Hess Ganken and H.H. Fisher, eds. Stanford, 1940.

Braunthal, Julius. *Geschichte der Internationale.* 2 vols. Hannover, 1961.

Brecht, Arnold. *Aus nächster Nähe: Lebenserinnerungen 1844-1927.* Stuttgart, 1966.

Brill, Hermann. "Karl Kautsky," *Zeitschrift für Politik,* N.S. I (1954), 211-240.

Buse, Dieter K. "Ebert and the Coming of World War I: A Month from his Diary," *International Review of Social History,* XIII (1968), 430-448.

———. "Parteiagitation und Wahlkreisvertretung," *Archiv für Sozialgeschichte,* Beiheft 3 (1975).

Carr, Edward Hallett. *The Bolshevik Revolution.* Vol. III. New York, 1953.

Carsten, Francis L. *Reichswehr und Politik.* Berlin, 1964.

Comfort, Richard A. *Revolutionary Hamburg.* Stanford, 1966.

Crothers, George D. *The German Elections of 1907.* New York, 1941.

David, Eduard. *Das Kriegstagebuch des Reichstagsabgeordneten Eduard David 1914 bis 1918.* Susanne Miller, ed. Düsseldorf, 1966.

Delbrück, Clemens von. *Die wirtschaftliche Mobilmachung in Deutschland 1914.* Munich, 1924.

Dittmann, Wilhelm. "Erinnerungen." Transcription in I.I.S.H.

Dokumente und Materialien zur Geschichte der deutschen Arbeiterbewegung. Institut für Marxismus-Leninismus beim ZK der SED, Herausgeber. Reihe II, Vols. 1-111. Berlin, 1957.

Ebert, Friedrich. *Kämpfe und Ziele.* Dresden, 1927.

———. *Schriften, Aufzeichnungen, Reden.* Friedrich Ebert, Jr., ed. Dresden, 1926.

Eichhorn, Emil. *Eichhorn über die Januar-Ereignisse.* Berlin, 1919.

Ein Leben für den Sozialismus, Erinnerungen an Karl Kautsky. Benedikt Kautsky, ed. Hannover, 1954.

Eisner, Kurt. *Der Geheimbund des Zaren.* Berlin, 1904.

Elben, Wolfgang. *Das Problem der Kontinuität in der deutschen Revolution.* Düsseldorf, 1965.

Epstein, Klaus. *Matthias Erzberger and the Dilemma of German Democracy.* Princeton, 1959.

Eyck, Erich. *A History of the Weimar Republic.* Trans. Harlan P. Hanson and Robert G.L. Waite. Vol. I. Cambridge, 1962.

Fall of the German Empire. 2 vols. Ralph H. Lutz, ed. Stanford, 1932.

Feldman, Gerald. *Army, Industry and Labor in Germany 1914-1918.* Princeton, 1966.

Fischer, Fritz. *Griff nach der Weltmacht.* Düsseldorf, 1961.

Gause, Fritz. *Königsberg in Preussen.* Munich, 1968.

Gay, Peter. *The Dilemma of Democratic Socialism.* New York, 1962.

Gegen Parteizerrüttung. Berlin, 1915.

Groener, Wilhelm. *Lebenserinnerungen.* Göttingen, 1957.

Groh, Dieter. *Negative Integration und Revolutionärer Attentismus.* Frankfurt, 1973.

Grossman, Stefan. *Der Hochverräter Ernst Toller, die Geschichte eines Prozesses.* Berlin, 1919.

Grotjahn, Alfred. *Erlebtes und Erstrebtes.* Berlin, 1932.

Der Gründungsparteitag der KPD. Hermann Weber, ed. Frankurt, 1969.

Haase, Ernst. *Hugo Haase.* Berlin, 1929.

Haase, Hugo. *Grundzüge für das Referat und die Resolution über Imperialismus und Schiedsgericht, Internationaler Sozialistenkongress in Wien, August 23-29, 1914.* Brussels, 1914.

————. *Haases Anklagerede in der Nationalversammlung in Weimar am Sonnabend, den 26. Juli 1919.* Berlin, 1919.

————. *Reichstagsreden gegen die deutsche Kriegspolitik.* Berlin, 1919.

Haenisch, Konrad. *Die deutsche Sozialdemokratie in und nach dem Weltkriege.* Berlin, 1916.

Halperin, S. William. *Germany Tried Democracy.* New York, 1965.

Hamburger, Ernest. *Juden im öffentlichen Leben Deutschlands.* Tübingen, 1968.

Harden, Maximilian. "Wieder Einer," *Die Zukunft,* CVII (1919), 229-240.

Haupt, Georges. *Der Kongress fand nicht statt.* Frankfurt, 1967.

Heine, Wolfgang. "Politische Aufzeichnungen." Transcription in Ba.

Herwig, Holger H. "The First German Congress of Workers' and Soldiers' Councils and the Problem of Military Reforms," *Central European History,* I (1968), 150-165.

Herzfeld, Hans. *Die deutsche Sozialdemokratie und die Auflösung der nationalen Einheitsfront im Welt-Kriege.* Leipzig, 1928.

Holzheuer, Walter. *Karl Kautskys Werk als Weltanschauung.* Munich, 1972.

Horn, Daniel. *The German Naval Mutinies of World War I.* New Brunswick, 1969.

Illustrierte Geschichte der deutschen Revolution. Berlin, 1929.

Der interfraktionelle Ausschuss 1917-18. Erich Matthias, ed. 2 vols. Düsseldorf, 1959.

Die Internationale und der Weltkrieg. Carl Grünberg, ed. Leipzig, 1916.

Jarausch, Konrad H. *The Enigmatic Chancellor.* New Haven, 1973.

Joll, James. *The Second International 1889-1914.* New York, 1966.

Das Kabinett Scheidemann-13. Februar bis 20. Juni 1919. Hagen Schulze, ed. Boppard am Rhein, 1971.

Kautsky, Karl. *Demokratie oder Diktatur.* Berlin, 1918.

————. *Das Erfurter Programm.* 17th ed. Berlin, 1922.

————. *Mein Verhältnis zur Unabhängigen Sozialdemokratischen Partei.* Berlin, 1922.

————. *Sozialisten und Krieg.* Prague, 1937.

Keil, Wilhelm. *Erlebnisse eines Sozialdemokraten.* 2 vols. Stuttgart, 1947.

Kessler, Harry Graf. *Tagebücher 1918-1937.* Wolfgang Pfeiffer-Belli, ed. Frankfurt, 1961.

Kluge, Ulrich. *Soldatenräte und Revolution.* Göttingen, 1975.

Knütter, Hans-Helmuth. *Die Juden und die deutsche Linke in der Weimarer Republik 1918-1939.* Düsseldorf, 1971.

Kolb, Eberhard. *Die Arbeiterräte in der deutschen Innenpolitik 1918-1919.* Düsseldorf, 1962.

Konnemann, Erwin. "Der Truppeneinmarsch am 10. Dezember 1918 in Berlin," *Zeitschrift für Geschichtswissenschaft,* X (1968), 1592-1607.

Koszyk, Kurt. *Deutsche Pressepolitik im ersten Weltkrieg.* Düsseldorf, 1968.

————. *Zwischen Kaiserreich und Diktatur.* Heidelberg, 1958.

Kotowski, Georg. *Friedrich Ebert.* Vol. I. Wiesbaden, 1963.

Krause, Hartfrid. *USPD.* Frankfurt, 1975.

Kuczynski, Jürgen. *Der Ausbruch des ersten Weltkrieges und die deutsche Sozialdemokratie.* Berlin, 1957.

Kurt Riezler, Tagebücher, Aufsätze, Dokumente. Karl Dietrich Erdmann, ed. Göttingen, 1972.

LaChesnais, P.G. *Le groupe socialiste du Reichstag et la déclaration de guerre.* Paris, 1915.

Der Ledebour-Prozess. Georg Ledebour, ed. Berlin, 1919.

Levine-Meyer, Rosa. *Leviné: The Life of a Revolutionary.* Farnborough, 1973.

Liebknecht, Karl. *Gesammelte Reden und Schriften.* Institut für Marxismus-Leninismus beim ZK der SED, Vol. VIII. Berlin (East), 1966.

————. *Klassenkampf gegen den Krieg.* Berlin, n.d. (1919).

Löbe, Paul. *Der Weg war lang.* Berlin, 1954.

Lösche, Peter. *Der Bolschewismus im Urteil der deutschen Sozialdemokratie.* Berlin, 1967.

Lucas, Erhard. *Frankfurt unter der Herrschaft des Arbeiter und Soldaten-rats 1918-1919.* Frankfurt, 1969.

Man, Hendrik de. *Gegen den Strom.* Stuttgart, 1953.

Matthias, Erich. "Kautsky under der Kautskyanismus," *Marxismusstudien,* II, (1957), 151–197.

Matull, Wilhelm. "Anfänge der Arbeiterbewegung in Ostpreussen," *Jahrbuch der Albertus-Universität zu Königsberg/Preussen,* XIV (1964), 220-241.

————. "Hugo Haase und Otto Braun," *Jahrbuch der Albertus-Universität zu Königsberg/Preussen*, XVI (1966), 171-195.

————. *Ostpreussens Arbeiterbewegung*. Würzburg, 1970.

Max, Prinz von Baden. *Erinnerungen und Dokumente*. Stuttgart, 1928.

Mayer, Arno J. *Politics and Diplomacy of Peacemaking: Containment and Counterrevolution at Versailles, 1918-1919*. New York, 1967.

Mayer, Gustav. *Erinnerungen*. Vienna, 1949.

Michels, Robert. *Zur Soziologie des Parteiwesens in der modernen Demokratie*. Stuttgart, 1925.

Militär und Innenpolitik im Weltkrieg 1914-1918. Wilhelm Deist, ed. 2 Vols. Dusseldorf, 1970.

Militarismus und Opportunismus gegen die Novemberrevolution. Lother Berthold and Helmut Neef, eds. Berlin, 1958.

Miller, Susanne. *Burgfrieden und Klassenkampf*. Düsseldorf, 1974.

————. "Zum 3. August 1914," *Archiv für Sozialgeschichte*, IV (1964), 515-523.

Mitchell, Allan. *Revolution in Bavaria*. Princeton, 1965.

Mommsen, Wolfgang. "Die Regierung Bethmann Holweg und die öffentliche Meinung 1914-17," *Vierteljahrshefte für Zeitgeschichte*, XVII (1969), Heft 2, 117-159.

Morgan, David W. *The Socialist Left and the German Revolution*. Ithaca, 1975.

Müller, Hermann. *Die Novemberrevolution*. Berlin, 1928.

Müller, Richard. *Vom Kaiserreich zur Republik*. 2 vols. Vienna, 1924.

Nadolny, Rudolf. *Mein Beitrag*. Wiesbaden, 1955.

Nettl, J.P. *Rosa Luxemburg*. 2 vols. London, 1966.

Niewyk, Donald L. *Socialist, Anti-Semite, and Jew*. Baton Rouge, 1971.

Nipperdey, Thomas. *Die Organisation der deutschen Parteien vor 1918*. Düsseldorf, 1961.

Noske, Gustav. *Aufstieg und Niedergang der deutschen Sozialdemokratie*. Zurich, 1947.

————. *Von Kiel bis Kapp*. Berlin, 1920.

Nowka, Harry. *Das Machtverhältnis zwischen Partei und Fraktion in der S.P.D.* Berlin, 1973.

Oehme, Walter. *Damals in der Reichskanzlei*. Berlin, 1958.

Osterroth, Franz. *Biographisches Lexikon des Sozialismus*, Part I, *Verstorbene Persönlichkeiten*. Hannover, 1960.

Prager, Eugen. *Geschichte der U.S.P.D.* Berlin, 1921.

Protokoll der Reichskonferenz der Sozialdemokratie Deutschlands vom 21., 22., und 23. September 1916. Berlin, 1916.

Protokolle der Sitzungen des Parteiausschusses (S.P.D.). Berlin, 1914-1918.

Protokoll über die Verhandlungen des internationalen Sozialistenkongresses zu. . . . Berlin, 1900, 1904, 1907, 1910, 1912.

Protokoll über die Verhandlungen des Parteitages der Sozialdemokratischen Partei Deutschlands. Berlin, 1898-1913, 1917, 1919.

Protokoll über die Verhandlungen des Parteitages der Sozialdemokratischen Partei Preussens. Berlin, 1904, 1907, 1910.

Protokoll über die Verhandlungen des . . . Parteitages der Unabhangigen Sozialdemokratischen Partei Deutschlands. Berlin, 1917, March 1919, November-December 1919, 1920.

Ratz, Ursula. "Briefe zum Erscheinen von Karl Kautskys 'Weg zur Macht,'" *International Review of Social History,* XII (1967), No. 3, 432-477.

———. *Georg Ledebour.* Berlin, 1969.

———. "Karl Kautsky und die Abrüstungskontroverse in der deutschen Sozialdemokratie 1911-12," *International Review of Social History,* XI (1966), No. 2, 197-227.

Die Regierung der Volksbeauftragten 1918-19. Susanne Miller, ed. 2 vols. Düsseldorf, 1969.

Die Reichstagsfraktion des deutschen Sozialdemokratie 1898 bis 1918. Erich Matthias and Eberhard Pikart, eds. 2 vols. Düsseldorf, 1966.

Ritter, Gerhard. *Staatskunst und Kriegshandwerk.* Vols. III-IV. Munich, 1968.

Roos, Hans. *A History of Modern Poland.* New York, 1966.

Rosenberg, Arthur. *Imperial Germany, the Birth of the German Republic.* Trans. Ian F.D. Morrow. Boston, 1964.

Rosenfeld, Günter. *Sowjetrussland und Deutschland 1917-22.* Berlin (East), 1960.

Roth, Gunther. *The Social Democrats in Imperial Germany.* Totowa, N.J., 1963.

Sammlung der Drucksachen der verfassungsgebenden Preussischen Landesversammlung, Tagung 1919-1921. Vol. XV.

Scheidemann, Philipp. *Memoiren eines Sozialdemokraten.* 2 vols. Dresden, 1928.

———. *Der Zusammenburch.* Berlin, 1921.

Schorske, Carl. *German Social Democracy 1905-17.* Cambridge, 1955.

Schröder, Hans-Christoph. *Sozialismus und Imperialismus.* Hannover, 1968.

Schröder, Wilhelm. *Geschichte der sozialdemokratischen Parteiorganisation in Deutschland.* Dresden, 1912.

Schüddekopf, Otto-Ernst. *Das Heer und die Republik.* Frankfruit, 1955.

Schulthess' europäischer Geschichtskalender. Vols. XLIX-LX. Munich, 1908-1919.

Schulz, Gerhard. "Die deutsche Sozialdemokratie und die Idee des internationlen Ausgleichs," in Alfred Hermann, ed., *Festschrift zum 70.*

Protokoll über die Verhandlungen des internationalen Sozialistenkongresses zu. . . . Berlin, 1900, 1904, 1907, 1910, 1912.

Protokoll über die Verhandlungen des Parteitages der Sozialdemokratischen Partei Deutschlands. Berlin, 1898-1913, 1917, 1919.

Protokoll über die Verhandlungen des Parteitages der Sozialdemokratischen Partei Preussens. Berlin, 1904, 1907, 1910.

Protokoll über die Verhandlungen des . . . Parteitages der Unabhangigen Sozialdemokratischen Partei Deutschlands. Berlin, 1917, March 1919, November-December 1919, 1920.

Ratz, Ursula. "Briefe zum Erscheinen von Karl Kautskys 'Weg zur Macht,'" *International Review of Social History,* XII (1967), No. 3, 432-477.

————. *Georg Ledebour.* Berlin, 1969.

————. "Karl Kautsky und die Abrüstungskontroverse in der deutschen Sozialdemokratie 1911-12," *International Review of Social History,* XI (1966), No. 2, 197-227.

Die Regierung der Volksbeauftragten 1918-19. Susanne Miller, ed. 2 vols. Düsseldorf, 1969.

Die Reichstagsfraktion des deutschen Sozialdemokratie 1898 bis 1918. Erich Matthias and Eberhard Pikart, eds. 2 vols. Düsseldorf, 1966.

Ritter, Gerhard. *Staatskunst und Kriegshandwerk.* Vols. III-IV. Munich, 1968.

Roos, Hans. *A History of Modern Poland.* New York, 1966.

Rosenberg, Arthur. *Imperial Germany, the Birth of the German Republic.* Trans. Ian F.D. Morrow. Boston, 1964.

Rosenfeld, Günter. *Sowjetrussland und Deutschland 1917-22.* Berlin (East), 1960.

Roth, Gunther. *The Social Democrats in Imperial Germany.* Totowa, N.J., 1963.

Sammlung der Drucksachen der verfassungsgebenden Preussischen Landesversammlung, Tagung 1919-1921. Vol. XV.

Scheidemann, Philipp. *Memoiren eines Sozialdemokraten.* 2 vols. Dresden, 1928.

————. *Der Zusammenburch.* Berlin, 1921.

Schorske, Carl. *German Social Democracy 1905-17.* Cambridge, 1955.

Schröder, Hans-Christoph. *Sozialismus und Imperialismus.* Hannover, 1968.

Schröder, Wilhelm. *Geschichte der sozialdemokratischen Parteiorganisation in Deutschland.* Dresden, 1912.

Schüddekopf, Otto-Ernst. *Das Heer und die Republik.* Frankfruit, 1955.

Schulthess' europäischer Geschichtskalender. Vols. XLIX-LX. Munich, 1908-1919.

Schulz, Gerhard. "Die deutsche Sozialdemokratie und die Idee des internationlen Ausgleichs," in Alfred Hermann, ed., *Festschrift zum 70.*

Geburtstag von Ludwig Bergsträsser (Düsseldorf, 1954), 89-116.

Schulze, Hagen. *Freikorps und Republik 1918-1920.* Boppard, 1969.

Sender, Toni. *The Autobiography of a German Rebel.* New York, 1939.

Severing, Carl. *Mein Lebensweg.* Vol. I. Cologne, 1950.

Spartakusbriefe. Institut fur Marxismus-Leninismus beim ZK der SED, Berlin (East), 1958.

Stampfer, Friedrich. *Erfahrungen und Erkenntnisse.* Cologne, 1957.

Stenographisches Protokoll der deutsch-französischen Verständigungskonferenz 11. Mai 1913 zu Bern. Bern, 1913.

Stern-Rubart, Edgar. *Graf Brockdorff-Rantzau.* Bonn, 1968.

Ströbel, Heinrich. *The German Revolution and After.* Trans. H.J. Stenning. New York, 1923.

Toury, Jacob. *Die politschen Orientierungen der Juden in Deutschland.* Tübingen, 1966.

Trotsky, Leon. *My Life.* New York, 1930.

Unterirdische Literatur im revolutionären Deutschland während des Weltkrieges. Ernst Drahn and Susanne Leonhard, eds. Berlin, 1920.

Die Ursachen des deutschen Zusammenbruches im Jahre 1918. 12 vols. Berlin, 1928.

Ursachen und Folgen vom deutschen Zusammenbruch 1918 und 1945. Vols. I-III. Herbert Michaelis and Ernst Schraepler, eds, Berlin, 1958.

Varain, Heinz Josef. *Freie Gewerkschaften, Sozialdemokratie und Staat.* Düsseldorf, 1956.

Verhandlungen des Reichstages. 1897-1919.

Victor Adler, Briefwechsel mit August Bebel und Karl Kautsky. Friedrich Adler, ed. Vienna, 1954.

Vidil, Charles. *Les Mutineries de la marine allemande 1917-1918.* Paris, 1931.

Vietsch, Eberhard von. *Bethmann Hollweg.* Boppard am Rhein, 1969.

———. *Wilhelm Solf.* Tübingen, 1961.

Volkmann, Erich Otto. *Der Marxismus und das deutsche Heer im Weltkriege.* Berlin, 1925.

Wachenheim, Hedwig. *Vom Grossbürgertum zur Sozialdemokratie-Memoiren ziner Reformistin.* Berlin, 1973.

Wheeler, Robert F. *U.S.P.D. und Internationale.* Frankfurt, 1975

Die Wirren in der Reichshauptstadt und im nördlichen Deutschland 1918-20. Kriegsgeschichtlich Forschungsanstalt des Heeres. Berlin, 1940.

Wistrich, Robert S. *Revolutionary Jews form Marx to Trotsky.* New York, 1976.

Zechlin, Egmont. "Bethmann Hollweg, Kriegs-risiko und S.P.D. 1914." *Der Monat,* XVIII (1966), Heft 208, 17-32.

Der Zentralrat der deutschen sozialistischen Republik. Eberhard Kolb and Reinhard Rürup, eds. Leiden, 1968.

Die Zimmerwalder Bewegung. Horst Lademacher, ed. 2 vols. The Hague, 1967.